NO TRESPASSING:
AUTHORSHIP, INTELLECTUAL PROPERTY RIGHTS, AND THE BOUNDARIES OF GLOBALIZATION

In this scholarly yet highly accessible work, Eva Hemmungs Wirtén traces three main themes within the scope of cultural ownership: authorship as one of the basic features of print culture, the use of intellectual property rights as a privileged instrument of control, and, finally, globalization as a precondition under which both operate. Underwritten by rapid technological change and increased global interdependence, intellectual property rights are designed to protect a production that is no longer industrial, but informational.

No Trespassing tells the story of a century of profound change in cultural ownership. It begins with late nineteenth-century Europe, exploring cultural ownership in a number of settings across both spatial and temporal divides, and concludes in today's global, knowledge-based society. Hemmungs Wirtén takes an interdisciplinary and international approach, using a wide array of material from court cases to novels for her purposes. From Victor Hugo and the 1886 Berne Convention to the translation of Peter Høeg's bestseller *Smilla's Sense of Snow*, Hemmungs Wirtén charts a history of intellectual property rights and regulations. She addresses the relationship between author and translator, looks at the challenges to intellectual property by the arrival of the photocopier, takes into account the media conglomerate's search for content as a key asset since the 1960s, and considers how a Western legal framework interacts with attempts to protect traditional knowledge and folklore. *No Trespassing* is essential reading for all who care about culture and the future regulatory structures of access to it.

(Studies in Book and Print Culture)

EVA HEMMUNGS WIRTÉN is an associate professor in Comparative Literature at Uppsala University, where she also holds a Swedish Research Council Postdoctoral Fellowship 2002–2006.

EVA HEMMUNGS WIRTÉN

No Trespassing
Authorship, Intellectual Property Rights, and the Boundaries of Globalization

UNIVERSITY OF TORONTO PRESS
Toronto Buffalo London

© University of Toronto Press Incorporated 2004
Toronto Buffalo London
Printed in Canada

ISBN 0-8020-8835-X (cloth)
ISBN 0-8020-8608-X (paper)

Printed on acid-free paper

National Library of Canada Cataloguing in Publication

Hemmungs Wirtén, Eva
No trespassing : authorship, intellectual property rights and the
boundaries of globalization / Eva Hemmungs Wirtén.

(Studies in book and print culture)
Includes bibliographical references and index.
ISBN 0-8020-8835-X (bound)   ISBN 0-8020-8608-X (pbk.)

1. Intellectual property.   2. Authorship.   3. Copyright.   I. Title.   II. Series.

Z552.W47 2004   352.7'49   C2003-903964-1

University of Toronto Press acknowledges the financial assistance to
its publishing program of the Canada Council for the Arts and the
Ontario Arts Council.

University of Toronto Press acknowledges the financial support for
its publishing activities of the Government of Canada through the
Book Publishing Industry Development Program (BPIDP).

To Minna, Rebecca, and Aurora

– for saving my day, every day –

CONTENTS

Preface   ix

Introduction:
The Pursuit of Property   3

1   Wearing the Parisian Hat:
Constructing the International Author   14

2   Inventing F. David:
Author(ing) Translation   38

3   The Death of the Author and the Killing of Books:
Assault By Machine   57

4   How Content Became King:
Economies of Print   76

5   From the 'Intellectual' to the 'Cultural':
Can There Be Property with a 'Difference'?   100

6   Genies in Bottles and Bottled-Up Geniuses:
Two Cases of Upset Relatives and a Public Domain   125

Notes   149
References   191
Index   215

PREFACE

Diva Revisited

Nothing strikes one as quite so embarrassingly outdated as relics of the recently transpired. Whether or not it was once deemed the height of fashion or considered an outlandish novelty by its contemporaries, hip grows old with a vengeance. I suspect this is why re-experiencing Jean-Jacques Beineix's film *Diva* from 1981 makes the sensation of witnessing hypertrendy gone charmingly hyperold as immediate as it is powerful.

Beineix's *œuvre* received widespread acclaim. Its tongue-in-cheek treatment of familiar generic ingredients instantly rejuvenated the hardboiled tradition of American movie classics and *film noir*. Briefly, the story revolves around a young postal worker's infatuation with opera in general and the singer Cynthia Hawkins – played by Wilhelmenia Wiggins Fernandez – in particular. He is so obsessed by her that he secretly records one of her performances, even though she refuses her permission to do so. No record of her voice exists; only the unduplicable immediacy of recital is on offer – irreplaceable, unique. As the story progresses and the couple become romantically involved, things get out of hand. Intended for personal use only, the pristine recording is aggressively hunted down by Taiwanese thugs representing the not-so-law-abiding music industry. Accidentally, it crosses paths with a surveillance tape disclosing the police commissioner as head of a prostitution ring, and suddenly our hero finds himself drawn into the dark underbelly of Paris, pursued from all quarters. The soundtrack made an odd international hit out of the aria in Catalani's *La Wally* (1892), and came accompanied by a scenography perhaps even more innovative, where colours, clothes, and interior decorating evoked the stylish 1980s to come, as if leaping directly out of one of the French much adored *bandes dessinées*.

Due to its cult status for a generation of which I was definitely a part, seeing *Diva* in Paris almost twenty years after its initial release produces exactly the nostalgic feeling of *déja vu* I had come to expect. Yet the film also triggers a rather different kind of recognition. In retrospect, my enjoyment is not tied only to lustful digging in the archeological bits and pieces of a period's form, narratology, and fashion. As I watch the account of a bootleg recording gone astray, I suddenly realize that *Diva* prophesied one of the more pressing concerns of contemporary cultural life two decades later – namely IPR, or intellectual property rights. Behind his extreme aestheticization of a pretty straightforward story, Beineix probed a territory about to undergo a dramatic reconfiguration: he showed us how a new infrastructure of ownership made possible by a fusion of technology, information, culture, politics, and economics could look like.

©

There is no doubt in my mind that the late-night screening of *Diva* in Paris in July of 2000 helped shape this book into its final form. When I began my work two years earlier, I envisioned a very different end product, one that would be an account of the changing conditions for publishing under globalization. I knew early on that intellectual property rights needed to be a part of that story, but somewhere along the way that summer in Paris I stumbled not only on *Diva*, but perhaps more importantly on Victor Hugo, and suddenly the perspective of one chapter grew into that of the entire six.

It is a great privilege to be able to follow such new directions and to witness how a project in some sense takes on a life of its own. 'Going with the flow' would not have been possible, however, if not for the support of a number of organizations and individuals. Through its committee 'Global Processes in a European Perspective,' the Swedish Council for Planning and Coordination of Research (today the Swedish Research Council) set things in motion by offering financial as well as moral support for the project in 1998–9. A generous Knut and Alice Wallenberg Foundation grant for recently graduated female scholars allowed me the luxury of time and travel when I needed it the most, and a postdoctoral scholarship from the Swedish Foundation for International Cooperation in Research and Higher Education (STINT) led to an invaluable stay at the University of North Carolina at Chapel Hill during the 2001–2 academic year. For their joint invitation leading up to that visit, I am deeply grateful to Professor Lawrence Grossberg at the University Program in Cultural Studies and Professor Joanne Gard Marshall at the School of Information and Library Science. Early encouragement from the Department of Literature, Uppsala University, where the project was originally conceived, must be recognized, and I acknowledge both the Centre for Cultural Policy Research and the Swedish School of Library and Information Science, Göteborg University and the University College of Borås, for support expressed in many different ways since 1999. In 2002 I was awarded a four-year postdoctoral fellowship by the Swedish Research Council, which facilitated the finishing touches on the book and above all, makes it possible for me to continue to explore a field that fascinates me and that holds so many challenging avenues to pursue.

During the past four years I have had the opportunity to present parts of my manuscript at various seminars and conferences in Sweden as well as abroad. Rather than list all such occasions, I extend a collective thanks to all who have given me the opportunity to vent a work in progress, a crucial, yet sometimes overlooked, element of academic research. Obviously, I have incurred the greatest debt to those persons who have carefully read and commented on the manuscript in its various stages of completion or simply given me faith that one day it would materialize into a book, particularly Jonas Ebbesson, Anders Frenander, Jenny Johannisson, Carl Josefsson, Lars-Göran Karlsson, Dick Kasperowski, Claes Lennartsson, Jan Nolin, Annika Olsson, Henry Olsson, Veronica Trépagny, and Geir Vestheim. My husband Per has, as always, been my most trusted reader. Any errors of judgment, lapses in style or content, should of course be attributed to me, and me alone.

As Peter Stallybrass and Allon White so accurately note: '"place" is not merely a name but something like a mode of discursive production.'[1] I am acutely aware of the fact that my own 'discursive production' owes a tremendous amount to some great places where I have been fortunate to spend time writing this book. They include the Bibliothèque Nationale de France, site François Mitterand/Tolbiac, and the UNESCO library in Paris; the Royal Library in Copenhagen; and the Stockholm University Library and the Royal Library in Stockholm. However, it was the impressive resources at the Walter Royal Davis Library and the Kathrine R. Everett Law Library at the University of

North Carolina at Chapel Hill, that really made all the difference to the way I was able to conduct my research.

Finally, credit where credit is most profoundly due. I dedicate this book to my three daughters, whose presence in my life makes everything possible to begin with.

NO TRESPASSING:
AUTHORSHIP, INTELLECTUAL PROPERTY RIGHTS,
AND THE BOUNDARIES OF GLOBALIZATION

INTRODUCTION

THE PURSUIT OF PROPERTY

The sequence of events depicted in the pages that follow unfolds in late nineteenth-century Europe and is then traced up to today's global, knowledge-based society. As I explore cultural ownership in a number of settings across both spatial and temporal divides, three overlapping interlocutory spheres serve as backdrop for my undertaking: *authorship* as one of the basic features of print culture; *intellectual property rights* as the privileged instrument of control exercised over the multifarious resources produced by the first; and finally *globalization* as the condition under which these two operate.

Before concentrating on each category and their mutual interconnections, let us consider some of the reasons for choosing print culture to frame the overall concerns of this book. An undertaking of this kind would perhaps be better served if it pivoted around more *Diva*-like topics, such as the challenges to the music industry à la Napster. Considering that so much of our cultural consumption no longer is limited to the offerings of print culture, why is it placed centre stage? Ousted, unseated, dethroned – why should we care about books, magazines, printed material at all when there are any number of other cultural forms poised much more centrally to deal with these matters? Few would probably disagree with the suggestion that if there ever were a privileged position for the printed word, then it is unquestionably one under fire. Am I attempting a search-and-rescue operation, then, looking to reinstate the printed word in all its old pomp and glory? Or is it rather the reverse – a final act of scooping soil on the coffin of something long ready for burial? Neither option sounds particularly desirable.

The counterarguments against print culture are attractive only on a superficial level. Even if we concede to the sidelining argument, print culture allows us, perhaps better than other media forms, to *historicize*. If this in turn needs further clarification, we can make a case that it is simply *because of* the historical legacy of print culture; *because* we may evaluate and follow its trajectories through time; *because* it is a slow medium where changes and transformations brought on by, for instance, new technology may work to highlight the conflicts and clashes of a long tradition in flux, that we are capable of saying something grounded in the experience of *the long haul*. Print culture and authorship insist on being understood historically; using this to our advantage will, in turn, add to our knowledge of globalization, as it demonstrates the need to put specific events seen as inherently contemporary into the necessary perspectives of time and place. The same arguments that can be launched against the validity of print culture can be used in its favour.

It is precisely the historical legacy, deeply imbued with questions of value, originality, hierarchization, imitation, and copying, that makes print culture so inviting as a field of inquiry. Not only is this relevant to publishing, authors, and critics, but in fact it applies to the entire field of print, including those who make it their business to study it – from a long-standing preoccupation with textuality in literature studies to the material concerns of book history. These scholars directly or indirectly devote themselves to issues of immaterial *and* material value, and hence also moral and economical worth and property.[1] To focus on print culture rather than any other cultural form is not to unduly favour it, but merely to underscore that a certain nucleus must be present in order for us to better understand the present from its past.

Forms of legal control in print culture long predate the arrival of the 'author' at what Michel Foucault famously terms a 'privileged moment of *indivualization.*'[2] Prior to such an appearance at the end of the eighteenth century, printers and publishers were generally the first copyright owners through the granting of privileges.[3]

If rights and traditions once mattered more than originality and personality, then the notion of the author as a self-contained, unique individual whose works must be judged by their intrinsic value alone is a new invention concomitant with the advent of the author as an autonomous legal subject. The penchant of the time for having personal names as book titles – *Pamela, Clarissa, Tom Jones, Tristram Shandy* – what Mark Rose labels 'the record of a personality,' is but one expression of how authorship and legal ownership began to coexist.[4]

Authorship and intellectual property rights are from the very beginning fundamentally paternalistic and gender-biased discourses that continue to appoint the owner, author, and proprietor as a man, a 'he.'[5] This strand of thought – authorship expressed in terms of a romantic, individualistic conception of *original* creation influenced by and separated from the mundane by inspiration that comes from within (a man) – is widely accepted as the very foundation of modern intellectual property doctrine.[6]

In order to understand the underlying principles behind modern intellectual property rights we must look to history. In chapter 1, Victor Hugo's opening speech at the Congrès Littéraire International in Paris 1878, which would subsequently lead to the formation of the Association Littéraire et Artistique Internationale (ALAI) and indirectly to the first multilateral treaty on copyright, the Berne Convention for the Protection of Literary and Artistic Works in 1886,[7] highlights a number of themes that will resurface during the following chapters. The rationale behind the international control of intellectual property rights that Hugo helped orchestrate is a tremendously important feature to address because it provides a structure by which we can understand the emerging internationalization taking place more than a century ago as a thing apart from, yet also reminiscent of, what we will encounter in globalization.

A major incentive behind the construction of these early international conventions was the question of translation. By taking a closer look, in chapter 2, at the two English-language versions of Peter Høeg's bestseller *Frøken Smillas fornemmelse for sne* (1992), I will highlight two major itineraries. The first relates to the question of where the limits of authorship are drawn and to whom the text belongs, translator or author or both. The second addresses the issue of intellectual property rights as an instrument of cultural imperialism, whether French at the end of the nineteenth century or Anglo-American at the beginning of the twenty-first. Yet, it is important to remember that as we look to the author for guidance we are dealing not only with an individual, a person. To be more precise, authorship should be interpreted, again drawing on Foucault, as a function profoundly 'transdiscursive'[8] in nature, supple enough to carry over into computer programming, software production, genetic and/or agricultural research, including individuals, corporations, collectives, even perhaps residing in prehuman creator ancestors.[9]

Clearly this function acts as an interpretative instrument allowing us to probe the many contradictory tenets of intellectual property rights of today, but it does not limit the possible uses and strategies to which authorship can be deployed. What is important in the end is therefore not so much the identification of authorship, but the varying and sometimes conflicting uses to which it is being put. The strength of authorship resides thus in its flexibility, its capacity to be used for different ends by different agents. One thing is certain: the relationships explored in the following chapters will routinely pit cultural and financial investments against one another. Our object of study can be Victor Hugo or the infrastructures of information technology, but *someone* is always claiming rightful ownership of the property in question, be it printers, booksellers, authors, readers, or TransNational Media-Corporations (TNMCs).

In chapter 3, the book moves forward to explore the critical feature of technology as an agent of change in reference to intellectual property, using the copier as a case study. Represented by Chester Carlson's invention xerography and the machine itself, this is not such a far-fetched choice as it might initially appear. Using the copier to illustrate how an instrument for reproduction functions to decentre the notion of text, reproduction, and copy enables interesting correspondences between technological innovation, textual categorization, and regulatory frameworks.

Under the influx of globalization, intellectual property rights takes on a new urgency. As a consequence, power in this field is assigned to those who have the ability to deny access to certain resources, or who may fence in specific types of valuable knowledge.[10] In chapter 4, I turn my attention to the relationship between conglomeratization, content, and convergence in order to describe the increasingly important economic motives behind intellectual property rights, arguing that content ownership and protection must be seen as one of the incentives behind the radical restructuring of publishing since the 1960s.

Why not then, in light of the subject matter and its historical legacy, use the more commonly known term copyright rather than intellectual property rights to denote the regulatory regime that safeguards content? There are two main reasons. Currently the scope of the Agreement on Trade-Related Aspects of Intellectual Property Rights (TRIPS), which together with the Berne Convention represents key international texts on intellectual property rights, includes copyright and related rights, trademarks, geographical indications, industrial designs, patents, layout designs (topographies of integrated circuits), protection of undisclosed information, and control of anticompetitive practices in contractual licences. By speaking of intellectual property rights we automatically include copyright, and while copyright indisputably has far more in common with print culture than, say, geographical indications and integrated circuits, what would seem an apparently obvious choice of words can still be debated. For one thing, while the differences between the French *Droit d'auteur* – *Urheberrecht* in German, *Upphovsmannarätt* in Swedish, *Diritto di autore* in Italian – on one side, and the Anglo-American *Copyright*, on the other, should not be exaggerated, they are often seen as two very different legal stances vis-à-vis intellectual property.[11] As they stem from the traditions of civil law and common law respectively, Paul Edward Geller instead speaks of *authorship norms* and *market place norms* to stress the differences in approach.[12] For example, the French and continental tradition recognizes the moral rights of the author,[13] and vests them almost exclusively in flesh-and-blood individuals; the common law tradition, on the other hand, allows legal entities to act as authors under the so-called work for hire principle.[14] Far from mere judicial cosmetics, the implications of *droit d'auteur* and *copyright* on the international agenda of intellectual property rights as well as being epistemological tools used to decipher the events that I discuss in this book must somehow be contended with. On balance, the relationship is better perceived as dialectical, providing a useful frame within which the various battles regarding intellectual property may be concretized.[15] As a consequence, intellectual property rights – *propriété intellectuelle* in French – denoting the legal rights which result from intellectual activity in the industrial, scientific, literary, and artistic fields, simply represents a more neutral choice of terminology.[16] Secondly, and as will become clearer towards the end of the book, many of the current tendencies in intellectual property rights must be rethought outside the realm of traditional copyright.

The conflicts that arise from the clash between a non-Western view of culture and the Western author-based romantic ideal is fertile ground for a number of questions regarding the limits and possibilities of intellectual property rights. That disagreements ensue when you seek to protect and preserve completely different assets from the ones held by the TNMCs is apparent if we consider the efforts of, among others, the United Nation's specialized agency World Intellectual Property

Organization (WIPO) to secure folklore and traditional knowledge (TK) within the framework of intellectual property rights and TRIPS. The international community here faces one of its most provocative challenges to date, which leads me to look more closely at the possibility of 'cultural' property rights in chapter 5.

One of the basic premises of intellectual property protection concerns the relationship between the immaterial and the material. Article 2 of the Berne Convention does not make fixation mandatory, but it is generally the case that expressions and not ideas as such are protected, and thus some sort of material conditioning becomes necessary.[17] While it would seem that my emphasis on the immaterial as the main asset sought for protection is problematic because of this proviso, this is only one of several inconsistencies that earmark intellectual property rights. Take music: not only records but also live performances are produced, something that makes it fundamentally different from the function of book/text, which is still consumed mostly individually and in silence. 'Although material objects (records, compact discs, cassettes) are indeed traded,' Steve Jones argues when, in a highly illuminating way, he illustrates the rapport between the material and the immaterial in respect to music and intellectual property rights, 'what gives those commodities value is the abstracted object of copyright – namely music.'[18] Paraphrasing Jones, content is the abstracted object of copyright in this book. In the end, both the term *intellectual property* and *copyright* fall short of rendering this important feature, which is more accurately captured by the Swedish term used for intellectual property rights: *Immaterialrätt* (law of the immaterial/intangible).

We can deem intellectual property rights the successful – or failed, depending on our position – administration of a set of contradictory tenets of which the correlation between the immaterial and the material represents only one part. A subset of other conflicting facets is the relationship between private protection and public good; the problematic balance between rights and obligations; the ambiguities surfacing as free trade treaties are elaborated on the basis of strengthening monopolies in the name of global free trade; and the question of piracy or copying infringements as either attempts to undermine a nationally important industry or simply as a form of flattery.[19]

In the final chapter, I will use two sets of upset relatives, the estate of Margaret Mitchell and a great-great grandson of Victor Hugo – the first of whom were engaged in litigation against the 2001 publication of Alice Randall's *The Wind Done Gone*, a rewrite of *Gone With the Wind*;

and the second stirring a debate in France over the publication, also in 2001, of *Cosette ou le temps des illusions*, a follow-up to *Les Misérables* – to recapitulate these conflicts in respect to one of the most important features Victor Hugo raised in his 1878 speech: 'le domaine public.'

©

The third and final sphere underpinning this investigation is *globalization*: the time-space continuum enveloping authorship and intellectual property rights. Despite the many options that come to mind when we set out to define its characteristics, one in particular overshadows the alternatives on where to begin peeling its layers. It concerns the importance of *spatiality*. Why is this notion of spatiality so central to globalization? The most obvious answer is that as we think of what we mean when we talk about globalization, we refer to various formations that may or may not be absolutely new to us but which are made possible by a rapidity, intensity, and scope of mind-boggling proportions. If pushed to be more specific, we will no doubt exemplify those with significant increases in flows of capital, culture, people, and labour, now organized, maintained, and developed independent of nation-state logic and in large part due to sophisticated technology. And as they take shape and come into focus, we will perhaps concur that all of these configurations demonstrate new kinds of spatial networks and interdependencies.

We can view it as a buzzword or agree that it is the cliché of our times,[20] but globalization undeniably denotes a very specific temporal experience in which increased migration, mobility, and transborder flows of money and culture are commonplace. We are presented with events that have substantial *spatial connotations, where questions of extended space, spatiality and place are foregrounded*.[21] In trying to come to terms with the repercussions of these processes, we are offered the possibility of *thinking differently about* the world. Hence the underlying assumption of this study, equally concerned then with the more measurable and tangible elements of globalization, as with their potential to create a theoretical matrix, a space made up by the importance of places.[22]

Working with globalization in this context means acknowledging that it actually denotes something very real while also remembering that it is a powerful epistemological representation that impinges on the way in which we have come to understand others and ourselves.

One of the reasons we can speak of globalization at all is because we think of ourselves as living in a globalized world. Seen from such an angle, there is hardly a discussion on globalization that is not related to a geopolitical framework of some kind. As I think will become clear, choosing this perspective means implementing new analytical tools for the understanding of the material conditions by which any cultural commodity and/or practice is produced, consumed, and regulated. But it will also alter our interpretation of the same processes. If we are to believe David Morley – and I think we should – the humanities and the social sciences have undergone a substantial epistemological reconfiguration in the last twenty years, from a primary concern with periodization and temporality, to arrive at the conclusion that events have not only a temporal but also a spatial form.[23] With a certain logic, this means that authorship and intellectual property must both be considered sites of temporal and spatial contestation.[24] Just as authorship must be understood in interplay with a multitude of influences, so will intellectual property be subjected to the work of cultural contexts.

To a large extent, the history of international intellectual property rights is one of expansion – in terms of subject matter, in terms of geopolitical reach, and in terms of the length for which the monopoly of intellectual property rights is accorded, something which has fluctuated substantially over time. The Berne Convention specifies the life of the author and fifty years thereafter. However, during the 1990s, two major adjustments relevant for the arguments that ensue occurred. The European Union extended copyright to the life of the author and seventy years thereafter from 1 July 1995 and in the United States in 1998, the Copyright Term Extension Act (CTEA), better known as the Sonny Bono Copyright Term Extension Act, extended copyright by twenty years from fifty years to seventy years for individuals, and from seventy-five years to ninety-five years for corporate authors, *even retroactively*.[25] Ensuring increased international harmonization is the one major raison d'être for the many conventions in the field, from Berne to TRIPS, and yet, intellectual property rights are still bound by territoriality and national laws.[26]

How then, more precisely, does globalization relate to authorship and intellectual property? James Boyle suggests that intellectual property bears the same relationship to the information society or globalization as the wage-labour nexus did to the industrial manufacturing society of the 1900s.[27] Thus, in a time of spatial interdependence, intellectual property regimes are seen as safety nets designed to protect the capital of our time, a capital which is not only increasingly immaterial rather than industrial, but which more importantly is *transborder and oblivious to nation-state regulation*. This means that the protection of assets that flow quite easily across and beyond borders becomes imperative, something which in turn drastically alters the basis of conduct for all those drawn into such an orbit.[28] Some of the basic building blocks of international conventions in the field, such as the crucial element of national treatment, are today pressured by the decreasing importance of the nation-state and the spatial complexities of globalization.[29] The inherent contradictions of intellectual property rights are therefore caused to bend and realign in new ways. Suggesting that those in control of this regulatory regime have the upper hand in the knowledge-based society is therefore hardly an exaggeration.[30]

Because of its critical importance in this spatial interdependency, intellectual property rights is an instrument – possibly the most important today – of what Susan Strange calls structural power, and of particular interest must therefore be the boundary between what is allowed to count as intellectual property at all, and what is not.[31] What determines this is a form of articulation that decides how things shall be done and how relationships and frameworks should be shaped, and it is continuously reworked on a borderline of interplay between states and markets. In this overall matrix, Susan Strange defines four structures of power: security, production, finance, and knowledge.[32] While she underlines that the knowledge structure might be the most important and least theorized, one could certainly argue that the distinctiveness of the knowledge-based economy is that in it knowledge has *become* production and vice versa and hence that the two should be viewed as fundamentally interrelated.

Globalization prompts us to recast this structural power into one of spatial power, one that binds together the very close with the far away in such a way as to cause both to operate within a complex logic of interdependency. It would be a major error to underestimate the presence of structural and spatial power, but equally dangerous not to surmise that there can be transformation or exchanges in the positions of those holding and vying for it. If we subscribe to a contextual historical analysis, we must accede that even power itself is a contingent thing.

©

Authorship, intellectual property rights, and globalization are the three main *topoi* around which the chapters of this book are organized. I have already posited these three as representing a contested terrain upon which the challenges concerning the ownership of contemporary key resources are played out.

As my work progresses, I hope to stay clear of at least two fallacies in thinking of them together. The first is not to perpetuate any false and unconstructive separation between these intersecting spaces. Because of the nature of the subject matter itself, which is equally fluid and changeable, this would be not only a mistake, but virtually impossible to pull off. Instead, I have tried to opt for a more holistic approach, underscoring the similarities, correspondences, and linkages between what on the surface might appear as separate and even contradictory systems of reference. My second manoeuver has been focused on not falling into the habit of oversimplifying the task of assigning power to any pre- and/or overdetermined apparatus. Having said that, I think there is evidence to suggest that the balance intellectual property is supposed to uphold between the right to access (public) and the right to ownership (private) is dislodged in the intellectual property regimes of the global economy and the information society. This is why it is important not only to remain in the realm of those *in* power, but also to consider the appropriation of intellectual property by groups striving for articulation. Very few things speak of power to the same extent as ownership, but in this case it should never be judged too quickly in an oversimplified or monolithically one-directional manner. The theoretical outlook of this study is substantially informed by Stuart Hall's particular use of 'above' and 'below,' which refers to the nation-state and can be seen as related to the concepts 'global' and 'local.'[33] From my own perspective, I would also like to think that it is possible to use the terms 'power' and 'agency' in the same manner and that these various levels must always be kept in mind.

In light of this, I hope I have made it clear at this point that what awaits the reader is not an exercise in legal scholarship. While clearly intellectual property is of paramount concern to the practice and theory of law, my own investigation is guided by a competence and raw material found elsewhere. Consequently I am indebted to a body of work concerned with the cultural, economic, and political significance of intellectual property.[34] Influenced by and hopefully contributing to this field in progress should thus be regarded as working within – and on the border of – a number of loosely neighbouring academic territories: studies in book history and print culture, cultural studies, literature studies, law, as well as the even larger and more fluid concepts of globalization and the information society. Undoubtedly, as we are dealing with a phenomenon that moves in and out of several interconnected yet at times also independent spheres, different disciplines and epistemologies contribute to an evolving critical perspective. Despite the drawbacks that might be involved, the most rewarding interdisciplinary work of all tends to surface when you have to, as Susan Strange once said, 'learn by looking over the fence.'[35]

The law – as in court cases, statutes, laws, international conventions, and the various external discourses relating to these – is treated as a social construct, contingent and interpretable, subject to the same type of interferences, manipulations, and appropriations as any text in the more conventional meaning of the word. The enduring popularity of court-room drama on television is but one simple example of the fact that the law (especially perhaps common law) also comes with a performative dimension, one which is difficult, if not impossible, to capture after the fact. The crucial point is that while we often find ourselves confined to documentary evidence in textual form in order to render certain events, the performative aspect of what happens in a courtroom and the relationships between those present, remains absent in this study. Yet I recognize that, as Shoshana Felman writes on the dramatic fainting of a witness during the Eichman trial, 'the dramatic can be legally significant.'[36]

In combining these approaches, I subscribe to a reading of legal doctrine as cultural text.[37] While 'text' therefore refers back to a number of various access points of which print culture, authorship, and intellectual property rights only represent three possibilities, my basic standpoint is to reject any idea of the law as fundamentally different in nature than any other construction that operates on the basis of language.[38] While it may seek to eliminate the slippages of interpretation and subjectivity and strive to obviate ambivalence, there is no secure position from where conventions or cases regarding intellectual property rights transcend into absolute objectivity. In this respect, law and literature are strikingly similar in their reliance and emphasis on the primacy of interpretation.[39]

I firmly believe that there is and needs to be a grounded focus and competence in an undertaking of this kind, but I am equally convinced that cultural texts of any kind – be they laws, novels, advertising copy, or policy documents – create a set of interpretable connections where, in Doreen Massey's words, 'the material and the discursive interlock.'[40] In the chapters that now await the reader I have tried to fuse both these perspectives into a coherent whole.

Chapter One

WEARING THE PARISIAN HAT:
CONSTRUCTING THE
INTERNATIONAL AUTHOR

Our story first begins on 17 June 1878, the year of the Exposition Universelle. The scene is Paris, and more specifically one of the numerous conferences hosted by that city during the year in question: the Congrès Littéraire International. Initiated by the Société des gens de lettres de France,[1] the honour of delivering the inaugural speech is set aside for one man and one man only: Victor Hugo. Now, trying to pinpoint the exact beginnings of major historical trajectories to a precise date and location constitutes of course a hazardous enterprise. We all know that history is not made up of temporal snapshots. Still, Hugo's speech is an excellent starting point from where the overall concerns of this book can be explored further. Not only is he about to articulate his concerns regarding the lack of an effective international regime overseeing *la propriété littéraire*, his stature as a respected internationalist makes this into an issue not only for authors, but for the civilized world at large. After all, who better to put into words the nascent comprehension of interconnectedness and interdependencies forming at the end of the nineteenth century than a man known, read, and respected on all continents? Who better to articulate the world?

Seventy-six years old, Hugo is so intimately intertwined with the turbulent history of nineteenth-century France that one can hardly tell where one begins and the other ends. Looking in the rear-view mirror of the past, Hugo can survey a career spanning every literary genre known to man: novels, essays, poetry, plays, speeches, an immense outpouring of creativity that included able artwork. Without a doubt, this is one of the first authors who truly steps into the light as a full-fledged cultural icon. Hugomania was a contemporary affliction that came in the shape of every odd, conceivable proof of flattery, from the import to France of foreign pirated copies of his books to the alleged spotting of fake Hugo's at various European cities.[2] Superhumanly idolized in a way inconceivable to any present-day author, the creator of *Notre-Dame de Paris* (1831) and *Les Misérables* (1862) is hero-worshipped almost beyond comprehension. Pascale Casanova claims that like Voltaire before him and André Gide after him, Hugo incarnates what she calls 'le mandarin intellectuel.' She continues to explain that such a person – empowered by a large audience to legitimize subjects ranging from the loftiest moral, cultural, and political order to the most banal of everyday matters – exercises influence far beyond what he actually knows, what he writes, and even beyond what he says.[3]

Accrued since his early thirties, his fame undoubtedly produced a very distinct consciousness regarding the value of his thoughts, actions, and words. He was motivated in equal parts perhaps by his keen sense of the demands of the book market and his self-inflated literary ego. If we are to believe his own son Charles, 'Nothing is lost. Everything ends up in print.'[4] Needless to say, the value of property – and especially literary property – is something Hugo can relate to.

Politically, Hugo's life is a chronicle of steadfast involvement in domestic and international affairs. Occasionally he sided with the establishment; in 1871 he became a member of the National Assembly and would in time even be titled Senator. Sometimes his position was more unorthodox: his lifelong opposition to the death penalty; his involvement in the John Brown/Harper's ferry incident in 1859[5] (rendering him status as a national hero in Haiti); and his largely self-inflicted exile following the 1848 revolution. Returning to Paris after nineteen years on the Channel Islands can be described only as a homecoming comparable to a public happening. History has it that because of the tumultuous reception awaiting him and the four public speeches demanded of him on his way, it took two hours to traverse the city on the day following the proclamation of the Third Republic – 5 September 1870 – from his arrival at Gare du Nord to his temporary quarters near the Étoile.[6]

Strikingly adept at managing a successful synthesis of his various traits – author, political activist, national superhero, and internationalist – into one coherent representation, Hugo is a chameleon who changes colours with the backdrop. But a better exponent of peace, progress, and the virtues of Western civilization celebrated by the World Fair than the white-bearded colossus chosen as keynote speaker by the organizers of the Congrès, is unthinkable.

I

Despite a gradual decline in the international importance and impact of the French language since the beginning of the century, late-nineteenth-century French literature and authors continued to be read and respected in Europe and beyond, in translation and in the original.[7] Making a living from that talent was something else entirely. From those who, like Hugo, profited greatly from their books to those who barely scraped by, authorship was a path one did not choose lightly. Some authors survived thanks to a second profession as civil servants, others were fortunate enough to secure patronage. Hugo's own trajectory on the book market and his ascendancy in cultural and economical standing matches the changing conditions of the market itself. In the early stages of his career he received financial compensation in the form of personal subsidies from Louis XVIII.[8] At that point primarily known as a poet, Hugo sees his earnings increase exponentially as the older system of literary patronage becomes less significant and a new liaison between author, publisher, and reading public develops into the business norm. The advent and gradual supremacy of the novel as the preferred literary genre of a new reading public benefits an entire generation of writers, and must be seen as coincidental with increased efforts at copyright legislation, and economic control.[9] This ultimate generic success story was, however, not limited to the balance sheets of publishers or the wallets of authors: the novel was the perfect vehicle for the nation-state to promote itself.[10]

It has been suggested that the two French writers who were most at ease with the workings of the book market at this time were Hugo and George Sand.[11] They were also, together with Balzac, notoriously disloyal and changed publishers without hesitation if they felt that their books were not promoted enough or sufficiently endorsed.[12] When Hugo's publisher Hetzel – a compatriot in exile who published *Napoléon-le-Petit* (1852) and *Les Châtiments* (1853) – offered a sum Hugo thought insufficient for *Les Misérables*, the author promptly took his business elsewhere.[13] Hugo and Sand knew how to profit from the conditions of the emerging mass market, as they were adept at using the many possibilities of reissues, magazine publication, and cheap editions now available to them. Perhaps they even had what we today would describe as media savvy. Both were extremely prolific, produced in several genres, and their financial and cultural careers were hardly worse off for the lucky fact that they lived long lives and managed to produce during an impressive period of time. Hugo made his debut with *Odes* at twenty in 1822 and he died in 1885; Sand, who debuted with *Indiana* in 1832, died in 1876 at the age of seventy-two.

With this new market and its well-known attributes – revolutionary printing technology, rising literacy, communication and transportation networks facilitating wider and better distribution – came the possibility of increased financial gain, at least to those who knew how to harness the capricious beast. Unfortunately, there was also the unpleasant side effect of very real financial *loss*. Lost revenues due to piracy or cheap editions produced outside France – Balzac complained vehemently in a letter that 'Belgium had ruined French literature'[14] – presented a bona fide predicament for French nineteenth-century authors. Before its publication in France, Flaubert's *Madame Bovary* first surfaced in a partial version in the *Revue de Paris*, and then in an equally incomplete German edition. Balzac as well as Mérimée saw their texts prematurely appearing in Belgium.[15]

Hugo is far from the first author in Europe to promote the moral and economic rights of the author in respect to his labour. Daniel Defoe raised the issue in *An Essay on the Regulation of the Press* in 1704, and England is also generally accredited with the first 'real' copyright law with the so-called Statute of Anne in 1709.[16] The almost uniform preference for the same best-selling writers – Scott, Bulwer-Lytton, and Dickens in England, and Dumas, Sue, and Hugo on the French side – showed how most of Europe read the same authors at roughly the same time.[17] No wonder then, that these successful novelists are highly invested in the quest *for* international copyright legislation and *against* infractions in whatever form. Together with Dumas, one of the most widely read and translated of the above, Hugo is no stranger to piracy. Hence, there is nothing remarkable about the fact that he should choose to speak of copyright.

As we know, there was no international copyright legislation in effect at the time of Hugo's speech. A general overview will disclose different national systems, or rather specific territorial frameworks. Bilateral treaties were becoming increasingly common, beginning with the German-Prussian agreements in 1825. When the multilateral Berne Convention was signed in 1886, a number of bilateral treaties were already in force: France led with thirteen, followed by Belgium with nine, and Spain with eight.[18]

In the absence of uniform regulatory frameworks, authors' dealings with publishers encouraged sharp business acumen. Hugo, Balzac, and

Sand all had contracts allowing the publisher the licence to publish a certain work *for a limited period*. This period could be quite brief, leaving the writer at liberty to renegotiate with the same publisher or with a new one for additional reprints. But it could also last for several years, as was the case with Hugo's *Les Misérables*. Hugo's contract ran for eight years and rendered the author a lump sum of Fr 250,000 (Fr 300,000 according to other sources), allowing the publisher to print as many copies as he liked during that period.[19] In 1835, Hugo signed an agreement with the publisher Renduel to receive Fr 60,000 for 11,000 copies of *Notre-Dame de Paris* for a period of three and a half years, a sum that included six volumes of plays.[20] Due to this contractual structure the exact remuneration for each individual book remains uncertain. Nonetheless, Hugo was unquestionably a wealthy man already in his late thirties. His best years lay ahead of him and paired with the fact that France had no income tax before the First World War, he was a well-to-do man indeed. At the time of his death in 1885, his estate was worth somewhere around four million francs.[21]

©

Hugo commences, not by alluding directly to the question of property, but by ascertaining temporality. He marks out 1878 as an exceptional year, one that will see war and strife defeated by progress. The overture paints a larger picture for the audience, relegating everything pertaining to more material concerns to the wayside. As we have already seen, the economic ramifications of being subjected to various forms of piracy presents a quandary to the international community of writers that must be resolved at all costs. But an *international legislation* on copyright is still an unattainable reality. Once again the call for such a legislation comes as a direct response to increased travel, expanding markets, new forms of distribution, more advanced production facilities, all of these logistical factors now altering the production and consumption of print. Given that the need for a regulative framework of this kind provides a strong incentive for Hugo, his speech is economically, legally, and culturally motivated. As all-important as this line of reasoning is, it is still downplayed. Hugo opts for another approach.

He opens by contextualizing, using all his personal understanding of the political past and present to stir the emotions of the audience. In many ways, it is a profoundly ideological address skilfully neutralized by the author's emblematic standing. Since Hugo is uncontested as a representative of France and utopian internationalism, no one would think to question his objectives. Considering that the 1878 World Fair was the first without any kind of official religious ceremony on the program,[22] Hugo steps in as a secular replacement substituting one message – intended to lure the masses into the opium-induced, trance-like state Marx had warned about – with another, where reason, level-headedness, and intellect are called for. But there is nothing remotely subdued or distanced in Hugo's presentation as he paves the way for his own outlook on literary property. He smooth-talks his listeners in order to secure their approval; those assembled in Paris are referred to as the most celebrated of talents, seen as the foremost representatives of their respective nations, even accredited 'ambassadors of the human spirit.'[23]

Before a word is said on property per se, Hugo introduces several recurring topics that form the basis of his programmatic declaration. First and foremost, his entire project rests upon the cementing of litera-ture and civilization into one bedrock foundation by which the progress of a nation can be measured by the quality of its literature. Effortlessly he then activates the idea of the *universal* and infuses it with a tremen-dously powerful connotation, as when he exhorts his audience to make it clear to legislators that literature is not something local, but some-thing universal.[24] There is a very particular spatial dimension to the centrality of the term, constructed on the repetitive interlacing of several components. One such piece in his giant puzzle is the rights of the author equated with universal rights, preceding an adamant sug-gestion of the undeniable and imperative affiliation between these two terms and that of copyright or literary property. The author as proprietor is analogous to the author as a free man. Deny the author the fruits of his labour, and you deny him his independence as a human being.[25]

Such a stipulation is conspicuously gendered, as Melissa J. Home-stead's study on female American antebellum authors shows. Their relationship to intellectual property rights was nothing if not schizo-phrenic; on the one hand, they were in many instances successful novelists who could claim authorship and thus a form of ownership; on the other hand, they could simultaneously be denied the right to own individual property. When Harriet Beecher Stowe in 1853 unsuccess-fully sought to stop an unauthorized German translation of *Uncle Tom's Cabin* published by F.W. Thomas for German immigrants in the United States in *Stowe v. Thomas*, her only access to the courts – despite being the acclaimed writer of the book in question – was by way of the true legal subject of the marriage: her husband.[26]

As words flow from the mouth of this French god-like father figure, not a hint of uncertainty can be detected as far as whom it all concerns; the universe of the universal is male. Hugo's opinions would not make sense to the audience unless they understood *property itself as universal*, and therefore it follows automatically: if the author is universal, so must his property be. The Congrès convenes for this very reason: to explore the possibilities of spatial organization and international collaboration, to make literary property into something geographically controllable. Finally, there is the complicated argument that the universal can be understood in terms of the national – Spain conjures up Cervantes, England Shakespeare, Italy Dante, France Voltaire – and of course, vice versa. The alliance between authors and nations rests on a complex binary logic. On the one hand, designated a heritage shared by us all, these consecrated authors are archetypically neutered, imperceptibly stripped of their individual nationalities. Concurrently and in a contradictory U-turn, they are infused with quintessential national qualities allowing Shakespeare to express the soul of England and Voltaire to embody Frenchness.[27]

Larger-than-life myths or flesh-and-blood individuals? The limelight position of the author in the construction of the nation-state is hardly accidental, and calling on the aforementioned writers is hence an ingenious move by Hugo. Such as it is, his appeal goes beyond the mere summoning of national pride and exaltation; it achieves the added benefit of underscoring to the participants that their presence is not motivated by base self-interest. They have a mutual goal: to defend and protect a legacy. The value of this heritage, Hugo argues, is perpetual and therefore it *cannot be measured*. In one instant, he diverts attention from or possible anxiety for the pecuniary aspects of their own ambition and redirects their interest to the elevated question of nation-state symbolism. As he establishes the overarching impetus of his invocation, the room fills with anticipation.

Hugo is on a roll. He continues to hammer in his idea that as individuals and as a collective, writers are special people, and they must be treated as such. Singled out as occupying a function outside the drabness of everyday life, they should be judged by a special yardstick. The extraordinary qualities that enable men of letters to put human experience and existence into words is what makes them more universal than everybody else – a logic of reasoning that will reemerge in other contexts pertaining to the history of international copyright legislation. The Kentucky senator Henry Clay, who stubbornly – and mostly in vain – lobbied the U.S. Congress in support of international copyright for many years during the mid-nineteenth century, once said: 'Of all classes of our fellow-beings, there is none that has a better right than that of authors and inventors to the kindness, the sympathy, and the protection of government.'[28] In Hugo's book the author is also someone with extraordinary powers, someone who can and should spearhead society's development, who must intervene to avoid war between nations, who stands as the ultimate promoter of rational progress and innovation. Because of Mark Twain's investment in American copyright legislation, Siva Vaidhyanathan dubbed him 'the champion of private publishing interests cloaked in the rhetoric of noble public service,'[29] a description almost tailor-made for Hugo as well. Many years earlier William Wordsworth expressed his concern for the way in which ownership and author's rights were being neglected by legislation, writing in 1819: 'It appears to me that towards no class of his Majesty's Subjects are the laws so unjust and oppressive.'[30] Using political connections and channels in order to influence the conditions for authors was an obvious course of action for successful nineteenth-century writers. Charles Dickens worked hard to convince both the British and American governments to legislate against the widespread and accepted use of piracy. During his first American tour of 1842, he failed, however, to engage the support of American authors in his cause against piracy and it has even been suggested that his crusade against the American publishing industry might have exacerbated the situation rather than helped to remedy it.[31]

On this day in question, the author materializes dressed in a very specific attire, arguing that his work should be understood precisely as labour, and thus inherently objectifiable into a very specific, fixed, determinable *thing*. It is intellectual and it is literary, but regardless of what you call it, property it still is. Any remaining essentialist notion of the author as a self-contained entity who perpetuates *l'art pour l'art* is an ideology impossible to maintain and contradictory to the objective of the gathering. The wish to safeguard and protect literary value, to keep the individualized, canonized author intact and the corresponding ambition to legislate, to seek international standards and treaties for the implementation of such an ideology is a dichotomy displacing the author in two worlds.

However, Hugo is asking for much more than the protection of the material object, 'the book.' He entices laughter from his audience when – playing on the solidness of the object – he makes a joke that 'the book is different from the thought; as book, it is seizable, so seizable as to be sometimes seized.'[32] Separating the book (material) from thought (immaterial) is a strategy consistent with the author/nation versus property approach allowing him to ask for the recognition of the author's right to *propertize himself and his ideas*. For all its materiality, property is becoming increasingly immaterial. And this is one of the more important moves in Hugo's address: to take what cannot be held and make it into matter, asking that it be recognized as such.[33]

That his own work would be singularly well suited for the transferral to screen and stage a century later, is a thing in the future. To late twentieth-century cultural consumers, *Notre-Dame de Paris* is perhaps best remembered in its incarnation as several Hollywood films, one of them a Disney animation, and *Les Misérables* as a musical fixture on Broadway and in the shape of more or less successful film adaptations. As we return to Victor Hugo in the final chapter of this book, we will see how such contemporary transformations of Hugo's works have stirred heated debate in France over the appropriate treatment of a national icon and his texts.

Up to this point in his solo presentation Hugo manages to deliver his speech in a somber tone, and then he seamlessly moves into the area of actual legislative suggestions. As if certain that the pill of what he has to offer will be infinitely easier to swallow if accompanied by passionate supplication, he now makes a halt in his proposals and the timbre of his voice changes once again. Quite abruptly, there is a high-pitched exclamation: 'Ah! Light! Always light! Light everywhere!'[34]

Obviously, we have no documentation of his movements; his facial expressions and gestures that day elude us. In the absence of pictures we can only guess how he came across on the podium. Perhaps he tilted his head, made a movement as if to indicate that he suddenly saw light seeping in through the windows, perhaps he simply let the audience imagine it for themselves. But in a remarkably eloquent shift, he bypasses all trace of materialistic Hugo, and every single hint of the subject matter (property) is instantly eradicated and forgotten.

Typical for the construction of the communication is that its tone often sounds deeply sentimental, sometimes crystal clear, and then suddenly turns ostentatious and embellished beyond belief. In some sense the result of the many sides Hugo tries to give his story, by and large the impression remains ambiguous. Old-fashioned, outdated, over the top – absolutely. A fascinating testament to a master orator at work, a pied piper who knew exactly how to work a crowd into a frenzy – yes, that too. Priscilla Parkhurst Ferguson describes his style as reliant on 'antitheses, the outsize, even grotesque images, the litanies of names and events' to create 'the linguistic resource by which he recasts history into legend.'[35] As he swings from one aspect of property rights – the undeniable rights of the author – to another – concrete proposals for remuneration to heirs and family – to a third – how can we learn from the experiences of the Paris revolutions to prevent them from ever happening again, this time on an international stage? – he is careful not to tip the scale too much in any direction. Balancing on a tightrope between the analytical and the megalomaniac, this combination – the masterful bringing together of incongruous parts – is precisely what makes his communication so powerful. Another description of its distinctiveness would be to say that the address tries uneasily to bridge the widening precipice between literary generations, descending romanticism on the one side and ascending modernism on the other. The romantic poet and the bourgeois novelist are both present in Hugo, and they struggle for space in his discourse.

The 'illumination' paragraph is without doubt one of the most openly allegorical parts of his speech. As such it illustrates well Hugo's ability to combine and build his case on electrifying and emotional metaphors. Slowly, his soliloquy gains momentum and places him firmly onto romantic soil. In a highly poignant frame of mind, he associates the anticipated beam of light with one nation: France. The luminosity of France guarantees not merely the projected success of international copyright legislation but that of human progress in general. His argument was backed up by action: France had taken steps in a decree from 1852 to unilaterally extend its laws to all works published abroad, without any demand for reciprocity in relation to the protection of French works in other countries. It was an inspired attempt to set the international agenda on literary property, claiming altruism and universalism while simultaneously 'shaming' other countries into following the French example.[36] Franco Moretti's suggestion that during the time 'England became an island' France proved less insular, is another argument in support of French internationalism. Moretti locates the (relative) disappearance of foreign novels to the British literary market in the 1790s and the late 1820s. In the first instance, the reason is due to the negative impact of the French revolution, and in the second, to the fact that a domestic literary production now represents strong competiton. Comparing the number of translated books in nineteenth-century English reading libraries with those in French equivalents shows that they develop in two diametrically opposed directions over time: the English reading library reduces the number of translations, whereas the French increases them. Moretti then accumulates more evidence to support his case by arguing that non-English language literature – and particularly perhaps French – arrives late into English translation; *The Charterhouse of Parma* appeared sixty-two years after its original publication, *Madame Bovary* twenty-nine. On the other hand, his examples of French translations of European writers – such as the Russian classics – show that they appear almost twenty years ahead of their English counterparts.[37] For Hugo, there is no doubt that France sets the standard for what it means to be cosmopolitan and thus for what intellectual property rights should be:

> France is in favour of the public good. France rises on the horizon of all peoples. Ah!, they say, it is day, France is here! (*Oui! oui! Bravos répétés.*) That one can have objections to France is surprising, but there it still is: France has its enemies. These are the enemies of civilization itself, the enemies of the book, the enemies of free thought, the enemies of emancipation, of examination, of deliverance, those who see in dogma an eternal master and in mankind an eternal insignificant.[38]

We are left with hyperbolic rhetoric and the obvious associations between France, the universal, enlightenment, and evolution. To be an enemy of France is to be an enemy of civilization. Hugo, saviour of the disenfranchised, draws blatantly on his personal myth to entice the congregation; the romantic cult of his self-promoted genius, his experience in exile, even his standing in the establishment, everything can be used to prove his point. To address the challenges of the international economics that now need to be harnessed for the author – and mankind – to profit, the crowd is once more placed on his emotional roller coaster. This time against war and famine: 'Let us deliver them blow upon blow. Hate against hate! War against war!' exclamations to which the audience responds with 'sensation.'[39] These are the measures, Hugo argues, by which we can do so much more than beat piracy and the appalling neglect for author's rights; we can actually clean up the sewers of modern society. If we are to believe the transcript, the crowd is ecstatic; frequent parenthical outbursts of approval punctuate key moments: 'Applaudissements prolongés,' 'Bravo!' 'Acclamation unanime.'

Behold an expert strategist at work. The economic and tangible parts of Hugo's agenda are made digestible by simple guilt-by-association. That there is a continuous use of elaborate contrast in the speech, a constant polarization of peace, prosperity, and progress with the notion of property, is clear. The combination of political agitation, literary analogies, and proprietary interests confirm that literary property is much more than merely something of concern to authors. It is important to the nation, and above all, it is essential if international cohesion is to take place. The images used are those that we will have occasion to return to during the course of this book: universalism, the national versus the international/global, the collective as opposed to the individual, private versus public.

In the following, I would like to continue by expanding the discussion on two fronts. First, by situating Hugo's speech in reference to the influential place from where it is launched: Paris. Following this line of thought, the final part of this chapter centres on a distinctly modern project partly resulting from his intervention: the international organizations and bodies that henceforth were to take charge of literary property.

II

Premièring in London's Crystal Palace in 1851, world fairs were by 1878 well established on the international arena. Exposition Universelle denotes in French the same thing as it does in English: a manifestation where innovations are introduced, nations demonstrate their accomplishments, New Worlds are put on display, and where the progress of the industrialized world in general can be admired. In its capacity to accumulate on a small piece of land the merchandise and communities of a world now so much larger, so much under the pressure of radical and rapid transformations, so alluring and frightening at the same time, the Exposition Universelle provides the ideal setting for Hugo's communication. It makes perfect sense to frame his invocation for national identity and international collaboration in surroundings inexorably drawing on the strength and weaknesses of both phenomena. Another reason why this is such a suitable arena is the convergence supplied between industry and art, visible not only in the underpinnings of the world fair as a whole, but in the proximity of these categories to one another as intellectual property forms into an entity comprising both elements. Innovations and trademarks may be differ-

ent from literature, but Hugo argued forcefully that industry and literature had common goals. The developments to come would also prove
that these two main clusters had distinct responsibilities and interests,
but also that their objectives would coincide.

A quick glance on the official map of the exhibition confirms the
suspicion that France dominates the event not only in spirit. England
may be second best as far as space is concerned, but the feeling that
Champ-de-Mars is a promotional zone celebrating the inherent cultural
supremacy of the French lingers persistently.[40] The world fair operates
on its own microcosmic level of Hugo's double matrix; the international seen in terms of the national. It places before us a world compressed, but compressed in such a fashion as to enable within its
transnational intentions the potential nationalisms of the same project.
The opportunity to display and promote a specific national identity
was to become more marked with each following exhibition, arguably
culminating in Paris 1937.[41] A wonderful picture taken that year from
the Trocadéro Palace facing the *Champ-de-Mars* show a group of visitors
leaning out over the railing, surveying the pre–Second World War
exhibition inquisitively. To the left they see the German pavilion,
designed by Albert Speer and crowned by an eagle. On the opposite
side they see the Soviet exhibition area, equally white and equally
recognizable in its respective iconography. But the picture is most striking for its centrepiece: the Eiffel Tower; an iron giraffe that finds itself
symbolically sandwiched in by two looming and gigantic effigies. Stag-
ing an abstract clash of what is to become horrible reality between the
two regimes a few years later, the picture also tells another story. It
spotlights the one monument that can pride itself on what appears to be
a permanent universality, the one symbol depicted in that black-and-
white picture still standing tall is the cultural capital of the world: the
city of Paris itself.[42]

The political turbulence of 1937 Europe is still a long time in the
future, however. When Hugo formulates his thoughts on property and
legislation, he does so by calling attention to a new experience, and its
successful decoding depends on the ability of his audience to make the
necessary connections between the international and the national. Since
the budding idea of nation is what enables them to think of something
as inter-national in the first place, the nation-state must be given a
prominent place in our discussion.[43]

Hugo's verbal eloquence reaches its powerful pinnacle when its
absolute placeboundedness is taken into account. We can hardly over-

estimate the importance of Paris and the particular spatial convergence of the triad *universal-international-Paris* to the overall impact of his address. Since there is only one city able to confer such power on those who visit and inhabit it, what the author suggests is that if the prominence of Paris is accepted as a universal bankable currency, true international understanding will follow automatically. There is wonderful precision in Hugo's challenge to us – appropriately put in terms of fashion – not to wear any hat other than the one originating in Paris: 'I defy you to wear any other hat than the one from Paris.'[44] Sporting such a headpiece is an antidote as good as any to the forces of evil, and the surest way to demonstrate a firm belief in the merits of rationalism and clear thinking.

Haussmann's incandescent French capital is the ultimate exponent of progress. The burgeoning world metropolis attracts an increasing number of international meetings towards the end of the nineteenth century; in 1861 the Union des Associations Internationales records a total of four international conferences. In 1878 the number has risen to sixty-three, and the Congrès Littéraire International is only one out of the forty-eight taking place in Paris. Perhaps not proof positive, but still evidence of the gravitational pull of that city, where the entire year is filled with international meetings, such as the congrès de météorologie, géologie, d'hygiène publique, postal, timbrophiles.[45] If London in the novels of the time is such a grimy and dark place that people prefer to leave, fictional and actual Paris is a magnet.[46] Just being there means partaking in a modern world, where infinite evolution and constant improvement of mankind comes with the territory. Hugo's personifies the city – its revolutions of 1789, 1848, and 1871 – and he ensures future uncluttered boulevards of the mind and body. Without fail, Paris denotes everything that is *modern*.

Few have captured the magnetism of the urban better than Walter Benjamin in his writing on the Paris *passages*. To Benjamin, the *passage* is nothing short of a miraculous transporter, a veritable cavity in which the image of modernity is created.[47] The shelter offered by the passageway does not only provide the *flâneur* with a roof over his head. It is in fact a nifty time machine. You enter in one period, and exit in another. As you pass through the world inside, modernity happens. Its plethora of symbols – restaurants, shops, glass ceilings, iron edifices suspended almost as if in mid-air – immerses the *flâneur* turned *voyeur* in an unstoppable torrent of newness. The surge either cleanses you or it carries you away. As a source of rebirth, it is intimately Parisian and profoundly aligned with the city as a fountain of youth. Paris is for the energetic and young at heart, nowhere more present than in the student-filled romanticized *rive gauche*.

The city provides its own frame of reference. Monuments, perfectly linear boulevards, mirrors and glass enlarging the cityscape everywhere is the architectural bricolage that makes Paris Paris. Modernity is germane to this place. It seeps in through the cracks of buildings, comes in the solidity of pavements, and even surrounds the small tables of the neighborhood café, where you are likely to consume the effervescent tonic of Paris. The walkability of the city's mythological topography creates a 'memory producing intoxication,' that in turn fosters the idea of Paris as the epitome of human progress and modernization.[48] The stamina with which Paris primacy endures cannot be reduced to anything but sheer power of representation. By virtue of dissemination, population, migration, and trade, many other cities could and would compete with Paris for this symbolic position, but the credence in Paris as being the cultural centre of the world remains surprisingly intact. Like few other cities, Paris in fact manages to continue to confer the sense of being urbane, of rubbing off an almost innate sense of what it means to be international on those who seek such consecration – an ideology disseminated in all wakes of life, from literature and language to fashion as well as in the omnipresence of French cuisine.[49] One of the strongest areas where this can be discerned is in epistemology and the continuous presence of French theory on the global academic scene, which can be constructed as a highly successful venture of this internationalization-universalization type.

The alleged universalism of Paris creates therefore two sorts of results; on the one hand, imaginary ones – continuously working to uphold the Parisian myth – and on the other hand, more corporeal ones, in the constant influx of authors and artists. Paris is therefore doubly universal: in the belief in its own universality and in the very real effects producing this belief.[50] The universal, which is French, is also the universal of 'high' culture, another important feature we will see reinforced in the French view on copyright, and one that will continue to differ from the Anglo-American one. To paraphrase Hugo: if the notion of literary property is a universal thing, the universal is international and as we know, the international is by default French. This is why the audience at the Congrès, after being courted, cajoled, and called upon as 'fellow citizens of the universal city' by Hugo,[51] readily accepts that at this particular time, at this specific place, there is nothing more international than being French, and nothing more universally desirable than the symbolic offerings of Paris. So persuasive was this imagery of cultural universalism that it even managed to make it seem attractive to be colonized by France.[52] To embrace Paris is by definition being in and of the world.

III

Thus far, we have considered Hugo's discourse primarily in view of his personal charisma and presence, his stubborn promotion of individualized universalism, and the absolutely vital position Paris occupies in the construction of this larger narrative. As suggestive as it might seem either to reduce his speech to a mere footnote in history or on the reverse end simply make too much out of it, at least one major aspect pertinent to intellectual property rights remains to be considered carefully in light of his oratory. For a more complete inquiry into the current dilemmas and conflicts facing intellectual property rights within globalized print culture in order to crystallize, we need to take into account a very specific dimension hitherto only hinted at. It concerns the arrival of a new agent: the international organization and its impact on the formalization of intellectual property as a question necessitating transnational control, supervision, and intervention.

Accentuating the spatial and the geopolitical should not dissuade us from recognizing the crucial impact of modernity on the institutions and practices of print. Nor should it lead us to believe that the spatial allows itself to be thought of as separate from the temporal. There is no arguing that vast geographical distances, people, and businesses were interconnected through the gradual supremacy of capitalism as early as the sixteenth century.[53] Countering all attempts to define globalization with comments to the effect that 'it has happened before' is perhaps therefore quite accurate, but represents nonetheless a cerebral cul-de-sac. This is because it falls remarkably short of enlightening us on what it is that strikes us as *new* about the occurrences and events placed under the microscope, and in what way it differs from whatever went on *before*. Globalization certainly did not become an issue on the economic and political calendar yesterday, and yet, its codependency with the institutions and technologies of the modern nation-state is irrefutable evidence in favour of a chronological classification that lies closer to our own time.

What are the reasons for judging Hugo's intervention an important temporal watershed? To some extent, the answer has already been given. First, it can be found in the insight that the world needs to be harnessed, that it even calls out for large-scale and strategic monitoring. Second, realizing the impact and consequences of being *international* predates and matches our present-day awareness of global relations. Closing this chapter by focusing on another ramification of Hugo's address – the consequences of what now stands forth as incipient cultural policy – is not intended to solve once and for all the ongoing dispute on where internationalism ended and globalization began. Rather, I would like to note the decisive importance of a particular novel addition – the international organization specializing in control and supervision of a specific field – to the general concerns of this book. It is essential to underscore that as we witness the formal arrival of international treaties and organizations with the express purpose of managing and creating sustainable frameworks for print culture and intellectual property in particular, these movements will fundamentally alter, structure, and partly redirect the flows established so far. The ordering of print culture into a new infrastructure will impact substantially on any future connection between culture and politics, and enters, as we shall see in chapter 5, a different stage post–Second World War. The point I am trying to make is that international legislation of intellectual property offers precisely such a distinctly modern institution, in turn reliant on a similarly modern logistics.

As personal as it is political, Hugo's plea is not only riding high on the individual stature of its speaker, but also summons the combined labours of a new collective. This chosen enclave thinks of itself partly in terms of distinct national qualities, and yet seeks to be created precisely on an international basis. Thinking and acting internationally is at the end of the nineteenth century becoming an economic, political, and cultural necessity. It would be impossible for the men present on that day in June 1878 to act on Hugo's appeal unless the means to do so indirectly and directly were available to them. Trade, education, culture, and politics are moving into transnational arenas where the coming struggles over intellectual property rights from now on will be played out.

©

From the second half of the nineteenth century and onwards, a veritable explosion in the setting up of international bodies, organizations, and treaties dedicated to the standardization and management of the world takes place. In respect to this expansion, Hugo's triple call for *universalism-internationalism-Paris* is heeded at least in two ways. As was the case with the Congrès itself, many of the international organizations established in this period stem directly from conferences taking place in the most universal of all cities, Paris. Second, French – patently obvious lingua franca of the European Union Hugo predicted – at least temporarily became just that: the preferred international language of these newfound alliances.

The speeding up in the flows of information, commodities, communication, travel, transnational business, and people fuels the arrival of vital infrastructural highways. It makes perfect sense that the first major international public unions, the International Telegraph Union (1865), soon followed by the Universal Postal Union (1874), are concerned with the intensification in international communications. Snowballing during the next decade, a myriad of regulatory bodies devoted to the management of international relations materialize. Their main area of expertise will differ, from the standardization measures undertaken by the International Bureau of Weights and Measures (1875) to the management of potential conflicts like the work of the International Labour Office (1901). Health, education, and human rights – the list of what now needs to and can be harmonized on an international scale goes on and on. Even that most elusive of life's ingredients – time – was standardized with the aid of the Greenwich meridian in 1884. More than thirty global intergovernmental organizations (IGOs) saw the light of day between 1864 and the First World War, where the close symmetry between the embryonic stages of these international organizations and the technological and industrial challenges of their respective age is incontrovertible.[54]

Visitors to the 1878 World Fair must have contemplated the corollary of the sharp increase in international mail services and the prospect of revolutionary innovations such as the telegraph. These novelties facilitated the exchange of ideas, they challenged the order of the nation-state in their capacity to overcome borders, and they stood as perfect technological paradigms of an ever-increasing world. Thus, industrial change and new technologies will push for legislative measures suitable to their needs and as expected, revisions to copyright treaties will attempt to respond to the requirements of evolving communication networks. New times will present new challenges. Technological breakthroughs exemplified by radio and later television elicited updated legislative reactions, as when the possibilities and problems of the first brought about the Universal Radiotelegraph Union in 1906. Closer to the concerns of our own time is the regulation of outer space leading up to the establishment of Intelsat in 1964. Faxes, cell phones, the Internet, every age has its own pet technological gadget and affixed decision-making structure. In the developing stages of the international public unions 'the issue was not the creation of a single authority to manage world affairs,' but rather – as Held et al. puts it – 'the establishment of regulatory regimes for, in principle, the predictable and orderly conduct of pressing transnational processes.'[55]

Let us for the sake of clarification and because of its intimate rapport with Victor Hugo and the issue of copyright look closer at some of the incentives behind the launch of the Association Littéraire et Artistique Internationale (ALAI), a direct result of the 1878 Congrès established on 28 June, only a few days following Hugo's opening speech.[56] Some form of international intellectual property rights is at the top of ALAI's agenda and the first number of the *Bulletin de l'Association Littéraire Internationale* reports in December 1878 that the work of the Congrès touched on questions of the 'highest possible order.'[57] Referring of course to the Congrès Littéraire International and Hugo's speech, ALAI identifies from its very inception the question of international copyright as one paramount to its future activities. Announcing in their constitutive remarks that Victor Hugo will be sought as Président D'Honneur, that the organization will be headquartered in Paris, and that its Comité Executif consists of forty-five members, fifteen French, and the rest 'étrangers,' each participating country naming two delegates, ALAI establishes its formal structure.[58]

Fully in accordance with his status as erudite sage and role model to the men who initiate the ALAI, a special commission gathers at Hugo's home on 5 January 1879 to present the work undertaken by them so far. No strain of the imagination is needed in order to picture the band of worshippers approaching their ailing idol with admiration, mindful of the fact that they rendezvous with history personified. Their account of this meeting is yet another testimony to the remarkable position Hugo occupied in his time. José da Silva Mendès Leal, ALAI's first president and ambassador of Portugal to Paris addresses Hugo as 'sublime master,' asks of him in the name of the organization to support its high goals, and implores him to shoulder the honorary title reserved for him from the outset.[59] Hugo accepts, assuring the men who have come to solicit his help that 'l'Association littéraire internationale will live.' Replying in a tone almost identical to his Congrès speech, Hugo cannot abstain from commenting on the uniqueness of authors, now even more passionately stressing a close to biological commonality: 'The race of authors, race rare, will lead; the people will follow. Universal peace will come from this immense spiritual brotherhood.'[60] Leaving the home of their preferred luminary, the small group appears triumphantly empowered with a profound sense of their own instrumental role in this glorious undertaking.

Hugo is the figurehead adorning ALAI's particular ship, but he is only one of many using personal authority and standing to promote international cooperation in a variety of forms. Count Serge Yulevich Witte, Pierre de Coubertin, Prince Albert – all were well connected in multiple public spheres; the political, economic, and cultural, and able to transfer private pet projects onto the international agenda because of it.[61] Their influence is important because – as Pascale Casanova has argued – they were powerful enough to set things in motion simply by being themselves. The budding collective still rotates around the individual and even if Hugo is the finest catch of them all, to augment the status of their organization even further the leaders of the ALAI add to their membership directory by recruiting other famous names to the honorary committee. The list of those approached to this end is impressive, including among others Emerson, Disraeli, Gladstone, Dostoyevski, and Tolstoy. The *Bulletin de l'Association Littéraire Internationale* regularly publishes replies from those being wooed and in a letter dated Paris, 7 July 1879, Ivan Tourgeniev accepts, offering a collection of his books and thanking the committee modestly for having thought of him in the first place.[62] A very different answer arrives in a letter dated ten days later, dispatched from Downing Street and Whitehall. Failing miserably to veil his annoyance, William Gladstone answers that his political and parliamentary duties force him to admit that he might not be able to give the ALAI the attention it merits. However, he ends his letter on a weary note, agreeing to fulfil whatever obligations the organization chooses to place before him.[63]

Ascertaining the moral support of the most consecrated writers around can perhaps be considered a glamorous side of ALAI's work. To mobilize public interest in the national literatures represented by its core members counts as a more down-to-earth activity. On 17 November 1879, a reading and presentation on the subject 'Camoëns et la littérature portugaise,' given by M. Santa-Anna Nery, vice-president of the organization is reported in the *Bulletin*.[64] This presentation was apparently the first in a whole series, and a year later a first advertisement announces lectures on contemporary literature each Monday, language classes in German on Wednesdays and on German literature on Fridays, all convening 8:30 p.m. at the premises on 51, rue Vivienne. Victor Hugo's name is prominently displayed at the top and the important information, 'Ladies allowed,' added in bold letters further down.[65] The ALAI was undoubtedly fully cognizant of the glory bestowed on them by their illustrious honorary president, but they did not shy away from using his name in advertisements furthering their cause whenever the opportunity arose. When the *Bulletin* acquires a logotype in 1882, showing two feather pens tied together holding a globe outlining Europe, North America, South America, and Africa, featuring prominently on both sides is – hardly surprisingly – the name of Victor Hugo.[66]

The burgeoning international organizations and their administrative structures emerge as constitutive features of modernity but are not ends in themselves. The high-level formalized contacts between nations also empower a new category of individuals, the professional civil servants. Rules and regulations are fine, but human beings need to interpret and carry out the conventions as well. Hence the growth of an 'expert system,' resulting from the increased specialization needed in modern society. In fact, the world is becoming so diversified and difficult to administer that specialists – in the sole business of managing and overseeing restricted fields of knowledge – are a logical outcome of the versatility of challenges confronting the international community. According to Anthony Giddens, experts are also inimical to modernity because they incarnate a new and abstract notion of trust; specialists 'know how' and they should essentially be relied upon to act in the best interest of others.[67] Civil servants and bureaucrats are professional labels denoting distinct functions in the emergence of this new political/cultural order. It is no coincidence that ALAI's officers are recruited from the diplomatic service or from the political scene. Authors, on the other hand, are consigned to a sphere of symbolic representation, essential to the cause but still distinct from the humdrum work of the expert.[68]

Rampant specialization and differentiation mean that the expert community continuously enlarges and that the potential fields of expertise also widen. One of the important spaces where these new experts can get together and meet with equals, is of course international conferences. Deciding to convene on an annual basis makes ALAI no different from any other organization coming into being at this time. London is settled on as the venue in 1879, Lisbon in 1880, Vienna in 1881, Rome in 1882, Amsterdam in 1883, and Madrid in 1884. The Lisbon conference in 1880 coincides nicely with the ninth Congrès International d'Archéologie et d'Antropologie, and in M. Mendès Leal's opening speech he emphasizes that 'all the sciences adjoin.'[69] Mendès Leal articulates a strong sense of being brother-in-arms with the archeologists and anthropologists present in Lisbon, of sharing a common cause, and yet at the same time he must underscore the absolute validity of their own distinctive area of interest. If not all men of science are interested in the same things, at least they must be enlightened enough to grasp that they share a symbiotic bond in the larger order of things – an order which they are very much themselves now in the process of creating.

Despite the implied and recurring idea of a worldwide camaraderie devoid of any kind of egotism – national or otherwise – the notion of national identity increasingly crops up alongside the international aspirations of ALAI's work. As one of the English delegates during the opening ceremony salutes the city hosting the fifth conference, Rome, he comes across sounding very much like Hugo: 'In the name of the fatherland of Shakespeare, I am happy to salute the fatherland of Dante.'[70] There is continual oscillation between on the one hand, affirming a fixed national identity – exemplified by the most canonized authors conceivable – and on the other, affirming the idea of literature as fundamentally international in nature.

Victor Hugo did not live to see his dream of literary property once and for all inserted on the international political and cultural agenda, but he must have been fairly sure of the impending success of his chosen enterprise. After the Lisbon conference in 1880, ALAI doubled their efforts to secure the successful construction of a multilateral copyright treaty, and to take advantage of what they perhaps felt were favourable winds, an extra conference is called for with the express purpose of serving as the base for a forthcoming 'Union de la Propriété littéraire,' in the same vein as the monetary and postal unions.[71]

In conjunction with increased lobbying on the part of the ALAI and others, an article by Numa Droz – minister of agriculture and commerce, member of the Conseil fédéral Suisse – is published in the May-June 1883 issue of the *Bulletin*. First printed in the Swiss *Bibliothèque universelle* and titled 'La Propriété intellectuelle,' it delineates among other things the reasons why Switzerland should become the central location for the administration of such an impending international convention. Concerned with intellectual property rights both in the artistic sphere but also as it related to industrial production, Droz concluded – perhaps prematurely and too optimistically – that 'an international convention on intellectual property offers much fewer difficulties than that of industrial property.'[72] Concentrated effort would nonetheless generate the desired results: the Berne Convention (signed by Belgium, France, Germany, Haiti, Italy, Liberia, Spain, Switzerland, Tunisia, and the UK) was finalized on 9 September 1886 and came into force on 5 December 1887.

Hugo had died two years previously – in June 1885. He staged a funeral worthy of his fame, masterminding to the very end the ultimate *hommage* to his own image. A hearse reserved for the poor carried the author to his final resting place in the Panthéon, a journey followed by two million people or more. A glorious way to go for someone who apparently tried to control his life down to the most minute detail. Priscilla Parkhurst Ferguson notes that the funeral was 'one of those rites of passage by which French literary culture celebrates itself and proclaims its existence to French society at large.'[73] Nonetheless, there is a certain irony in the fact that the man who so expertly promoted the universality of France and the brilliancy of Paris, and who set in motion the events leading up to the Berne Convention by his 1878 speech, could not intervene from the crypt to secure Paris as the future host of the treaties, conventions, administrative offices, and professional networks waiting around the corner. That honour would go to Switzerland, a country that became the site for the first multinational treaty on intellectual property rights and the future headquarters for an impressive number of international organizations in the years to come.

That the forward thrust of the matter had shifted from resting on the individual to the collective with Hugo's passing is much too theatrical a suggestion, and even if the rules and regulations of intellectual property rights did receive their first formalization in the shape of the Berne Convention, international intellectual property rights at the end of the nineteenth century is still only in its infancy. What Victor Hugo suggested in his speech was something more significant; he claimed universality for intellectual property rights and above all, for authorship. In late nineteenth-century internationalism, there is unquestionably a geographical reach of impressive proportions, and an accelerating interdependency between nation-states and other geopolitical entities, but these connections are essentially erected on a traditional centre-periphery model, molded on the colonial division of the world. It makes sense for Hugo to speak of universality from the vantage point of France and Paris simply because the value system perpetuated through these discursive markers have not yet been called into question. So deep-seated is the acceptance of their significance to the world that it allows him full rein to articulate what is seen as optimal in culture and society. Things that fall outside this frame, in particular distant places and experiences, partake in this universality not in their own right but as an appendage, as something possible to remould. Hugo's universality encompasses the margins simply because they are part of an international economic, political, social, and cultural organism whereby they cannot *avoid* being included but it still places them in the fringe. They are present, but not represented.[74] As intellectual property rights continue to evolve and be contested up until today, all the questions that were either directly addressed or implicit in Hugo's speech – power in respect to authorship, the role of the nation-state, international flows in communications and how it was to be met through international agreements and conventions, and the relationship between private and public interests – would face a number of challenges unforeseen by either Victor Hugo himself or the men who listened to him talk in Paris on 17 June 1878.

Chapter Two

INVENTING F. DAVID:
AUTHOR(ING) TRANSLATION

Victor Hugo's spectacular international success was to some extent made possible by readers for whom the French language did not constitute an insurmountable linguistic obstacle. And yet, in the long run it would owe even more to another feature by which literature travels: translation.

Spanning from vacuum-cleaner manuals to Nobel Prize winning poetry, translation is also one of the necessary components of the international conventions, recommendations, and agreements that govern its protection.[1] Despite its creative, financial, moral, and legal implications in the matrix of print culture, the question of how translation interacts with authorship in intellectual property rights has warranted scant attention, while authorship has been extensively theorized and, as I tried to show in the introduction, its status as a critical facet in the analysis of intellectual property rights is today largely taken for granted. Put in somewhat different terms, those who study translation seldom consider its legal repercussions, and those who analyse intellectual property rights on the basis of authorship, rarely consider the translator as author.[2] No doubt this is because the first tends to be considered a derivative of the second, without valid claims to either intent or originality, and thus to contend with the translator is in some sense to unwittingly destabilize the category of authorship necessary for the analysis of intellectual property rights.

There is no question that to the men of the ALAI, translation was a top priority. Upon their return to Paris following the 1880 Lisbon conference, the participating delegates share their accounts of the event at a meeting at the École Polytechnique, where the discussion swiftly turns to translations. A report delineating ALAI's policy on the matter by Louis Ulbach, president of the organization between 1885–8, gains considerable attention. In the proposed conclusion, translation is described as 'this sort of transfusion of a foreign blood into the veins of a nation' that 'should be made with care, knowledge, and honesty.'[3] Referred to in terms bordering on genetic determinism, translation was equated with an exchange of bodily fluids whereby national literatures and hence also qualities blend into the bloodstream of other countries by way of a biological, self-regulating apparatus. More a metaphorical than literal view, it was nonetheless articulated in the same emotionally charged tone that earmarked much of the discourse pertaining to intellectual property rights at that time. Behind this flamboyant rhetoric lurked more down-to-earth motives: since translation provided the key to any widespread textual diffusion of literary property, international intellectual property rights were clearly of little use to authors if they did not somehow address the legal side of linguistic conversion. Although a variety of solutions had already been set in place on the level of individual nation-states, translation proved that it was a major stimulus behind the search for international cooperation in the field of intellectual property rights at the end of the nineteenth century when it became the first right recognized in the Berne Convention.[4]

Not all members of the ALAI unreservedly approve of the report, and if my account in the previous chapter suggested a rosy picture of an international fraternity united in their acceptance of the innate superiority of French culture, nothing could be further from the truth. One participant even suggests that the report is coloured by that exclusionary frame of mind Germans always have noticed in the French, bluntly adding that he finds it too narrowly, if not altogether, focused on translations from a French viewpoint.[5] As if to lend support to his biting comment, George Conrad, despite his English-sounding name one of the German members of ALAI's Comité Executif, recapitulates a meeting with a Portuguese man in Lisbon. On being asked about his possible participation in the conference, he had answered Conrad: 'How would you have me take part in the work of the Congrès? At the end of the day, doesn't l'Association Littéraire Internationale work exclusively for the profit of French authors and playwrights, whose productions dominate the world market to the great detriment of other literatures?'[6]

©

Two conflicting sets of problems converge when translation is considered in the light of intellectual property rights, historically as well as in the present. The first concerns the ambivalent role of the translator and translations, which posits both in an inconsistent relationship to the author. Article 2(3) of the Berne Convention states: 'Translations ... shall be protected as original works without prejudice to the copyright in the original work,' a recognition potentially at odds with the ensuing Article 8, where the author is provided with the exclusive right to make and authorize translations. The legal subject designated proprietor of the intellectual property in question resides here in two camps, offering us (at least) two entities whose claims to the text may in effect be equally valid, yet possibly also in dissonance with one another.

The second larger consideration is structural. It connects translation and intellectual property rights with what we – for want of a better word – can call cultural imperialism. The main reason given by George Conrad's Portugese acquaintance as to why he cannot partake in the Lisbon conference is because he thinks its agenda is exclusionary, catering only to French interests, interests he sees as overshadowing those of other nations. What is being referred to is an underlying, basic manifestation of structural and spatial power inherent in intellectual property rights, namely its construction as an instrument of control primarily serving the purposes of those who, at a given historic moment, can be seen as exporters/producers of assets deemed intellectual property, and not the interests of the importers/consumers of the same assets. The pattern that evolves from this basic cartography logically places the translator/translation on the side of importers/users and not the other way around. From the very beginning of international intellectual property rights, being an exporter rather than an importer implies not only a discursive upper hand, but a competitive *trade-related advantage*. Translations are central in this construction because at the end of the nineteenth century – before the vast media and communications explosion that is to come – they facilitate international cultural flows.

Today, English has replaced French as the international language par excellence, and the Walt Disney Company is the most translated 'author' globally. Whereas pre-1989 statistics put Vladimir Illyich Lenin in first place with the current translations of Lenin's works estimated at 3000, United Nations Educational, Scientific, and Cultural Organization (UNESCO) also concludes that new ones are at a standstill.[7] Everywhere and nowhere at the same time, translation is an uncanny barometer of changing cultural flows. And yet, as Lawrence Venuti argues, its very omnipresence renders both the activity itself and the those who execute it 'invisible.'[8]

In the following, I would like to frame my arguments around the two

English-language translations of Peter Høeg's novel *Frøken Smillas fornemmelse for sne* (1992) (*Smilla's Sense of Snow* [1993] and *Miss Smilla's Feeling for Snow* [1993]), the first by Tiina Nunnally and the second by F. David.[9] An unlikely international bestseller, it qualified in 1997 as the most widely sold novel by a non-English-speaking author in the United States to date.[10] Twenty-four countries, from Brazil to South Korea, had at that time published the story of the angry, stubborn, Euclid-loving Smilla Qaavigaaq Jaspersen, and at least ten more had bought the rights to do so in the future.[11] *Smilla* anchors my discussion precisely because it operates so well on the two levels of subject and structure. First, the troubled question of textual ownership resonates in the account of two conflicting translations, and second, the Danish-Greenlandic colonial experience that was such an important part of the story suitably mirrors the material conditions the book encountered in its global circulation. Drawing on these two versions of *Smilla* should not be interpreted as a normative approach attempting to uncover which text is the most 'accurate' or 'faithful.' Excavating on a lexical level still tends to be a favoured approach when comparing different translations, but I will keep such dissection to a minimum. One of the reasons is that it has already been done in this particular case, and while interesting, the most revealing potential of translation studies lies, not in the infinitesimal, but in providing a larger canvas upon which cultural codes of intellectual property rights and authorship are reinscribed in new and unexpected ways.[12]

I

Numerous components mutually benefited *Smilla's* worldwide triumph, not least of all the swift sales of rights to the American publisher Farrar, Straus and Giroux, even before the book was published in Denmark.[13] Elisabeth Dyssegaard, a Danish editor working for the publisher initially pushed for Høeg's novel, saying: 'I had been following his career and reading him [*sic*] his work. I was quite excited about an earlier book but I was waiting for something to come along that would travel.'[14] Her comment suggests that for a Danish book to be able to succeed internationally, some sort of special je ne sais quoi is needed in order for it to warrant attention in the great onslaught of competing titles. As one of the most powerful textual vehicles shaping our image of a culture, translation is a process that relies on navigating and keeping the 'exotic' elements that come with a book such as *Smilla* as much as it does recasting the same 'foreign' into the expectations of another language and culture.[15] André Lefevere calls this intervention 'refraction,' an activity that is never ideologically neutral, but encoded with the desires and expectations always present in cultural transpositions.[16]

Asking whether or not a book will travel well remains squarely the prerogative of the dominant, since it is seldom asked of representatives of a major language to what extent they possess the appropriate characteristics facilitating a reversed trajectory. Stuart Hall describes this phenomenon when he speaks of the 'English eye' – an eye surveying everything and everyone, placing everybody, and yet being incapable of understanding or looking at itself.[17] Such an inspection is always rooted in the bias that comes with the unreflected belief in one's own universality, taking the success of journeys, such as the one from English to Danish, simply for granted.

What was it then that Dyssengaard saw in a first-person account of a thirty-seven-year-old Danish-Greenlandic leading lady who, in her quest for a boy's murderer, unravels a conspiracy of epic proportions taking her back to Greenland, an ice cave, and a meteor with prehistoric killer worms, that made her think this particular book has the prerequisite qualities? Smilla herself, nonconformist and with a huge chip on her shoulder, was perhaps one of the reasons. Half Greenlandic on her mother's side, half Danish on her father's, her home is the mental and physical exile provided by Copenhagen. Expelled from boarding school, never finishing her university education but with a track record of political activism on the far left in the *Inuit Ataqaatigiit*, her life is a mess, professionally and personally. Uprooted from a Greenland she never ceases to desire, her true passion is snow. Its texture, power, and predictability make it a faithful partner that can be trusted to be both consistent and reliable. Something of a recluse, she has never excelled at either making or keeping relationships. She has no colleagues to speak of, her brother committed suicide, she is alienated from her father, and her lover The Mechanic turns out to be a dubious character, easily swayed by the forces of evil. Her only successful emotional bond of any kind is with the boy Isaiah, and it can hardly be thought of in traditional adult-child terms. Although she provides him with basic physical needs – food, clothing, and care – when it comes to bedtime reading, she displays an eccentric preference for Euclid's *Elementa* or Lewis and Carrisa's *Detection and Classification of Ice*.

Greenland provided an original setting and background for this postcolonial critique, especially in combination with a cynical protagonist acting out an unconventional crime yarn, and *Smilla* raised high hopes. To begin with, the marketing and promotion lavished on the book by Farrar, Straus and Giroux was remarkable for a translation. In Canada, Doubleday Canada reportedly pursued the rights, largely based on the marketing strategies deployed by the U.S. publisher. Early expectations hovered around a modest print run of 5,000 to 7,000 copies at best, but once the translation reached all those involved in the economics of print culture (sales people, buyers at the chains, book club editors) it apparently soared to an initial 40,000. As a result, U.S. marketing included a massive advertising campaign to the amount of $50,000 and a Book-of-the-Month Club selection in September 1993.[18] When the paperback version hit the stands in August the following year, the promotional paraphernalia included not only 'Think Snow' baseball caps and snow pillows, but also a reader's companion with sample group discussion questions for booksellers. The mass-market version was at that time expected to hit the two-million-copy range, and the in print total was 770,000. *Publishers Weekly* noted that the paperback sales pattern copied that of the hardback version, with strong sales at the independents. Major advertising campaigns in *Vanity Fair, Entertainment Weekly*, and the *New York Times* were scheduled.[19] And apparently they paid off. The Danish daily *Politiken* reported with barely concealed national pride on 16 October 1993 that Høeg's American success was a fact, and that *Smilla* was headed for the number seven spot on the *New York Times* bestseller list.[20]

Critics were divided over the merits of the book, especially in Scandinavia, where major issues at stake were conflicting views on style/form and content, a critique against Høeg's writing as 'too perfect,' and an apparent anxiety in the face of bestsellerdom. From a postmodern perspective, the story was primarily considered a pastiche, toying with all the high and low elements previously compartmentalized and now fused by the author into a melting pot of irony so typical of postmodern lack of respect.[21] Some subscribed to this view and did so favourably, others judged *Smilla* a mere play with words, genres, and conventions – too superficial, too neat, too flirtatious. There were those who claimed that the ease with which the story was assembled showed signs of literary engineering. At worst it was a skilful fabrication born out of market considerations, offering the reader a smorgasbord of everything and nothing.[22] Others viewed Høeg as nothing but a professional con man, an author deliberately setting out to construct an American bestseller, something seen as definitive proof of the 'speculative' nature of the book.[23] Anglo-American reviews were more favourable, led by the *New Statesman and Society*, where John Williams spoke of 'an arctic tale worthy of Conrad,'[24] and *Time Magazine*, where it was voted Best Book of 1993. Stressing its generic angle, *Publishers Weekly* called it an 'absorbing suspense novel,'[25] Brad Leithauser coined the term 'techno-thriller' in the *New Republic*,[26] and 'brooding detective thriller' was John Skow's choice of phrase in *Time*.[27] However, not all critics were as easily won over. Jim McCue, who in the *Times Literary Supplement* accused the author of writing 'like an escapologist,' felt that 'Smilla is as resourceful in the face of extinction as James Bond, and this story too has implausible, entertaining shifts – of gear, tone, direction, genre – whenever a premature ending has to be avoided.'[28] Even so, most took to Smilla herself. A new kind of female protagonist had arrived; quirky, angry, yet vulnerable and still not quite housebroken, she was even compared to a Danish Pascal.[29]

Peter Høeg's own observation that 'Miss Smilla is every bit as tropical as she is polar,' is equally important to consider when trying to understand the extraordinary fate of the novel.[30] In making a case for his heroine as a *condition* rather than simply as that of a straightforward fictitious character, Høeg suggests a universality turned upside down, voiced from the vantage point of difference. The advent of a common denominator linking hot and cold, allows the author to hint at the possibility of a *postcolonial universality*.[31] Connecting ice and heat bears witness to the way in which Smilla's story offers an experience now seen as 'universal' precisely by virtue of its particularity. The exotic locale, the cold, and the ice, may be important, but when it was paired with the ironic style and wit of a postcolonial outsider Dyssegaard knew she had a best-seller: a novel behind which superficial geographical nodes masked more general concerns that came with globalization.

Switching between irony, sadness, and biting postcolonial critique with ease, Smilla's 'dustbin' (147) identity struck a cord with readers who perhaps recognized the constant negotiation of 'otherness,' its function of incorporation and negotiation. A part of her identity is transformed as her proficiency in Greenlandic slowly withers into oblivion, this while she stacks up her encyclopedic knowledge of luxury brand names. As if to confirm her own claim that 'it's always easier to explain away things if you're nicely dressed' (69), Smilla likes Burberry's, packs Louis Vuitton bags, and wears custom-made trousers made from kidskin, fluctuating wildly between Smilla 'Greenlander *de luxe*' (120) and 'Smilla the fake Greenlander'(155). The simultaneous strength and weakness of this hybrid, transformative identity is precisely its incorporated dichotomies, its internalized polarities. Smilla is colonized and colonizer in the same body. As half Greenlandic, half Danish by birth, she is Greenland and Denmark at the same time, margins and centre in one body; oscillating between two geographical points and between two epistemological ones.

II

The novel is in three parts: *The City* (Byen) precedes *The Sea* (Havet), and the novel ends with *The Ice* (Isen). Although these three places mark out a very real journey from Copenhagen to Greenland, they are also indicative of different moods, tempos, and concerns. Approaching Greenland and the truth about what happened to her young friend, Smilla's movements become more restricted in *The Sea*, where she finds herself confined to the perimetres of the icebreaker, *Kronos*. Seeking vengeance for a child that could be a mirror image of herself – Isaiah is killed at the same age as Smilla was when she was brought to Denmark by her father and where she encountered a different sort of death – she explores the ship and its menacing crew with a screwdriver as her only defence. 'Wounded children killing wounded children, wounded children avenging wounded children,' Mary Kay Norseng succinctly comments, 'is the underlying *modus operandi* of *Frøken Smillas fornemmelse for sne*.'[32] The *Kronos* strips Smilla of her need for style and fashion, and the well-dressed Copenhagen persona quickly withers away. This segment has her body no longer dressed to kill, but rather dressed to be killed, as she is constantly attacked, beaten, and threatened.

As Paul Gilroy notes in *The Black Atlantic: Modernity and Double Consciousness* (1993), the ship is a useful metaphor for the relationship between the empire and the colonies, wherever they may be located. In this respect, even the North Sea comes with its own colonial problematics. Despite the ever-presence of Greenland in Copenhagen and Copenhagen in Nuuk, the condition that Smilla seems to be analogous to, even conjoined with, is that of the *Kronos*. It was from this in-between, the no man's land at sea predicated on the necessary correspondences and dependencies between Greenland and Denmark, or between the British Empire and India, or any other such relationship that involves those submitted to colonialization and those implementing its power, that some saw as the book's ultimate strength. In the Swedish daily *Dagens Nyheter*, Sara Danius argued that those who liked the book but were content to underscore its allegorical potential as well as those who criticized *Smilla* outright had failed to recognize the most important feature of the book – its contemporaneous quality. *Smilla's* generic identity as a crime story is essential, but resting there only means skimming the surface. According to Danius, *Smilla* is first and foremost a text about the contemporary conditions of postmodern uncertainty and postcolonial ambivalence, and only second a literary pastiche.[33]

Thus, the sorry bunch of half-petty criminals, mad scientists, and corrupt physicians bound for the Gela Alta ice tells a modern-day parable of travels that historically went in very different directions. We should hardly be surprised that Smilla in her mind's eye compares her own journey on-board the *Kronos* to other ominous transits: 'Isn't this an example of history repeating itself? Hasn't Europe always tried to empty out its sewers into the colonies? Isn't the *Kronos* once more the convicts on their way to Australia, the Foreign Legion on its way to Korea?' (279).

©

If the *Kronos* returned Smilla to Greenland in the text, then the equivalent vessel that contributed to the success of the book on a larger scale was its translation. John North visualized the hurdles facing *Smilla* when he wrote in his *Toronto Star* review: 'What are the odds of a translated novel by a relatively obscure Danish author and featuring a part-Inuit female scientist/detective living in Copenhagen succeeding in the crowded North American book market?'[34] Overcoming the barriers meant first of all speaking in a language other than either her mother tongue or that of her adopted Danish. Later, when the novel was successful enough to motivate the transfer from paper to celluloid, international, well-known actors were considered necessary for a major motion picture with a budget of $35 million and so was the choice of language: English.[35]

Despite the scale and ambition of Bille August's 1997 film, which included Julia Ormond as Smilla, Gabriel Byrne as The Mechanic, and Richard Harris as evil Hviid, critics this time around proved merciless. Brian D. Johnson wrote that *Smilla's Sense of Snow* is 'a profoundly unintelligent movie, a pedestrian thriller with a congested plot that creaks to its climax with the pacing of pack ice,' and Lee Bacchus was even more outspoken when he described the result as 'La Femme Nikita Meets the X-Files.'[36] Reports from Greenland were much more positive. When the movie premiered at Nuuk's very first cinema in 1997, more than 3,500 tickets had been sold in advance, an impressive number considering the size of the population. Spontaneous applause was noted as the first icebergs came floating and as Julia Ormond started talking with a Greenlandic accent.[37]

Returning to the time of the U.S. hardback publication in 1993, Tiina Nunnally, a respected translator whose credits include the three-volume translation of Sigrid Undset's *Kristin Lavransdotter*, for which she received the PEN/Book-of-the-Month Club Translation Prize in 2001, was asked to undertake the translation. Entitled *Smilla's Sense of Snow*, Nunnally's work received numerous accolades. 'Nunnally has outdone herself,' wrote Brad Leithauser in his *New Republic* review, underscoring that this book was no fluke, but rather the crowning achievement of an already impressive career, stressing that the book 'must have been ferociously difficult to translate, not only for its length and wealth of technical detail but for its diverse subtlety.'[38] Robert Nathan seconded his opinion in the *New York Times Book Review*, calling her work 'engaging.'[39] Nunnally won the Lewis Galantière translation prize from the American Translators Association in 1994 for *Smilla*, and she continues to be favourably noticed in reviews of the Scandinavian literature she translates.[40]

Yet, when I was trying to locate the book and, pressed for time, had to rely on the first version I could find – a British paperback version from 1996 entitled *Miss*[41] *Smilla's* <u>*Feeling for*</u> *Snow* and not *Smilla's* <u>*Sense of Snow*</u> – Nunnally's translation was nowhere to be found. Instead, the cryptic F. David was listed as the book's translator. Not until Thom Satterlee's article, 'A Case for "Smilla,"' appeared in *Translation Review*, did the reasons for the two versions become clear. Knowing Danish, Satterlee read the Tiina Nunnally and the F. David versions alongside the Danish original, and found that they were remarkably alike. Perplexed enough to pose as 'the Colombo of the publishing world,'[42] Satterlee contacted both publishers asking for further clarifications and the identity of F. David. Only Guido Waldman from Harvill Press replied, and did so in the following way:

Farrar, Straus and Giroux commissioned an English translation by Tiina Nunnally. The author went over it with his Danish publishers, both of them highly proficient in English usage, and made a number of sugges-tions on it. Some of these the translator accepted, some she rejected. The American publishers chose to go with their translator's version, while

Harvill [the British publisher], working more closely with the author and his Danish publisher, chose to accept the text as it was approved by them. The translator therefore repudiated the version to be published by Harvill and asked for her name to be removed from it. Therefore the Harvill edition has gone out with a pseudonymous translator, F. David.[43]

As downplayed and discreetly formulated as it is, Guido Waldman's comment cannot hide the apparent: a major rift must have taken place, a conflict that sets in motion two different strategies by author and translator. Objecting to Nunnally's translation, Peter Høeg chose to collaborate with his editor in order to mould the book into a different linguistic form, a teamwork I have referred to elsewhere as 'transediting.' Combining translation with editing, 'transediting' indicates instances when an editor – with or without the participation of author or translator – rewrites a text for the purpose of achieving a more fluent or, in his/her eyes a more suitable translation. Høeg and his editor formed such an alliance, adding the latter into *Smilla's* brew of authors. Generally, major textual interventions involving editing or translation, such as deleting passages or inserting new text, are considered less acceptable in 'high' literature than in popular literature. The second category tends to be constructed as both 'author-less' and 'text-less' in some sense, which in mass-market publishing – such as the enormous amount of translations that make Harlequin Enterprises' romances truly global literature – usually means that both author and translator are subsumed under the work-for-hire principle. Global mass-market publishing of this kind instead indicates a reversal of roles whereby the translator – who needs to rework the text in order to accommodate it to the local market – may in fact be given much broader leeway in terms of creativity, and it is instead the author who finds herself/himself subordinated to the demands of the 'importing' market.[44]

Authors who take an active part in the translations of their own texts are not altogether uncommon. Nobel Prize laureate Rabindranath Tagore's own translations of his Bengali poetry into an English that would conform to expectations has been well documented,[45] as has Milan Kundera's struggles with the English-language translations of *The Joke*. In his note to the fifth – and last, according to him – English-language translation of *The Joke*, Kundera retells his experiences with previous, unsatisfactory versions, and describes his own work with his editor on the now definitive translation in a way that substantiates the collaborative nature of the undertaking.[46] As Alison Stanger notes, both the French and English texts that Kundera promotes as definitive reworkings/translations, share a number of deletions from the original Czech version, making her question just how final and complete we should consider such 'definitive' versions.[47] When Harriet Beecher Stowe went to court in *Stowe v. Thomas* to fight a translation, she was concerned, not only with the moral or abstract right to her own literary property, but with protecting the market for the translation she *had* authorized.[48]

Although she was paid by the word and received no royalty for her translation,[49] Tiina Nunnally's decision to back away from the U.K. *Smilla* published by Harvill Press is a radical and dramatic choice. Nunnally is asserting authorship by removing her name from the version she no longer considers hers, becoming visible by choosing total invisibility. In the Farrar, Straus and Giroux edition, the copyright is attributed to the U.S. publisher, but Farrar, Straus and Giroux and Harvill Press hold the British version jointly. This conflict pushes to the fore the previously mentioned tension in intellectual property rights which posits the translator as both an infringer *and* an author of a derivative work, protectable in its own right. Sam Ricketson explains: 'While the person making a derivative work may be an infringer of the rights in another work, he has altered the form of that work in such a way for him to be regarded just as much an author as the author of the primary work.'[50] It would seem then, that as far as translations are concerned, there are two kinds of authors recognized in the Berne Convention, and that the balancing act between them is sometimes dislodged to the extent that extraordinary consequences ensue.

Considering this dramatic turn of events in the translation of *Smilla*, what is the outcome of Satterlee's reading? Locating all those differences that tend to emerge the moment you scrutinize and compare a translated text word for word with its original, he tries to assess which text feels the most 'English,' or the most truthful to the Danish language, weighs one option against another, and returns in intervals to the standard question in any undertaking of this kind: is the book best served by fidelity or betrayal? At the end Satterlee sides with Tiina Nunnally, concluding that Høeg's efforts at having the translation stay as close to the original Danish as possible in fact work in just the opposite way: 'By offering British readers a less readable version of his novel, Peter Høeg betrays his own work.'[51] Siding with the U.K. version, Kirsten Malmkjær takes the opposite stance and argues that the F. David version gives a clearer picture of the book and that the American

translation fails to do complete justice to the original. In his correspondence with Malmkjaer, Guido Waldman provides this time a somewhat
different chronology of the events than in his letter to Satterlee, stating
that the changes to the Harvill Press edition were undertaken by the
British publisher and then agreed to by the author and his Danish
editors.[52] Finally, while both Satterlee's and Malmkjær's readings provide valuable clues to how texts are localized, they largely limit themselves to the interpretation of linguistic, rather than cultural choices.

Whether or not the appreciation of the novel will differ or if the
pleasure of reading it will somehow be diminished depending on which
version you read is, of course impossible to uncover, but the fact that
there existed two translations of the book did attract the attention of the
readers who discussed *Smilla* online in the so-called Book Group List in
1997.[53] Although their discussion did not officially start until 1 May and
continued for two weeks, the earliest posting in regard to *Smilla* sur-
faces as early as 8 January. In this, one of the readers informs the others
that there is more than one translator of the novel into English, and
continues: 'If I recall correctly ... which one you read does make a
difference.'[54] Immediately there is a follow-up question sent out, asking
if she recalls which translator was the better.[55] To this she replies: 'My
recollection ... is that some thought the translator of *Miss Smilla's
Feeling for Snow* was closer to the Danish as opposed to whomever
translated *Smilla's Sense of Snow* (the version I read – which I really
liked).'[56]

Translations are generally thought to be superior when they seamlessly
bridge source- and target-language. This particular reader does raise
the issue, saying that, although she believes *Miss Smilla's Feeling for
Snow* (approved by Høeg but repudiated by Nunnally) was closer to
the Danish, she really liked *Smilla's Sense of Snow* (Nunnally's translation), the version she read. Yet her posting makes it clear that she has no
idea that F. David is an invention and that Tiina Nunnally withdrew her
name from the British version, since she speaks of 'the translator' in the
first case and 'whomever' in the second. Inclined to consider the U.K.
version executed by a professional and the translation important enough
to reflect on it as a crucial part of her reading experience, in both cases
the translator is unknown to her, cancelled out, without name and yet
somehow still of critical importance.

During the ensuing two weeks much of the discussion continues
to have this preoccupation with translation at heart. In no part of
the discussion log, however, is there any mention of F. David's non-

existence. Comments such as 'It had great potential but maybe it would have been better in Danish' suggests that translation is a handy scapegoat when a foreign book offers its reader resistance.[58] Another participant is having so much trouble that she completely loses track of the original language, saying 'I kept thinking that maybe something was lost in the translation of the book from Dutch to English.'[59] Others concur, but then there is a crisp message consisting of one word only that same day from another participant who tries to set the record straight by coldly asking, 'Danish?'[60]

Sometimes used as a scapegoat, translation can also take on a different function. In one of the reviews published at the amazon.com web page, *Smilla* receives five stars out of five: 'This is one of our finest thrillers for lots of reasons: the plot and characters of the story are very well characterized, there are lots of clever twists, *and it is written by an author from far away from USA and England*' (my emphasis). This reader, allegedly from Brazil, expresses a kind of deep-seated satisfaction with the success achieved by a minor-language bestseller, clearly prompted to give such a favourable review at least in part *because* Høeg does not write in English.[61] Taken together, these comments suggest that translation operates in a kind of double mode; its amorphous nature and invisible 'author' allows it to be filled with whatever meaning the reader requires at the time of her/his reading. On the one hand, translation can be seen as a nuisance, hindering a good read because a book needs to be accessed in its original language in order to capture its most essential elements of style. On the other hand, a successful minor-language translation can be construed as close to a subversive act, to which all sorts of high hopes and promises are attached. *Smilla* proved the impossible: a Danish book could conquer obstacles raised by the Anglo-American book market.

The fact that there had been a certain controversy surrounding the translation was enough for me to begin to look closer at the various versions. Locating the British edition but still having difficulties finding the American, I turned to the Swedish translation, and above all the Danish original. My own project was somewhat different from Satterlee's and Malmkjær's. In juxtaposing larger chunks of text, bits and pieces I felt could not be reduced to single words but that stood out as segments particularly persistent in the context of postcolonialism and globalization, I was searching rather for key moments in the text and their transformation in translation. Moving through *Smilla* I noticed something that neither Satterlee nor Malmkjær, despite their detailed readings, apparently had not seen. In the part where Smilla stands on the *Kronos*, thinking about those other convoys, the British version was incomplete. In the Danish original – and in the Swedish translation I already had in my home – the sentence does not end with the Foreign Legion being en route to Korea, but actually with a reflection on 'engelska commandosoldater på vej til Indonesien?' (English commandos on their way to Indonesia?).[62]

If the English commandos are deleted from the British *Smilla* – authorized by Høeg – but certainly remain in the original, in the Swedish translation, and in a few other translations I have consulted since,[63] the pressing question was what the American edition would reveal. Finally getting my hands on the book, and looking up the by now so familiar passage, I read that this time, Smilla thinks to herself: 'Hasn't Europe always tried to empty out its sewers in the colonies? Isn't the Kronos a repeat of the prisoners on their way to Australia, the foreign legion off to Korea, and *British commandos going to Indonesia?' (Smilla's Sense of Snow*, 319; my emphasis).

III

When *Smilla* undertakes her international journey, she does so in a very specific linguistic and cultural setting. According to UNESCO, almost 50 per cent of all translations are made from English into various languages. But only 6 per cent of all translations are into English.[64] A mere 2.96 per cent of the books published in the U.S. in 1990 were translations; in Britain the number was 2.4 per cent that same year.[65] In 1994, 1,418 of the 51,863 books published in the U.S., or 2.74 per cent, were translations.[66] Between 1968–92, only 2 per cent of the books on *Publisher's Weekly* annual list of bestsellers came from non-English-language authors.[67] In Sweden on the other hand, the number of translations falls somewhere around 50 per cent annually.[68] A comparison of book translations in so-called SIACS (States in Advanced Capitalist Societies), France, Germany, Japan, the Netherlands, Spain, Sweden, UK, and the United States between 1983–5, substantiates these findings. English is the language from which most translations occur, a tendency of domination additionally corroborated by the reciprocally minimal ratio of translations going the other way. TV programming presents a similar picture, where the level of imported programming on the major American television networks hovered between 1 and 2 per cent in 1973–83.[69] Although we see tendencies that the number of web sites in English on the Internet decreased from 80 per cent at the end of 1995 to about 57 per cent in August 1999, the Internet still largely communicates in English.[70]

If we look for statistics in express terms of export/import, our options are severely limited. *The UNESCO Statistical Yearbook*, one of the few sources available anywhere as far as information on the global production of books is concerned, is a notoriously dicey instrument.[71] Based on the 1999 edition, most countries have a negative trade balance when it comes to import/export of print culture, and if we should accept these numbers at their face value, we can basically conclude that the entire world engages in the importation of what the U.K. and the U.S. exports. There are compelling reasons why our understanding of these statistics must be more nuanced. We can almost certainly discern tendencies of exclusion, whereby entire continents such as Africa, almost to a fault, display negative trade balances over time, whereas the U.S. and the U.K. consistently display positive trade balances.[72] In addition, the merits and disadvantages of being an 'importer' as opposed to being an 'exporter' suggest far too sweeping generalizations on the part of both categories. The idea that cultural trajectories have one direction only can be refuted by the strong presence of local and regional cultural flows that cut across sweeping geopolitical assumptions of sender and receiver.[73]

When we frame this situation in the light of *Smilla's* particular travels, two main points should be made. The first would seem to suggest that at any given time in the conflict between author and translator, the author prevails. However, nothing demonstrates as clearly as translation the immense changes, refractions, alterations, and new identities that texts take when they are transported into new cultural contexts. So what if the author has the final legal say-so? The text is still free to do what it wants, just as much as we are free to use it in the way we see fit. With this in mind, does it matter if *Smilla* is translated with or without British commandos? And what is the role of the author and/or the publisher in such a situation? Did Høeg deliberately lose the British commandos because he thought that sales would suffer if they were left in? Why not then get rid of the Foreign Legion in the French version? And what relevance, if any, has the replacement of the 'engelske' in the original Danish text with 'British' in the American edition?

Lew Gloin, reporting on *Smilla* for the Associated Press, noted that the translation encouraged 'publishers in nine other countries to jump on the bandwagon for a Danish novel they couldn't read in the original.'[74] I would argue that the most profound question that needs to be raised by the disappearance of the British commandos is this: if English has become a sort of 'clearing-house' language and the British F. David translation is the gate through which subsequent translations into other languages pass, then the British commandos *do not exist* in those translations. Even if much indicates that Nunnally's translation was the one from which *Smilla* made her passage into other international markets (and I have based my argument on the disappearance of five words), we are still faced with the fact that the Danish original – where there are commandos – by now has lost its importance in the wider circulation of the text. I am not suggesting that Danish needs to be widely mastered, just this: *any* language running the risk of becoming, or already being established as the vernacular of the world, will enable *and* disable interpretation at the same time. This is not only an issue of linguistic competence, it is a question of perspective and epistemology and as relevant for translation as it is for the understanding of the implicit perspective that must follow when all or nearly all scholarly work – all *visible* scholarly work, that is – must take place in English. We should not make too much of this, but we should understand that the dominant position of the English language takes on its most crucial immediacy when considered in relationship to the so-called cultural industries, and the knowledge-based economy as a whole.

While the global economy thrives on increasingly complex flows that no longer can be outlined in a straightforward connection between language and nation-state, and several of the most powerful TNMCs today are non-U.S. based and owned, they are still building their empires on the presence of the English language – in research, in entertainment, in literature. If all we needed in order to prove linguistic power were numbers, then Chinese would do just fine. As it is, English is the vernacular of the world because power is assigned in the interstices between linguistic supremacy *and* control of the industries that capitalize on content, information, knowledge, or other assets of intellectual property *in that language.*

©

Let us in conclusion return to the ALAI and their position on translation, a contentious enough issue to solicit profound disagreement within the ranks of the organization. As we saw, reactions to the way in which translation was presented in the report following the 1880 Lisbon

Conference expressed serious concerns for the hegemonic position of France and the French language, connecting them to cultural imperialism of the highest order. It is clear from Victor Hugo's speech and the claims the French language could make in the domain of symbolic representation at that time, that France wanted translation inserted in the Convention because it was considered an indelible asset in the wider dissemination of their own intellectual property – the universal literature of Hugo, Sand, Balzac – and thus also in the larger project of exporting French culture.

During the 1884 and 1885 Diplomatic Conferences in Berne, France sought therefore to subsume translations under the right to reproduction, whereas the Scandinavian countries resisted such a move, arguing that their relative isolation made them depend substantially on translations.[75] If further circumscribed, domestic education, reading, and wider access to knowledge would be seriously impeded and these countries would find themselves at a distinct disadvantage at a time when the new infrastructures of communication and information were laid out. Not until the Berlin Revision Conference in 1908 did translation rights become completely assimilated under reproduction rights and former opponents, notably the Scandinavians, relented.[76]

The Scandinavian countries relied on a discursive weaponry almost identical to the one that newly decolonized nations would launch during the tumultuous Stockholm Revision Conference in 1967, where they argued that the straightjacket imposed on them by the intellectual property laws of their former colonizers effectively delayed their participation in the international community. After the 1960s provided the temporal backdrop for a wave of new technology and communication networks to emerge, developing nations asked for special provisions in the Berne Convention so that they could have any chance to achieve equal terms with developed countries in the face of these challenges.

Even the United States perceived itself as a developing nation for a long period of time. Widespread piracy of British books was legitimized by the special demands of a country that had cast off its colonial shackles comparatively recently. No doubt, this position contributed to the reluctance of the United States to adhere to international conventions, and left the country a bystander to the Berne Convention until 1986. The complex and pivotal role of the United States in respect to the development of international intellectual property rights will be explored in detail in chapter 4.

What this chapter demonstrates is that the importance placed on intellectual property rights is related to (contingent) forms of market dominance and the discursive (also contingent) right to name the symbolic and material resources classified as such. M. Friedmann argued that the French were in a unique position to do this in 1880; today it is articulated in English and from the strong U.S. position in intellectual property rights. Both draw their relative strength in different historical eras based on their position as exporters/producers. If we rethink this in terms of one of the basic dichotomies in intellectual property rights – between the French emphasis on the author and the Anglo-American emphasis on the market – then we can see that both rely on colonial prowess to organize the world according to an economic, political, and cultural infrastructure that serves its interests. Pierre Bourdieu brilliantly describes the relationship between France and the United States as 'a confrontation between two imperialisms of the universal.'[77] To Bourdieu, France and the United States are similar in the sense that they have managed to use specific forms of symbolic capital in the service of specific forms of imperialism, something we can see in respect to intellectual property rights.

As this power balance has shifted during the last century, France has come to reinforce what could be described as a position based on 'high' culture, one which includes protectionism in the shape of an isolationist linguistic policy and the active promotion of cultural quotas, in many cases to counter what is being perceived as a mass-market assault by the U.S. cultural industries.[78] The United States on the other hand, blissfully amnesiac when it comes to its previous role as both a pirate nation and a developing nation in intellectual property, aggressively pursues a very distinct intellectual property rights policy defined in terms of global free trade, all while constructing its own market protectionism on the domestic front by, among other things, the marginalization of translations.

Translation is a profoundly destabilizing activity, not only because it can make us question who a text's owner really is, but also because it was and is a major incentive behind the ordering of intellectual property rights into an export/import matrix in which authorship and colonialism interacts textually as well as materially. As French supremacy in this particular form of cultural imperialism declines, the American, and in particular, the English-language based, ascends. Both, however, have put the intrinsic belief in the universality of their positions to good use in respect to intellectual property rights, and in that project, translation was and is a pivotal key.

Chapter Three

THE DEATH OF THE AUTHOR
AND THE KILLING OF BOOKS:
ASSAULT BY MACHINE

When it comes to intellectual property rights and copyright especially, the ability to reproduce, duplicate, and, of course, copy is a given, but far from uncontroversial, feature. Even translation, as we saw in the previous chapter, occupies the imagery of the derivative, a copy made from an original.[1] As something to be revered and later, feared, the act of copying is appropriately enough also part of the history of literature. Thus, material and immaterial changes go hand in hand: the meticulous transcription by hand taking place in convents and monasteries during the Middle Ages morphed into the mass production of the printing press. The praise once bestowed for centuries on those who were able to recast old traditions and legends into new forms, became overshadowed by a romantic author and a modernist aesthetic where search for innovation and novelty took centre stage and any hint of imitation was to be abhorred. Drawing on the complexities of copying, my primary goal in this chapter is to consider what happens to authorship and intellectual property rights as they *meet the machine*. The Internet is perhaps the most current example of how reproduction of content is facilitated on an unprecedented scale by technology. At the same time, intellectual property regimes put in place years before anyone could even consider the possibility of such a global network lag behind. Consequently, a number of ever-increasing volumes produced within widely disparate academic disciplines have addressed the possible fate of the book and the text, as well as the ramifications posed by the World Wide Web in respect to free speech, access to information, and ownership.[2] However, for reasons of obvious shortsightedness, it remains difficult to ascertain to what extent these predictions of dystopia or utopia are realistic. Because of this, and because the fundamental importance of the technological impact in respect to intellectual property still remains to be considered, I have chosen to turn my attention to a technological revolution every bit as significant for intellectual property rights as the Internet, albeit one that offers the advantage of historic hindsight: the copier. Taken for granted in schools, offices, and even homes, we seldom consider that the photocopier once caused the same anxieties to surface in respect to print culture as the Internet gives rise to today. Controversial enough to be banned in the Soviet Union until 1989, the most problematic aspect of what is now a cheap and readily accessible piece of office equipment is perhaps its capacity to be a 'killer of books' – as the small ad on the back of French publisher La Decouverte's books suggests in the form of the portentous warning: '*DANGER. Le Photocopillage tue le livre.*' The Internet may be the most advanced device of reproduction the world has seen to date, but it was the copier that brought both author and text into the Information Age.

I

Perhaps it was to be expected that the man who invented the technology that later materialized as the copier, did so because of inconveniences he encountered as a patent attorney. Chester F. Carlson, whose grandparents emigrated from Sweden, was born in Seattle on 8 February 1906.[3] Both parents were sickly and the family moved around until they finally settled for a warmer climate in California. Ellen Carlson died of tuberculosis in 1923, leaving seventeen-year-old Chester to care for his father. While he managed to earn a Bachelor of Science degree in physics from the California Institute of Technology in 1930, this also landed him in debt during the Depression. Desperately trying to find work he sent out eighty-two job applications, none of which resulted in an offer. Carlson finally found employment at the laboratory of the Bell Telephone Company in New York, but was laid off as the Depression worsened. He went on to secure a position at the patents department of the electronics firm P.R. Mallory, attending night school at the New York Law School between 1936 and 1939 to become a patent attorney. When he ended up as head of the company's patent office, his dealings with the many documents and drawings needed for patent applications made him realize that there was always a shortage of copies. The process of making duplicates was laborious; either they were photographed, or they had to be copied individually and then proofread carefully.

The need for facsimiles of correspondence and office documents was not recent; it had been filled by hand by copy clerks, copiers, or scribes until the mid-nineteenth century. Until the 1870s there were basically only two options available if you wanted to make numerous copies: either use the services of a commercial printer, or buy a small printing press. Nonetheless, there were several attempts to invent useful copying devices. James Watt patented a copying press in 1780, which could, either by roller or in a screw-down version, allow for reproduction of writing on a damp sheet of thin but durable tissue paper that was placed under pressure. Thomas Jefferson was known to have liked Watt's press and used it during his stay in Paris, but he favoured the polygraph. Today more associated with the lie-detector tests seen in movies, the polygraph was a sort of multi-pen apparatus, in which the writer would use one pen as a master pen, and then by a set of mechanical arms another pen would simultaneously copy the writing. Jefferson relied on it for many years but it was never successfully marketed and sold in the United States.[4] The stylograph with carbonated paper followed, rendering, as Jefferson wrote, a room 'pestiferous' with its smell.[5] Because it was both messy and unreliable, use of carbon paper did not really advance until the typewriter became a fixture in offices and carbon paper came coated on one side only. Stencil duplicating machines were launched towards the end of the nineteenth century; Gestetner introduced the first self-inking stencil duplicating press in 1890; rotary duplicators first came on the market in 1898.[6] Nevertheless, the question of how to make single copies that would be of use to corporations as well as individuals was still not solved by the 1930s.

Trying to come up with a solution to his copying problems, Chester Carlson began in 1935 to spend time at the New York Public Library, poring over scientific articles. He turned his attention to the field of photoconductivity, setting up his laboratory in the kitchen of his Jackson Heights, Queens, apartment. A number of failed experiments later, his wife suggested that he instead use an empty room in the back of a beauty parlour owned by his mother-in-law in Astoria, Queens. Together with an unemployed refugee physicist from Germany named Otto Kornei, Carlson managed in 1938 to successfully complete an experiment in what he would call 'electrophotography.' First he wrote the now famous date and address '10–22–38 ASTORIA' in ink on a glass slide; then a metal plate coated with sulfur was rubbed with a cloth to give it an electrical charge. He positioned the slide against the plate, placed both under a powerful lamp for a few seconds, removed the slide, and sprinkled powder on the plate. His inscription appeared. To finish off the experiment, waxed paper was pressed against the plate, and the image transferred to paper.[7] While the process would require many more years of additional refinement before it could be put to commercial use, the technique he perfected that day basically remains the same today in modern photocopying.

Between 1939 and 1944, more than twenty of the largest U.S. companies turned Carlson down when he approached them with his invention, including IBM, Kodak, General Electric, and RCA. Continuing to work for P.R. Mallory, Carlson finally succeeded in soliciting the interest of one investor: the Battelle Memorial Institute, a non-profit organization funding technological research. In 1944 Battelle agreed to help him develop his invention by extending $3,000 for research and the rights to 75 per cent of royalties.[8] Three years later, in 1947, Battelle signed a licensing agreement with a small Rochester company by the name of Haloid, giving them the rights to the basic patents in return for an 8 per cent royalty on the proceeds. From the same town as the better-known Kodak, Haloid too dealt in photographic products, and their investment in xerography was a major gamble. In 1948, the name 'Xerox' was trademarked, and xerography – combining the Greek word *xeros* for 'dry' and *graphis* for 'writing' – replaced 'electrophotograhy' as a description of Carlson's process. The first of Haloid's copiers, the Model A, known as the 'Ox Box,' came on the market in 1949. Not particularly effective, it took a total of thirty-nine manual steps in order to perfect a copy,[9] following instructions in a manual of painstaking detail:

> Dry the plate surface by striking it lightly and briskly with a clean, dry, UNTOUCHED portion of cotton ... With a spoon, carefully spread one-fourth of a teaspoon of XeroX Toner over the developer ... When mounted in the process tray, the four tabs of the electrode should protrude no more than approximately 1/64" above the level of the side gaskets, nor should they go below the side gasket.[10]

The Model A was a disaster. Fortunately but quite unexpectedly, it could still be used as a maker of paper masters for offset printing presses. Continuing to improve on xerography, Haloid realized that the 8 per cent Battelle share might in the future present a serious impediment to their chances of funding continued research. In return for stock that was to bring many millions to Battelle, effective from 1 January

1956, the Institute conferred all rights to the basic xerography patents to Haloid.[11] In 1958 Haloid officially changed their name to Haloid Xerox; in 1959 all worldwide patents on xerography were purchased from Battelle, and in 1961 the company – inspired by the way in which the name Kodak was constructed around the same first and last letters – became Xerox. In the first ad presenting the new corporate name in *Fortune* in July 1961, Xerox emphasized that there was nothing ancient and Greek about the corporation, stressing instead its commitment to meet what already then was seen as 'the sheer mass of information.'[12]

Chester Carlson became a consultant to Xerox but was never involved in its day-to-day business. His 40 per cent share of the Battelle royalty had made him a millionaire whose 1964 royalties amounted to 3 million dollars and increased by circa 1 million a year. Most of his substantial private fortune was however donated to charities and universities.[13] He died while watching a movie in a New York theatre on 19 September 1968.

©

Xerox's first major breakthrough came with the launch of the model 914 – so called because it could copy sheets as large as 9 by 14 inches – which was first shown to the public at the Sherry-Netherland Hotel in New York on 16 September 1959. Two copiers were on hand that day. One caught fire.[14] When the 914 was scheduled for its first live television appearance, the print proved so faint that it did not even register for the cameras. Since there was no toner to be found in New York, some had to be flown in from Rochester, arriving five minutes before the demonstration was to air.[15] The unfortunate tendency of Xerox copiers to ignite at inopportune moments forced the company to add fire extinguishers to the machines. Sales representatives declared that it amounted to corporate suicide suggesting to customers that the copiers could cause a fire in the office; they recoiled at the use of the word 'fire' under any circumstances. Hence, the fire extinguishers became known as 'scorch eliminators.'[16] One of those who publicly decried the unstable 914 was Ralph Nader, who claimed that his Washington office machine had caught fire three times in four months.[17] A later model, the 3600–3, would burst into flames in the White House.[18]

Although Xerox was doing well on the copying market with its Copyflo, a machine that enlarged prints on a continuous roll from microfilm originals introduced in 1955, there were also serious competitors in the field. 3M had their Thermo-Fax unit, Kodak the Verifax, and a number of other companies tried their hand at various copying processes. Although these machines were small enough to fit on a desk, and also modestly priced at around $500, they came with major drawbacks. Either they were somehow limited in function – the Thermo-fax did not reproduce all colours – or they involved time-consuming and careful handling of the documents. Neither machine made copies that were permanent, nor could they operate without specially treated and expensive paper.[19]

The 914 revolutionized copying for several reasons. Despite the fact that it was huge – in the beginning only five machines a day, each the size of a small truck weighing over 650 pounds, rolled off the assembly line – it was marketed as a machine anyone could handle. In a 1960 TV commercial promoting the 914, Xerox made their point by showing a businessman sitting at his desk. He asks his daughter Debbie to make a copy of a letter. When the little girl returns with two papers in her hand, he wants to know which one is the original, to which she replies, 'I forget!' One angry viewer demanded proof from Xerox that Debbie was not in fact a midget, since the idea of a small child operating such a complicated piece of machinery seemed out of the question. Fuelled by the Debbie success, Xerox relied on a trained chimpanzee to demonstrate the 914 in their next commercial. This time their strategy backfired. Calls poured in from irate customers the day after its premiere. Secretaries who normally operated the machine complained that they had found bananas on the copiers and were ridiculed by male employees who argued that since a monkey could do the job just as well, why did they have to pay the women salaries? The commercial was pulled and never reappeared.[20]

'Anyone is an *expert* the first time he uses the XeroX 914 Copier,' trumpeted the glossy, colour foldout advertisement introducing the 914 in *Fortune* in March 1960.[21] That the 'he' was somewhat of a misnomer is proven by the print ads, where all those working with the copier tended to be women. Confirming the secretary as the true mother of the machine, John Brooks wrote in a 1967 article for the *New Yorker*; after having spent a day in the company of a 914 and its female 'caretaker,' he could report that he had witnessed the closest relationship between a woman and a piece of office equipment he had ever encountered. He ruminated that the copier 'had distinct animal traits: it has to be fed and curried; it is intimidating but can be tamed; it is subject to unpredictable bursts of misbehavior; and, generally speaking, it responds in kind to its treatment.' The secretary Brooks interviewed went on to say that she had been warned by the Xerox technical representative not to be afraid of the 914 because the machine would sense her fear and, like a mischievous child, misbehave.[22] Portrayed in a 1963 *Fortune* ad as a costume-clad, crew-cut young man with a briefcase, the Xerox man was, according to the company, not only 'educated,' but well prepared to change the toner, fix the so-called mispuff that tended to cause paper jams, and generally oversee the performance of the copier.[23] From the start, the copier had almost taken on a life of its own, and since many within the corporation took the view that it was a contraption 'mere mortals could not develop,'[24] it needed to be treated like a living entity. In the movie *9 to 5*, the copier was used to make precisely this point of the unpredictable and unstable relationship that existed between humans and machines. Playing a divorcee employed outside the home for the first time, Jane Fonda is depicted in one scene in the 'Xerox room,' about to oversee what looks like a simple process of copying. Without apparent reason, the machine goes berserk, sending copies flying across the room. Failing to end the chaos, the distraught woman is forced to watch her chauvinist boss turn the thing off with the confidence of one who knows the key to comporting oneself in the presence of technology: not to be scared. Perhaps she had her showdown with a Xerox 9200, a copier marketed in a highly successful series of TV commercials known as 'Brother Dominic.' These featured a monk – Brother Dominic – who, when Father Superior wants him to produce five hundred more sets of the illuminated manuscript he has been toiling with turns to the 9200 for help.[25]

In addition to the fact that the 914 could be operated by almost anyone, causing unlimited copies to flow at the simple push of a button, these copies came on ordinary paper. For several years, the ease of use and the idea of making a copy so close to the original as to make it impossible to see the difference between them was an important advertising strategy. When the company in a September 1963 advertisement in *Fortune* displayed a Picasso original next to a Xerox copy of the same picture asking readers if they could spot the original, they promised anyone who guessed correctly a Xeroxed copy of the painting.[26] Drastic but effective, it was the culmination of a number of similar ads on the same theme. All stressed that the copier could manage important originals without destroying them, that the copies were almost as good as the originals, and that all of this wizardry was within the reach of everybody.

The second decisive element in the success of the 914 was the pricing policy. In fact, the 914 was so expensive that the company was in serious doubt that it could be sold in any numbers at all. Early versions reached $4,000 in production cost alone and in 1966, it came with a retail price tag of $27,500. In a stroke of genius, the company came up with a metred pricing-policy, based on the licensing, not the buying, of the machine. For $95 a month for the first 2,000 copies and 4 cents per copy thereafter, the idea was to charge for copies, not for the machine.[27] That way, not only did Xerox own the machine and therefore the depreciation and write-offs that came with ownership, they were secured a steady income long after it had paid back its initial cost. In large part, this became one of the reasons for the subsequent success of the copier, since no one could have anticipated that the number of copies made by those who rented the machine would explode in the years to come.

Answering the hitherto unknown needs of the market, the 914 was used to produce not 2,000 copies a month but rather 10,000, and some went as high as 50,000 copies a month.[28] People made not only copies from originals as Xerox had expected – and built much of its advertising on – they made copies of copies.[29] Such unexpected possibilities did the copier present in terms of dissemination of information, that when *Business Week* wrote about Xerox at the time of the 914 launch, they felt compelled to spell out to their readers what possibilities the copier really provided, listing a department store that copied invoices, an importer who copied letters written in foreign languages for further distribution to its banks, and a Detroit engineering firm, copying specifications sheets.[30]

The number of copies made annually in the U.S. went from some 20 million in the mid-1950s, to 9.5 billion in 1964, and 14 billion two years later.[31] Xerox, who had hoped to place 5,000 units of the expensive and cumbersome 914 within three years of the 1960 launch, had instead shipped 10,000 by 1962.[32] That same year, when production was up to forty machines a day, there was a twelve-week wait for delivery.[33] What Xerox had stumbled on was a licence to make money, and the company went from sales of $32 million in 1959 to $1,125 billion in 1968.[34] Profits rose from $2.6 million in 1960 to $134 million in 1968. Staff were recruited at a pace of fifty to a hundred people a month.[35] What could possibly go wrong?

©

Things could and would go wrong. The many patent protections surrounding xerography benefited both Chester Carlson and Xerox, making it possible for the company not only to prosper during the 1960s, but basically to secure a monopoly on the copier market. However, at the beginning of the 1970s the old patents were beginning to expire and the following years would prove a 'lost decade,' every bit as disastrous as the preceding one was successful.

It began in 1972, when the Federal Trade Commission (FTC) sued Xerox for violating antitrust laws. The FTC claimed that Xerox had 60 per cent of the overall copier market, and 95 per cent of the plain-paper copier market, demanding among other things that the company start licensing off its patents. The FTC suit was not settled until 1975, when Xerox agreed to some of its demands and made an estimated 1,700 patents available to its competitors.[36] From 1976 to 1982, Xerox's share of American copier installations dropped from around 80 per cent to 13 per cent.[37] In the early 1980s margins plummeted from 70 per cent to 10 per cent.[38] So used to ruling the market, the company did not even include formal market share information in its reports. They had always amounted to 100 per cent.[39] Hubris reigned as some expected the metre on the back of the copiers to count, not copies, but money forever.

One stunning example of how far corporate complacency would lead was the widespread fear of Xerox engineers of damaging the original document in any way. Subsequently, they were convinced that it was impossible to build a copier in which the original could be fed *into* the machine. When, in the midst of Xerox's crisis Kodak introduced a recirculating document handler in 1976, the Xerox people were incredulous. They simply did not think it could be done.[40] The Japanese posed another threat, since they not only built better copiers, but did so more effectively and at half the cost. Moreover, the Japanese had targeted the small copier, a mushrooming market Xerox ignored and which proved an immense success.[41]

The instability created by these combining factors would also lead to what some consider the worst blunder of all; the missed opportunities of Xerox PARC (Palo Alto Research Park). When Steve Jobs, founder of Apple, was quoted as saying that Xerox could have owned the entire computer industry today, and that it could have been a company ten times its current size, he was no doubt thinking of PARC.[42] PARC researchers developed the Alto, the first personal computer; constructed the Ethernet; came up with the user-friendly interfaces of menus, pop-up windows, and desktops now so familiar to all computer users; designed the first word-processing programs; developed the laser printer; and even toyed with what was called a 'worm,' or what we more commonly refer to as a 'virus.' Xerox managed to capitalize on and turn only one of these into a successful product: the laser printer.[43] Because of a corporate bureaucracy sometimes referred to as 'Burox,'[44] internal conflicts, clashes between east-coast and west-coast approaches to technology, Xerox never fully came to exploit the potential for in-house innovations and was left behind when the time came for the copier to be surpassed in its capacity to circulate information by the personal computer and the World Wide Web.

II

In 1966, at the peak of Xerox's success, Marshall McLuhan stated that xerography was the most startling and upsetting electric innovation to date. In his rambling style he went on to describe why what he later would call 'every man's brain-picker'[45] posed such a tremendous challenge to the status quo:

> Xerography is bringing a reign of terror into the world of publishing because it means that every reader can become both author and publisher ... Authorship and readership alike can become production-oriented under xerography. Anyone can take a book apart, insert parts of other books and other materials of his own interest, and make his own book in a relatively fast time. Any teacher can take any ten textbooks on any subject and custom-make a different one by simply xeroxing a chapter from this one and from that one ... [But] Xerography is electricity invading the world of typography, and it means a total revolution in this old sphere.[46]

If we are to understand the copier and photocopying, not only as a tremendous corporate success story during the 1960s, but also as a revolutionary invention promoting textual as well as legal interventions impacting on authorship and intellectual property rights alike, McLuhan's comment sends a revealing message from the past. However, before we look more closely at the copier, it must be said that any technological leap forward – and the copier did represent one such breakthrough – that enhances the possibility for reproduction, and places that capability in the hands of a larger and *different* audience has the potential to impact on *all* functions of print culture and is not only limited to the refinement of reproductive techniques alone. We know that the printing press acted as an agent of change that enabled not only a different and more effective way of manufacturing books, but spurred changes in ownership, authorship, reading habits, and distribution.[47] The copier, and now more recently the Internet, must be interpreted in the same light. The most basic of presuppositions regarding long-standing cultural relationships are questioned when we are forced to contend with the definitions of what a book really is, and what it means to be an author, a reader, or a publisher. Such questions are always present within print culture, but they insist on being addressed more directly at a time of drastic technological changes.

McLuhan is obviously concerned about the arrival of xerography and the copier because he expressly singles them out, but he is perhaps even more focused on the consequences of new technology per se, especially as it relates to print culture and authorship. He was not the first to worry. In 1935 with the world teetering on the brink of war, Walter Benjamin questioned the modern machine's ability to strip the work of art of its aura. Granted, Benjamin was more interested in the visual than the textual, but his argument did not hinge on that distinction alone. Just as Marshal McLuhan many years later would lament the upheaval of tradition so did Benjamin predict that the mass market and commodity capitalism would sever the ties between the author and the public, mapping out a new territory in which the reader was about to turn into writer at any moment.[48] This suggests a dramatic revolution in the ordering of intellectual property, as tumultuous and radical a change as when eighteenth-century writers went from primarily considering themselves craftsmen, to promoting and viewing themselves as authors.[49] Both McLuhan and Benjamin used the machine to suggest that such a reversal of roles was imminent; Xerox relied on commercials and print ads to illustrate the outcome of their prophecies. Since women, children, and chimpanzees could operate a machine that served the purpose of instantaneously reproducing texts, *anyone* could become author and publisher by bypassing the traditional functions of print culture. The copier and its new users collude to *demystify* and to question the roles previously assigned to producer, distributor, and consumer in print culture, roles that until the 1960s mostly had been occupied by men.

While the copier operates as a printing press of sorts, it is still a far cry from actually producing new *books*. The function of the copier is precisely the reverse: it negates the book; it takes it out of the equation. It does so because the technique of reproduction embodied in the copier 'detaches,' as Walter Benjamin writes, 'the reproduced object from the domain of tradition.'[50] This is a perfect description of a material and immaterial transformation – you need only visualize the process: place a book or a journal under the lid of a copier, press a button, the light turns on inside the machine, and a few seconds later out comes nothing remotely resembling what was placed there to begin with. Smudged and unintelligible at times, the papers containing the information you need can be, and often are, too dark or too light; with not enough or too much enlargement or reduction; or they are simply not forthcoming at all because the machine is broken, and so on. The copier is the perfect machine for its time because it emphasizes, not form, but content, and because it suggests that authorial power has been placed in the hands of the person using the machine. Both these critical elements in the understanding of the copier can be related to an upsurge in information and an increased emphasis on and awareness of education and knowledge as resources both in political and monetary terms. In his *New Yorker* article on Xerox from 1967, John Brooks succinctly raised the complicated question of copyright, and the potential for the copier to effortlessly reproduce text for swift distribution.[51] He did so by noting that the copier had penetrated libraries and universities to the point where the technology was taken for granted, if not by publishers, then by the public. Therefore, at the time when Xerox's sales seemingly could only go up, and the photocopier became part of the corporate, educational, and public landscape, it was a lawsuit about to happen.

©

One of the first cases testing the subversive capacity of the copier was *Williams & Wilkins Co. v. United States*, involving on the one hand Williams and Wilkins – publisher of a number of medical journals – and on the other the United States government through the Department of Health, Education, and Welfare and its institutions the National Institutes of Health (NIH) and the National Library of Medicine (NLM).[52]

On 17 February 1968, Williams and Wilkins filed a complaint against NIH and NLM, arguing that the library's unauthorized photocopying of articles from journals published and copyrighted by Williams & Wilkins amounted to copyright infringement. The plaintiffs claimed that they faced loss of revenue because photocopying now substituted for subscriptions and they charged that the fair-use doctrine – allowing for the photocopying of certain parts or extracts from books and/or journals for scholarly purposes – never was intended to cover complete works, which was the case in this instance. The defence argued that

NIH and NLM as non-profit agencies was well within the bounds of fair use when they assisted individual researchers with photocopying and that the amount copied was not a decisive factor against the practice. They also stated that the copyright was not, in fact, the publisher's but the author's, authors who had received no financial compensation from Williams & Wilkins, and who furthermore did not object to being photocopied, since they knew how vital it was to gain access to new information themselves. Nonetheless, the 1972 district court decision went in favour of Williams & Wilkins. With the least possible majority of 4–3, the appellate court reversed the decision in favour of the defendants the following year, concluding that the case had failed to prove significant economic detriment to Williams & Wilkins, but that it did demonstrate 'injury to medical and scientific research if photocopying of this kind is held unlawful.'[53] Once again appealed, this time to the Supreme Court, an equally divided court of 4–4 meant that the previous ruling would stand.[54]

Williams & Wilkins Co. v. United States had made it abundantly clear that the copier would need to be contended with in legislation. As we have seen from Xerox sales and advertising, the criticism of xerography by McLuhan, John Brooks's long essay on Xerox in the *New Yorker*, and even from the very basis of the *Williams & Wilkins Co. v. United States* case, the impact of the copier and the phenomenal success of Xerox were not in dispute. If the decision in *Williams & Wilkins Co. v. United States* favoured the defendant's interpretation of fair use and sided with the NIH and NLM, part of the reason behind this was that the U.S. Congress for many years had been trying to pass a revision to the 1909 Copyright Act.[55] At the time of *Williams & Wilkins Co. v. United States* there were simply no provisions in the Copyright Act for accommodating the new possibilities of reproduction provided by the copier, which undoubtedly prompted the court of claims's comment that there was a pressing need for Congress to treat the problems of photocopying.[56] The same call for a rejuvenation of intellectual property regimes suited to a new digital environment both nationally, regionally, and globally would be brought on by the arrival of the Internet and the information society.[57]

When the new Copyright Act from 1976 became law, section 107 codified fair use based on four factors; the purpose and character of the use (if for commercial or non-profit reasons); the nature of the copyrighted work (factual or non-factual with more leniency for the factual); the amount of the work copied in relation to the whole work (less or more); and the effect of the use upon the potential market for, or the value of, the copyrighted work.[58] When, in 1985, another case – *American Geophysical Union v. Texaco Inc.* – provided the battleground for a new confrontation involving the copier and fair use, the legal framework and the mechanisms ensuring intellectual property rights enforcement were therefore radically different from what had been the case during *Williams & Wilkins Co. v. United States.*

American Geophysical Union v. Texaco Inc. involved six scientific and technical publishers who sued Texaco because its in-house researchers had photocopied articles without paying licence fees to the publishers in question. The case came to rest on the example of one such researcher, Dr Donald Chickering, and his copying of four articles, two letters to the editor and two notes, from the *Journal of Catalysis.* While AGU claimed that he was violating fair use, Texaco and several other *amici* would argue that as a researcher who used the articles for his own research, laboratory work, or even for future reference rather than for profit, he was not in breach of fair use. One of the authors of an article Chickering had copied, Professor Schwarz, testified for Texaco, saying that both his colleagues and his students viewed photocopying as an important and essential part of their education, 'a natural [act] much like breathing.'[59] As in *Williams & Wilkins Co. v. United States,* the publishers vehemently disputed this 'natural act,' and insisted that photocopying hurt business. Two cases, of which *Williams & Wilkins Co. v. United States* was the first, seemed to add support to Texaco's position on fair use. The second, the famous *Sony Corp. v. Universal City Studios, Inc.,* had on similar grounds ruled that 'time-shifting,' that is, private home video recordings of copyrighted material shown on television, taped for later viewing, was to be considered fair use.[60]

Despite these forerunners, the 1992 decision by the United States District Court for the Southern District of New York held that Dr Chickering was in violation of fair use when he copied the articles.[61] From the four criteria set down in section 107 the judgment was weighed as follows; the for-profit motive of the company paired with the fact that the articles were placed in an archive rather than used directly went in favour of the plaintiff; the second criteria, where the nature of the copyrighted material is deliberated, found in favour of Texaco since the texts were factual; on the third count, which considered the amount copied, the court found for the plaintiff since entire articles were copied, and fourth and perhaps primarily, since prior cases had signalled the importance of this last of the four considerations, the court found that the publisher had indeed suffered financial loss because of lost subscriptions. The decision was appealed to the 2nd circuit court of appeals, where the ruling, despite many interventions on the part of organizations in the library community, prevailed in October 1994. In his dissenting opinion, Judge Jacobs insisted that he viewed Dr Chickering's copying reasonable and well within what fair use was intended to allow for. The fact that the articles were placed in Dr Chickering's file did not contradict their intended purpose of research. Drawing on findings in Bruno Latour's study *Laboratory Life: The Social Construction of Scientific Facts* from 1979, Judge Jacobs argued that 'photocopying of journal articles, and the use of them, is customary and integral to the creative process of science.'[62]

The publisher's claim of lost revenue due to photocopying was not such a relevant factor as the plaintiff would have it sound, because as he pointed out, the publishers charged a much higher subscription rate for the institutional subscribers, of which Texaco was one. The most interesting contention in his opinion can, however, be read as a blow against the very underpinnings of intellectual property rights. Judge Jacobs noted that the reward from writing for these journals was miniscule, if any. Like the authors involved in *Williams & Wilkins Co. v. United States*, the researchers who published in the *Journal of Catalysis* did not receive a fee or any royalty. Instead, their contribution awarded them another form of capital: tenure, research grants, graduate students, and peer appreciation, a form of remuneration primarily sought not for reasons of economic profit. If it was true that, as Judge Jacobs argued, '*the level of copyright revenue is not among the incentives that drive the authors to the creative acts that the copyright laws are intended to foster*' (emphasis mine), then his statement meant a serious blow to one of the fundamental building blocks of copyright, namely that it exists to protect and reward authors in order for them to keep producing.[63]

Stressing that copyright law is supposed to uphold a balance between a fair return for the author while permitting creative uses of that author's work, Judge Jacobs expressed his fear that what the future would hold was a bloated apparatus of intellectual property protection, something that would only hinder, not ensure further research by putting 'a transactional scheme' in place that 'would seem to require that an intellectual property lawyer be posted at each copymachine.'[64] Before the case could continue to the Supreme Court, Texaco settled with the publishers, agreeing to pay a seven-figure settlement, plus a retroactive licensing fee to the Copyright Clearance Center, signing also an agreement with the CCC for future licensing.[65] The Copyright Clearance Center, founded in 1978 to secure and oversee licensing agreements primarily in regard to photocopying, did not exist at the time of *Williams & Wilkins Co. v. United States,* and was now used against Texaco to demonstrate that there was a forum in place by which obtaining a licence for the kind of copying Texaco had engaged in would only be a formality. Judge Jacobs disagreed in his opinion, holding that while these licensing fees undoubtedly benefited the copyright holder (i.e., the publishers), they did not necessarily stimulate creativity.[66]

The third and final case pursuant to the copier is *Basic Books, Inc. v. Kinko's Graphics Corp.,* where eight publishers sued the photocopying shop chain Kinko's for printing so-called course packs for use at universities. Since the mid-1980s Kinko's had been offering a program they called 'Professor Publishing,' which involved copying excerpts from books and making course packs without acquiring permission from the publishers involved. These packs were then sold to students for a profit. Although Kinko's relied on a fair-use defence, the court found for the plaintiff, and Kinko's was enjoined from selling the packs and ordered to pay statutory damages in the order of $510,000 as well as attorney's fees and costs.[67]

III

The differences between these three cases are evident. *Williams & Wilkins Co. v. United States* as well as *American Geophysical Union v. Texaco Inc.* revolved around the copying of specific, individual articles for use in a research or educational environment. While also intended for educational purposes, the copying at issue in *Basic Books, Inc. v. Kinko's Graphics Corp.* instead involved the multiple copying of chapters and articles for subsequent 'course-packaging' and resale for profit. The cases were also judged differently, partly on the basis of the for-profit motives of Texaco and Kinko's as opposed to the non-profit agencies of NIH and NIM.

What is most striking about all three is, of course, the common denominator setting off the complaints to begin with: the copier. Furthermore, all of them implicate research institutions, libraries, and universities, thus squarely setting the problematics within an expanding and increasingly important realm of information and knowledge. All three cases consequently problematize the relationship between the uses of content and the owning of it, establishing a gap between the interests of two major players in print culture, publishers on one side, and libraries and universities on the other.[68]

I want, however, to stress one shared characteristic that I think is the most crucial: the power of the copier to act as an instrument of selection and sampling. In *Williams & Wilkins Co. v. United States* as well as in *American Geophysical Union v. Texaco Inc.*, the publishers emphasized strongly that a loss of revenue occurred because instead of first subscribing to a journal and then reading it, researchers were photocopying articles from journals in-house and then reading them (or not). The court did not find evidence of financial detriment in the first case, but in the second the majority did. However, the most important aspect of Dr Chickering's behaviour was that he proved how essential it had become to *select* within the 'mass of information' Xerox so aptly had identified many years earlier and that faced him daily as a researcher. He needed the *Journal of Catalysis*, not in its entirety, but in bits and pieces. The Kinko's case only takes this particular characteristic to the next level. Making the course-packs under the 'Professor Publishing' program constituted precisely the kind of activity McLuhan predicted in the quote above when he stressed: *'Any teacher can take any ten textbooks on any subject and custom-make a different one by simply xeroxing a chapter from this one and from that one.'*

The copier enables the swift compiling of information; the collecting of one chapter here, another one there, not only in order to simply redistribute them to a class of expectant students, but to recombine them and make a new, more useful tool. In one stroke, the copier makes the old author extinct, while at the same time laying the foundation for another to appear. To compile, to combine, to accumulate, to 'sample,' is a new form of authorship that proved to be the copier's most transgressive function. Not only did it make copies, it reproduced authors. The capacity of 'sampling,' was identified by Roland Barthes in 1968 when he spoke of the ability to 'mix [mêle] writings,' as the only true power that the modern author possessed.[69] Although the consequences of the 'author'-compiler are clearly present in *Basic Books, Inc. v. Kinko's Graphics Corp.* to a much larger extent than in the other cases, it is equally clear that while poststructuralist thought might allow and even give the author-compiler a justification for existence, the legal framework does not condone such forms of authorship, a problematics I will return to in chapter 5 when discussing intellectual property rights in relation to traditional knowledge and folklore. That a new value is created by the recombination of existing material is not self-evident in any way.[70] Sampling is at the base of hip-hop music, the file-sharing activities on the Internet, and the downloading and subsequent burning of new, individually selected and compiled CDs, all of which are driven by the same logic as we see enabled by the copier.[71] It makes sense that devices such as the copier and the MP3-player emerge in a knowledge-based society, not only because technology makes them possible, but because they are directed at the selection and reconstruction of information.

As the copier made the exchange of information possible in a radically new way and opened the floodgates for its dissemination, it became increasingly obvious that such a lucrative commodity would necessitate some form of control. As soon as we see new technological modes enabling access, we will see a direct response on all levels to delimit and police that possibility. Such strategies include not only revisions to most treaties and national laws, but also the emergence of new agencies, in this particular case so-called Reproduction Rights Organizations (RROs), that licenses reproduction of copyrighted material on a collective, rather than individual basis. RROs were specifically constructed to meet the problems of photocopying, but the principle of collective administration of rights is much older and generally credited to the difficulties involved in ensuring proper control of music performances. While the International Federation of Reproduction Rights Organizations (IFRRO) is the international umbrella organization for RROs, the French Société des Auteurs, Compositeurs et Éditeurs de Musique (SACEM) is generally regarded as the first example of such a *collective administration organization*.[72] Reproduction rights were not secured as a minimum Berne Convention right until the 1967 Stockholm Revision Conference,[73] and different nation-states have treated the dilemma of photocopying differently. In Germany, a statutory levy based on reproduction capacity is imposed on the sale of all reprographic equipment and another levy, based on the number of pages reproduced, is imposed on the operator.[74] In Sweden, the Swedish Writer's Union uses the revenues collected from licences by the RRO BONUS to administer a special fund called 'Fotokopieringsfonden' (The Photocopying Fund), from which any author and translator may apply for grants once a year.[75]

Thus, the copier gave us more than the possibility to distribute, to sample, and to create new texts, and more than the possibility to make copies of copies; it also gave us new instruments of control. In 2000 Xerox, the company that once saw itself in the vanguard of building the 'architecture of information,'[76] launched a company called Content-Guard, Inc. in cooperation with Microsoft. Developed at Xerox PARC, ContentGuard has designed a Digital Rights Language, XrML (eXtensible rights Markup Language), or, as the company puts it 'a universal method for specifying and managing rights and conditions associated with digital content as well as services.'[77] Allowing you to access copyrighted material such as music, images, or text on the Internet, Content-Guard epitomizes Marshal McLuhan's 1966 conjecture that 'there is no possible protection from technology except by technology.'[78] Paradoxically, with the launch of ContentGuard, the company that forty years earlier had produced a machine revolutionizing the diffusion of content, now focused, not on wider dissemination, but on the enhanced protection of the same resource it once helped distribute in an unparalleled manner.

Chapter Four

HOW CONTENT BECAME KING: ECONOMIES OF PRINT

If we transport ourselves outside the more immediate realm of the technological and textual, we can begin to discern another, less philosophical perhaps but equally influential arena bordering that of the previous one: the economic. There are several reasons why intellectual property catapults to the forefront of contemporary attention, but the most patently obvious and most tangible of all is by virtue of money, pure and simple. Based on three interrelated concepts – conglomeratization, content, and convergence – this chapter suggests a possible framework within which we can understand this *ménage-à-trois* as an expression of an increasingly powerful economics of intellectual property rights.

Such an approach warrants first of all that close attention be paid to one of the crucial developments in post-1960 publishing and media in general: its so-called *conglomeratization*. This term is mainly used to denote the apparently haphazard amalgamation of disparate corporate entities under the umbrella shelter of one huge corporation buying everything in its way. Gulf + Western was one such well-known example of a company caught in a purchasing frenzy, owning land in the Dominican Republic, insurance companies, racehorses, sports teams and lingerie manufacturers, as well as the publisher Simon and Schuster and Paramount Pictures, comprising an odd collection of companies.[1] Gulf + Western did not focus on media until 1989, when 100 unrelated businesses had been shed from the corporation and it was rechristened Paramount Communications.[2]

Cross-media and later cross-border Mergers and Acquisitions (M&As) and their close companion Divestitures are second nature to the global media market, where any buying spree initiated by a TransNational Media Corporation more often than not necessitates the forced or voluntary shedding of other assets in order to secure a more lucrative deal. Strategically motivated on the part of the corporation, divestitures may also be needed in order to circumvent anti-trust legislation.[3] As United Nations Conference on Trade and Development (UNCTAD) notes, M&As are more likely to be As rather than Ms, and thus in practice M&As means 'acquisitions.'[4] Today a norm rather than an exception in the global economy, not all proposed fusions will succeed. In 2001 the European Union stopped two proposed mergers because of anti-trust concerns. In May that year, Bertelsmann and EMI announced that they would abandon their plans to combine their respective companies rather than meet the demands of the EU, which would have required EMI to dispose of interests such as Virgin Music. Even more controversial was the decision a few months later to block what would have become the world's largest industrial takeover: GE's $43 billion bid for Honeywell.[5]

In this context, I will use conglomeratization as a more general indicator of a specific phenomenon beginning in the 1960s. To a substantial degree, the consolidation of the U.S. corporate landscape is an ongoing rather than a new phenomenon. Both structurally and financially, some major nineteenth-century deals were quite as impressive as those made a century later.[6] To an accelerating extent present in all conceivable types of businesses, the events outlined below are consequently by no means unique to media or publishing. However, the 1960s is clearly an important starting point for major changes in publishing, particularly when it comes to increased concentration of ownership. The topography of this changing media landscape which publishing has had forty-odd years to acclimatize to, is by now well-chartered territory, and has brought into play a profound conceptual disarray in the tradition of the book as business, which some claim has wreaked irreparable damage on print culture as a whole and publishing in particular.[7] Their argument? Where once there was a publishing house relentlessly searching for quality or a bookshop with an owner passionate to promote a good read there now stretch desertlike corporate spaces of major multinational media conglomerates whose understanding and appreciation of books and reading is tantamount to nil. This is no doubt an oversimplified account of the current state of affairs, if for no other reason than that it surmises too much, both of the present *and* of the past.

While Bertelsmann and Vivendi Universal both represent the increasing presence of non-U.S. TNMCs in global media and, as we have already noted, the nation-state figures less significantly by the day in the operations of these corporations, the following account will be skewed towards an emphasis on U.S. publishing. The major reason behind this choice is that the dominant role occupied by the United States in intellectual property regimes today must be understood against a backdrop of profound alignment with its cultural industries. The history of how substantial investments are made to ensure content protection by intellectual property rights is one in which U.S. publishing interests have played and continue to play a major, but historically ambivalent part.

In light of the more general concerns of this book, I would like to relate these events to one feature in particular: the recognition of and emphasis on *content* as a strategic corporate asset. Media conglomerates such as Bertelsmann frequently favour an image of the company as a 'content powerhouse,' where 'the opportunities for cross-promotion become virtually inexhaustible,' presumably referring to the endless synergies derived from comprehensive cultural ownership.[8] In contrast, the validity of this belief in content is also questioned, particularly considering the economic, technological, and social ramifications we have come to expect from the World Wide Web and a new digital environment, which some suggest prefer connectivity to content.[9] However, as *an idea of an entity worth increased protection,* content ownership must be recognized as a major incentive behind the conglomeratization and concentration in media and publishing in the first place. My prime concern in putting this emphasis on content should not be interpreted as directly related to whether or not corporate predictions will hold true; rather I take the position that the interesting thing is the way in which content is *represented* as a key asset, believed to be critical to the well-being of the company, and the arguments used to sustain that belief.

Finally, it is the component of *convergence* that will allow the possession of content to reach its highest evolutionary stage to date. While convergence tends to be conceptualized as primarily a technological term indicating the erasure of traditional boundaries between media forms and the commingling of diverse platforms in media, telecommunications, and software, the issue of ownership and control is just as important.[10] Convergence, together with conglomeratization and content, promised to coalesce the compounded assets achieved by years of consolidation in a hitherto unprecedented manner.

I

We have already witnessed the accuracy of Richard Ohman's claim that books are a highly adaptable market commodity that prospered from the booming market conditions of mass production, but he is perhaps even more correct when he continues to say that 'one might almost as convincingly hold that book publishing was the last culture industry to attain modernity. Not until after World War II did it become part of the large corporate sector, and adopt the practices of publicity and marketing characteristic of monopoly capital.'[12] Being subjected to the malicious as well as benevolent whims of the market presented an unwelcome reality check that took many publishers by surprise. Thomas Guinzburg, who sold Viking to Penguin in 1975, definitely expressed a sense of lost innocence when taking stock of the deal, which looked so ideal on paper, but quickly turned sour in real life. Penguin did not understand, Guinzburg said after being ousted from the company, that 'our *instinct* for books was always central.'[12] As it evolves during this time period, the identity crisis of the business can be related to this built-in dichotomy where publishing – and trade publishing in particular – on the one hand, is seen as an entity that needs to make a profit, and on the other hand, clings to a die-hard self-image as a unique undertaking operating according to its own, inverted economic law. This shapes the general layout of the field and the positions available within it, making the publisher's *personnage double* that of a collective Dr Jekyll and Mr Hyde – either falling in the category of those who know how to 'read,' or being placed in the technological-commercial corner of those who know how to 'count.'[13] The position of publishing and the way in which altered conditions for media in general have changed during this time-period will differ between nation-states and be crucially dependent on various contextual parametres involving not only cultural identity, but also political legislation, economic incentives, and social demographics. Even accounting for all the disclaimers above, much suggests that what has taken place during these years can be described as a strategic shift shared by countries diametrically different in social, economic, and political outlook and structure.[14]

While publishing has never in any time or place presented us with a homogenous and harmonious field – quite the opposite in fact – it is generally assumed as a truth of sorts that it used to be an endeavour where profit margins were low but steady and thus offered you a line of business you hardly entered for profit but because you had some sort of relationship with books and reading.[15] Building a reputable stable of writers was a long-term rather than short-term commitment, where investments were made in authors based on what they could achieve down the line and dividends put on hold until they eventually one day would – many years in the future perhaps – provide a return on that initial investment. As ideal an equilibrium as this might seem, it hardly resulted from an economic vacuum. One of the basic premises that made such reasoning possible was that publishing operated on a principle of swings and merry-go-rounds. If the publishing house was fortunate enough to secure a best-seller, then the substantial revenues that could be expected from that book would subsidize the losses incurred by less successful and perhaps even at times controversial books, books that nonetheless were judged important as part of the overall publishing program.[16] Although the individual jackpot in securing a best-seller was crucial, it was the offerings of the house in its entirety, as well as a well-managed backlist that was to be sought after, a backlist that in some cases could represent about 60 per cent of the annual business by a serious publisher.[17] Logically, the rewards you could hope to reap in such a system were intangible, coming to you in the shape of cultural and social capital. In André Schiffrin's words publishing was 'run by its editors rather than its accountants.'[18]

Even if we are compelled to subscribe to this description in broad strokes, it is one in dire need of additional clarification, primarily because publishing has always been two things at once: a commercial activity as well as a cultural one, balancing between a system of economics that is as much symbolic as it is economic.[19] When publishing went from being a largely privately owned small-scale business into becoming part of a larger corporate sector by way of M&As, some even ventured to describe the former as a backwards, inefficient, and perhaps even at times unprofessional business.[20] It was a trade marked not only by bursts of eccentricity but also by distinct gender biases and equally apparent class distinctions that operated to strengthen rather than eradicate the difference between what it meant to consume the 'high' and the 'low.' Perpetuating a nostalgic longing for mythical times when this was a gentleman's profession is a stratagem that clearly feeds off the disintegration of clear-cut classification borders, and therefore increases in strength as the market pressures from consolidation and concentration transforms the global media landscape. In his survey on the symbolic boundaries marked out in French and American publishing, Daniel Weber notes that French publishers were more prone to 'justify a desire to launch a bestseller as a means of subsidizing a more difficult or experimental work' than their American counterparts. In general, the American publishers Weber interviewed were more utilitarian in their approach to literature, relying on the market to distinguish a good book. The French interviewees, on the other hand, were more sensitive to the possible effects of recent publishing trends such as conglomeratization and they expressed concern for the possible fate of French literature and language in the wake of importation and translations.[21]

Despite the critique that can be raised against the retrospective idolization, there is no doubt that major changes have come to bear on what Alain Gründ, president of the International Publishers Association (IPA) in 2000, referred to as 'a trade which is not totally like others.'[22] Publishing is, however, less than ever a means to itself. Once perhaps allowed to operate according to charming idiosyncrasies it is at present rather a cog in the wheel of an entire media machinery that in the end is supposed to enhance the total value of the parent conglomerate. Books are by and large expected to meet much higher profit margins. Since it is equally desirable that they perform well individually rather that in the context of a complete publishing program, internal subsidization and long-term investments are no longer considered pillars of a viable publishing strategy. Backlists are relegated to very real backseats, but may reappear as valuable property if e-books ever become a business reality. In the summer of 2001, Random House sought an injunction against the e-book publisher RosettaBooks, who had signed contracts with authors such as William Styron and Kurt Vonnegut for digital rights to books that were not covered by the ordinary contract with Random House. Random House based their claim on the fact that the old contracts gave them the exclusive rights to issue the author's work in 'book form'; however, district court Judge Sidney Stein denied the injunction and centred his argument on the crucial formulation 'book form' which he found not necessarily needed to include e-books. Random House appealed to the second circuit court of appeals, where the 8 March 2002 decision also went in favour of RosettaBooks. In a press release from 4 December 2002, both companies announce that they have entered into a licensing agreement and ended their ongoing litigation.[23]

In addition, a new economy also introduced new players to the field, not necessarily because they desired to work with books, but rather because they were equipped with the preferred know-how demanded of a new type of market. The agent knew better how to negotiate and promote the deals that some authors now could expect. The subsidiary rights race that began with paperback publishing but would branch out into major licensing deals from movies to bedding in the wake of a truly successful book also required new expertise; business managers had the advantage now of technological breakthroughs of inventory control and the arrival of computerized systems that would tell if a book did well or not. The idea that everything could be tracked, understood, and made profitable by the new gadgets of surveillance certainly made an impact on the industry.[24] Add to this that the product itself – the book and the text within that paper-bound receptacle – stood to face massive challenges in the shape of things to come: e-books, hypertext, and more; and it all added up to a reconfiguration of a business that had existed without fundamental changes since the mass market of Dickens and Hugo once took off.[25]

Trying to summarize these developments, one finds pros and cons at all ends. Despite the fact that they made independent booksellers go out of business, the arrival of the multistores Barnes & Noble and Borders have helped to create a new form of public space in the United States. The technological advances of print-on-demand and e-books might permanently solve the dilemma of keeping seldom sought-after titles in stock, but looked at from another perspective this technological wonderland can be counterproductive as well, hindering public accessibility to literature under the pretext of individual choice. The mushrooming of the TNMCs have not been an obstacle to a simultaneous growth of small publishers, and the Internet holds the potential for fostering new, niche presses. But few things are as prone to politics as statistics; while some say that the title output has never been so impressive – growing 256 per cent in the U.S. between 1960 and 1989 – others argue that since a handful of companies control the market this is only a smoke-screen argument, since it hides the fact that true publishing clout of the kind only available to the media conglomerates is necessary in order to sell and display your books.[26]

Perhaps the most accurate description of what has taken place in this highly volatile business is to say that it illustrates an ongoing but also an inherent polarization: between centralization and decentralization, between consolidation and diversification, between expansion and contraction, between art and business. Add to this the dimension of increased transnational and global implications and you have a situation where conglomeratization, content, and convergence rearrange positions and possibilities.

©

The integration of publishing into larger conglomerates begins in the 1960s and can be described as a three-stage process.[27] Although close scrutiny will prove that we are not witnessing a perfectly chronological sequence but rather seeing a fluid process in which some of these broader tendencies overlap in time, we can still describe it as 1) beginning with the buying of textbook publishers by companies who had little or no previous investments in books, 2) continuing with the buying of trade publishers by larger media corporations, and 3) the vertical consolidation and globalization of the contemporary TNMC inclusive of their holdings in print.[28]

The acquisition of textbook publishers by corporations like IBM, ITT, Westinghouse, and Xerox was initially prompted by an anticipation that buying software or content would – in combination with the hardware already at their disposal – serve as the ultimate tactic at a time when teaching and education increasingly was perceived as a new market of Klondykian proportions. John Dessauer, head of the Research and Engineering Division at Xerox during the boom years of the 1960s, wrote in his memoirs that in 1965, more than $43 billion flowed into U.S. education, making it a highly attractive investment.[29] Much of this corporate activity strikes one as unmotivated and far-fetched in retrospect, such as the ultimate failure of Western Pacific Industries – owner at that time of, for instance, the Western Pacific Railroad – to buy the publisher Houghton Mifflin in 1978.[30] That a former water company named Compagnie Générale des Eaux twenty-three years later and under the new conglomerate name of Vivendi Universal would purchase the same leading U.S. textbook publisher for $2.2 billion, making Vivendi Universal Publishing the world's #2 educational publisher after Pearson, demonstrates how contemporary media conglomerates may come about, but also, as we shall see later in this chapter, how quickly they can disentangle themselves from such alliances.[31]

Xerox began their inroads into education and publishing by acquiring University Microfilms Inc. in 1962; the American Education Publications Inc. in 1964; R.R. Bowker Company with its reference publishing program, publisher of *Publishers Weekly* in 1967; and Ginn and Company the year after. When John Brooks wrote his *New Yorker* piece on Xerox in 1967, he appropriately described the company almost in terms of a modern-day media conglomerate, observing that Xerox's acquisitions in publishing made it into a publisher as well as a copy-machine firm.[32] Publishing also provided Xerox with more unexpected benefits. The Xerox PARC researchers, who developed the Gypsy, or what later was to become one of the first word processing programs, used the editors at Ginn and Company as guinea pigs. In front of a nonfunctional dummy machine the editors were asked to enact and describe their routines. The 'cut' and 'paste' technique, which today is one of the most useful elements of word processing actually stems from watching the Ginn and Company editors use scissors and paste pots to rearrange manuscripts on paper.[33] By 1985, however, Xerox had sold six of its publishing companies, including the ones mentioned above.[34]

Xerox was only one company partaking in the prevalent optimism of what 'teaching machines' might accomplish, even acquiring the manufacturer Basic Systems. Black-and-white pictures from the 1960s show children intently focused on large screens, with a teacher/instructor watching over them as they use the cumbersome machines in the classroom. Although teaching machines would prove to be only one of many misguided hopes about what the technological future would hold, one must note that once the connection between content and technology was made, it was here to stay. Much corporate activity forty years later in the educational sector is deeply enmeshed in the ability to package and deliver information and content online, on CD-ROMs, and through other channels that make teaching machines seem like prehistoric dinosaurs. Two of the largest companies in this sector – the Dutch Wolters Kluwer and the Dutch-British Reed Elsevier – sold almost $2.4 billion worth of books and journals in 1990, equalling at that time sales figures of the two largest American publishers, Simon & Schuster and Time Warner.[35]

Together with trade and professional books, education represents one of the three major publishing segments. While much of this discussion centres on trade publishing – mostly for its cultural rather than financial significance – professional and educational publishing can hardly be discounted in a world where information is the mantra on everybody's lips. Textbook publishers are targets for acquisitions and major businesses in their own right, displaying signs of concentration and consolidation similar to those in trade publishing. Testament to their strategic role is the fact that the largest acquisition in printing and publishing history is the sale by Viacom of Simon & Schuster's textbook unit to Pearson PLC in 1998.[36] With a steady and reliable flow of consumers, education is considered as presenting a higher profit range, between 15 and 25 per cent as opposed to the previously mentioned one-digit numbers for trade publishing.[37]

The second wave of corporate inroads into publishing is the one whereby corporations such as RCA, CBS, and Gulf + Western begin to purchase trade publishing houses. The story of Random House is an example indicative of the buying and selling pattern typical of this consolidation. When 30 per cent of Random House's stock went public in October 1959, it resulted from a need to ensure the continued existence of the company. First-generation publishers had few options; some viewed possible cooperation with a major company as something beneficial to both parties, while others, faced with tax laws making it prohibitively expensive to buy a partner's share in case of his death, chose, like Random House, to go public.[38] Bought by RCA for $40 million in 1965, Random House had already at that time purchased Knopf in 1960 and Pantheon in 1961. Sold to the Newhouse group (Advance Publications) in 1980, who in turn traded the company to German Bertelsmann for $1.4 billion in 1998, today Random House acts as the corporate umbrella of over 100 publishing houses in thirteen countries, owning imprints such as the previously mentioned Knopf, but also Ballantine Books and Bantam Books in the U.S., Plaza & Janés in Spain, and Goldmann in Germany.

The third stage – which is mostly of interest here – can perhaps be described as a further consolidation of stage two, in that we now face these developments operating on a distinctly transnational media market. Not only is this market global, but also its power centres are highly concentrated, both in geographical terms and in terms of ownership.[39] Several of the largest players are still American, most notably AOL Time Warner, Disney, and Viacom. The main market for these companies also is still the United States; in 2001 AOL Time Warner had 85 per cent and Viacom 83 per cent of their sales in that country.[40] The increasing transnational nature of the media market also means that many of those companies who have risen to global prominence are located outside the United States, but with substantial investments in American publishing, leading to a growing recognition that the United States is by no means immune to what Barnet and Cavanagh call a 'takeover' by European interests.[41] In fact, between the years 1985 and 1992, the United States became a prime market for Foreign Direct Investment (FDI) in media properties.[42] Bertelsmann made two acquisitions in the U.S. in 1986, buying Doubleday Publishing ($475 million) and RCA Records ($330 million), crowning their American presence with the

1992 purchase of a $200 million office building – known as the Bertelsmann building – on Broadway.[43] Major players based outside the United States at the beginning of the twenty-first century are Rupert Murdoch's News Corporation, German Bertelsmann, Dutch-British Reed Elsevier and Dutch Wolters Kluwer, the Canadian Thompson, British Pearson PLC, and the two French giants Lagardère and Vivendi Universal. It is striking to note that all of the above non-U.S. corporations have a history with print culture, several of them starting out as publishing houses, whereas the U.S. firms such as AOL Time Warner, Disney, and Viacom have stronger ties to movies, music, and television.[44]

The intracorporate aggrandizement by M&As is even further exacerbated by the many alliances between the conglomerates themselves.[45] Joint ventures, exclusive deals, alliances and licences – the Disney Corporation worldwide licenses 16,000 items of merchandise[46] – are part and parcel of a market that can safely be described as increasingly oligopolistic. Although Ben Bagdikian's fear that there would be ONE, giant media owner in the mid 1990s proved to be exaggerated, even the more modest prediction of a handful or so vertically integrated media giants is perhaps concentration enough.[47]

One of the distinguishing traits of this market, increasingly oblivious to national borders, is the growth in cross-border M&As, succeeding the consolidation to that effect already established on a national level. The total number of all M&As worldwide (cross-border and domestic) has grown at a rate of 42 per cent annually between 1980 and 1999. At the same time, the value of M&As as a share of the World GDP rose from 0.3 per cent to 8 per cent. The majority of M&As are still horizontal, but vertical M&As have increased in recent years, possibly the result of the search for long-term strategic control.[48] In 2000 two major deals with clear impact on the global media market took place – the acquisition of Time Warner by America Online,[49] and the arrival of Vivendi Universal, created through the merger between Vivendi, Seagram, and Canal+, valued at $42.8 billion.[50] The creation of Vivendi Universal is a good example of the structural incentives of the cross-border M&As of the global economy. On 8 December 2000 Vivendi – the result of the 1998 merger between Compagnie Générale des Eaux and Havas, one of the largest publishing groups in France; Seagram, owner of, among other things, the Universal Music Group and Universal Studios and ranked 23 among the world's 100 largest TNCs in the *World Investment Report 2000*; and Canal+, one of Europe's largest pay television providers – announced the merger, naming the new company

Vivendi Universal.[51] Almost immediately, the new company announced its intention to divest itself of the Seagram's Spirits, Wine, and Beverages business since it was a 'non-strategic asset of Vivendi Universal.'[52]

In conjunction with the purchase of Houghton Mifflin in 2001, Agnès Touraine, CEO of Vivendi Universal Publishing, declared the company's full intention to increase its international markets.[53] The present concentration in French publishing resembles that of the United States and the rest of Europe. The 'duopole' Vivendi Universal and Lagardère[54] dominate the scene and are followed by a group of independent publishers (Albin Michel, Gallimard, Flammarion, and Le Seuil), who in turn precede a large number of smaller publishers.[55]

The contemporary TNMC looks very much like a Russian babushka doll, where the largest doll holds a smaller one, which holds even smaller ones, until the most miniscule is reached. As we have already seen, Random House comprises a number of well-known imprints; at the time of its merger with Générale des Eaux, Havas had reached its position by overtaking a number of publishing companies, such as Laffont, 10/18, and Plon; and HarperCollins (owned by News Corporation) harbours imprints such as Avon and William Morrow. Within these conglomerates, books constitute more or less important segments, with Bertelsmann arguably being the most book or print oriented. Bertelsmann executive Peter Olson, Chairman and CEO of Random House Inc., has been quoted saying: 'Books publishing is not a stepchild here ... It is our focal point.'[56] In 2000 Time Warner Trade Publishing's contribution to Time Warner's total revenues stood at a mere 1 per cent. HarperCollins provided 7 per cent of its parent company News Corporation's total sales, and Simon & Schuster's contribution to the Viacom total revenue was expected to decline as a result of the purchase of CBS in 2000, from 5 per cent to 3 per cent. In 2000 Random House had sales of $2 billion, representing approximately 12 per cent of its parent company's total revenues.[57]

If HarperCollins is a doll within a larger conglomerate, hiding a number of even smaller ones, then let us for the sake of perspective attempt to place the media conglomerates themselves in the framework of the largest of them all: the transnational corporation (TNC). From the perspective of *The World Investment Report 2001* and its official listing of the world's 100 largest TNCs in 1999, only a handful are categorized as media/publishing. Four corporations fit the bill: Seagram at place 23, Rupert Murdoch's News Corporation at place 31, Vivendi SA at place 47, and Thompson Corporation at 57.[58] Take the example of Thompson

Corporation, placed in the lower half of the 100 largest TNCs but top-listed in terms of the transnationality index (TNI), which intends to capture the foreign dimensions of a firm's total activities by calculating the average of three ratios: foreign assets to total assets, foreign sales to total sales, and foreign employment to total employment. As the *2001 Report* points out, transnationality varies substantially between businesses, with the media industry the most transnational of all with an average TNI of 87 per cent in 1999, compared with, for instance, pharmaceuticals at 62 per cent and trading at 18 per cent.[59] The second important feature of the largest TNCs in terms of transnationality is that they tend to originate in countries with small domestic markets.[60] Among the ten largest such TNCs in 1999, Seagram is placed 9, and other companies in the top ten include Swedish Electrolux, Swiss ABB, and Dutch Akzo Nobel NV.[61]

The TNMCs are in turn part of a much larger context of transnationalization and globalization. Moreover, if publishing has been affected especially since the beginning of the 1960s, the rise of the modern TNMC must be seen as concomitant with the rise of TNCs in general. From 7,000 at the end of the 1960s to 40,000 in the second half of the 1990s, the growth of TNCs has been dramatic in the developed countries.[62] With the exception of three companies – Hutchinson Whampoa Ltd from China (48), Petróleos de Venezuela (84), and Cemex SA from Mexico (100) (in that same order the top three of the fifty largest TNCs from developing economies in the *World Investment Report 2001*) – all TNCs are found in developed countries.[63] TNCs are one of the driving forces in the knowledge-based economy and are as such at the 'core of the process of globalization.'[64]

What I have described so far is a structural reconfiguration. The mergers and acquisitions will no doubt continue, just as assuredly as the players and corporations involved will have different names. What remains a constant are restructured premises for the global economy in general: a deregulation of the market, increased transnational markets and capital flows following the continued free-trade doctrine elaborated since the Second World War, the ascendancy of English as a global language. As we have already seen, the economic importance of publishing in pure monetary terms borders on the insignificant. Its impact reaches, however, far beyond what the comparison between media conglomerates and other transnational corporations suggests, and we must rather search for the reason behind the continued importance of print properties elsewhere. Albert Greco's point that 'the U.S. book industry was the prestigious keystone of the entire mass communications industry, primarily for the "content" it generated,' is therefore an interesting one to consider.[65]

II

In July 2000 Bertelsmann appointed Rolf Schmidt-Holtz as new Executive Board member with the title Chief Creative Officer, or CCO.[66] This was a logical step in light of the new corporate organization, which rested on three strategic sectors: Content Network, Media Services and Direct-to-Customer Business. The units of the so-called Content Network – the five divisions Random House, BMG, Gruner + Jahr, the RTL Group, and Bertelsmann Springer – were described as striving towards one common goal: *excellence in content*.[67] Very few words are used by TNMC executives with the same frequency or with similar self-assuredness as *content*. Its definition in my daughters' *Oxford American Desk Dictionary and Thesaurus* as 'what is contained, as in a ... book' immediately reveals a genealogy from print culture. Contrary to what the critical embodiment in material form suggests, controlling one of the highest valued kinds of contemporary property is not so much dependent on the familiar physical object we consult seeking entertainment, knowledge, or information, but rather reflects a desire to own what André Schiffrin calls the 'profitable tip of the information pyramid'; the expressions, ideas, stories, and thoughts currently found in an array of forms, but that used to be, as he continues laconically, 'available simply by consulting a book.'[68] At first sight, such a valuable resource would seem to require authors – in the sense of physical persons – but what I intend to trace next is the importance of content as a thing produced, owned, and protected by corporations. As should have become clear by now, the author in this chapter is consequently not the individual as much as the legal entity of the publishing house.

©

Exports from the cultural industries became crucial sources of revenue for the United States following the Second World War. Apparent in film and music, U.S. exports of books also grew from $12 million in 1945 to $50 million by 1960 and $175 million by 1970.[69] The movie industry had prospered abroad since the beginning of the twentieth century and as early as in 1914, 85 per cent of the world film audience watched Ameri-

can films.[70] Hollywood's European exports – films, television programming, and videotapes – increased by 225 per cent between 1984 and
1988, to some $561 million annually. Worldwide exports doubled in
value between 1987 and 1991 from $1.1 billion to $2.2 billion, whereas
film and television *imports* totalled a modest $81 million in 1991. The
United States enjoyed a trade surplus with Europe in media fare of
$6.3 billion in 1995, more than tripling the media trade surplus between
the U.S. and Europe for 1988.[71]

Even if awareness of the contribution made by the cultural industries
in securing this economic preeminence must have been apparent with
the arrival of mass-produced moving images and records, intellectual
property rights as explicit *policy* is a fairly new phenomenon in the
United States, and it was the sea change of the global economy that
made it possible. Interconnected, technology-driven, and above all,
knowledge-based, this economy was stimulated by products the United
States had or could manufacture plenty of in elite universities, research
parks, or Hollywood studios; subsequently, U.S. companies were likely
to benefit from the deregulation of global markets and the increase in
transnational trade, whether their business was in pharmaceuticals,
software, or sitcoms. As a major exporter of intellectual property products – be they patented or copyrighted – two simultaneous market
movements further underwrote the drift towards increased emphasis
on global protection; at home, domestic markets were in some cases
nearing saturation; abroad, foreign markets represented the potential
for substantial new revenues, but on the downside many of these
provided inadequate intellectual property protection.

As a consequence, U.S. business interests resolutely rallied around
the cause of international intellectual property rights, demonstrated in
part by the launch of organizations such as the International Intellectual
Property Alliance (IIPA) in 1984. Add to the brew the fact that IBM,
General Electric, Disney, and other companies worked hard to ensure
that intellectual property became an important part of the GATT Uruguay round,[72] and you have a comprehensive tactic Peter Drahos describes as leading up to the global period in intellectual property
regulation.[73] IIPA claims that those industries who 'create copyrighted
materials as their primary product,'[74] continue to be one of the fastest
growing segments of the U.S. economy, and that the annual growth of
these so-called core copyright industries has been more than twice that
of the economy as a whole.[75] According to IIPA the foreign sales/
exports of these corporations – growing from $36 billion in 1991 to $89

billion in 2001[76] – exceed almost all other major sectors in the U.S. economy, including aircraft, cars, and chemicals.[77] Because this industry represents such a vital segment of the U.S. economy, any potential loss due to unauthorized use – estimated in IIPA's 2002 'Special 301' Recommendations at $838 billion in 2001 – indicates considerable adverse effects.[78] Another member of IIPA, the Business Software Alliance (BSA), put the world piracy rate at 37 per cent in 2000, predicted their loss for that year at $11.75 billion,[79] and concluded in a survey together with the Software and Information Industry Association (SIIA) released in 1999, that the United States and Canada were the two nations most severely hit by piracy, leading every other world region with 26 per cent of the total.[80] In 1995, it was estimated that China produced $1.8 billion, Russia $726 million, and Italy $515 million worth of U.S. films, books, and recorded music without compensating originating firm or artist.[81]

Not until the mid-1980s would a revamped trade policy put an end to the ad hoc approach favoured up until then and secure intellectual property rights the full attention of the U.S. government. The financial importance of copyright in relation to the export industry had created a 'copyright super lobby' in Washington, whose concerns fell on the favourable ears of industry-insider-incumbent President Ronald Reagan.[82] His era of liberalization and deregulation could not have provided a better climate in which to fortify the connection between trade and intellectual property, laying the foundation of what appears to be a strong bi-partisan consensus in support of intellectual property as the 'engine driving U.S. economy into the 21st century.'[83] A clear link between intellectual property, trade, and export was established, one that has only been reinforced as the export market surpassed the domestic in importance.[84]

The basis for these changes is section 301 of the Trade and Tariff Act of 1974 giving the President the right to enforce U.S. interests in trade agreements, and allowing industries, trade associations, and individuals to petition the United States Trade Representative (USTR) if they feel that U.S. commerce is somehow jeopardized by unfair practices and piracy. Established in 1962, but renamed the Office of the United States Trade Representative in 1980, the USTR is the chief trade negotiator for the United States and its representative in major international trade organizations. In a 1984 amendment by Congress, the USTR's authority was extended so that it could initiate cases on its own accord, and for the first time, failure to adequately protect intellectual property was deemed actionable. Another important incident at this time was the accession of the United States to the Berne Convention. After substantial lobbying from the core copyright industries and after a century of congressional debate, Congress quietly and with the presence of only five members signed the Convention in 1986, the same year that the Uruguay round was launched.[85]

Additional muscle came with the enactment of H.R. 4848, the Omnibus Trade and Competitiveness Act of 1988 and the new amendments to section 301. The USTR was permitted to identify unfair practices, but could now also introduce trade sanctions as retaliatory measures in response to insufficient intellectual property protection. Under the 'Special 301' and the 'Super 301' the USTR must annually identify intellectual property priority countries, thirty days after which the agency must self-initiate an investigation, determine if action is warranted, and decide what sort of action is to be taken.[86] In the 2002 Special 301 Report issued by the USTR, the Ukraine is designated Priority Foreign Country for the second year running, with an estimated level of piracy of 80 per cent in the category Motion Pictures (down from 99 per cent in 2000) and 85 per cent in Records and Music (down from 95 per cent in 2000), leading to continued U.S. sanctions – valued at $75 million – that were initially imposed on Ukrainian products in January 2002.[87] Together with the so-called Generalized System of Preferences (GSP), which accords preferential duty-free entry into the U.S. market for about 140 designated beneficiary countries and territories, the United States enacted between 1984–8 a powerful set of trade instruments which could act as leverage in order to ensure and enforce the interests of the core copyright industries.[88] Mexico and Brazil – the former a signatory of NAFTA and the latter one of the strongest opponents to U.S. trade policy who suffered retaliatory tariffs for two years because of lack of protection for pharmaceutical patents – have even been suggested as 'natural laboratories,' furnishing goldmines of information on how the U.S. may further implement its global IPR policies.[89]

The discourse on 'piracy' takes on a more sinister tone as the contribution of the core copyright industries to the national economy is applauded. Many of IIPA's member organizations feature prominently the opportunity to report infringements on their web sites.[90] Industry insiders such as Sergio Robleto, managing director at the corporate security firm Kroll Associates, compare infringements in intellectual property with drug trafficking, concluding in close to paranoid terms that 'the bandits are everywhere.'[91] Organized crime in the shape of the

Italian Mafia and the Russian mob, as well as the IRA and Middle Eastern terrorists are said to prosper from counterfeit rings and piracy,[92] and the British Alliance Against Counterfeiting and Piracy (AACP) refers to a 1995 confirmation from the Royal Ulster Constabulary that counterfeit videos represented a major source of funding for the IRA.[93]

©

Under the chairmanship of former Congresswoman Patricia S. Schroeder, the Association of American Publishers, Inc. (AAP) is one IIPA member actively supporting the agenda for increased copyright control.[94] However, the very vocal call made by the publishing industry in favour of trade sanctions, retaliatory measures, and increased intervention to ensure stronger protection in the light of the new digital environment, is a point of view illustrative of a particular and contingent position of power. Urging publishers to back all measures protecting content by intellectual property rights or face certain extinction[95] provides, in the perspective of history, a fascinating insight into the memory loss of an industry that once could not have persevered let alone reached its present position *without* recourse to piracy. Indeed, prominent historian John Tebbel suggests in his monumental exposé on the history of American publishing that international copyright would have been a hindrance to book publishing in the United States had it been enacted before the Civil War.[96] Publishing novels without rights being bought or awarding foreign authors any compensation was an activity considered illegal from an official European standpoint, but completely above board in the United States, where only domestic writers were protected by copyright law. Interestingly enough, this did not apply to The Provisional Congress of the Confederacy, which, in an 1861 act, extended copyrights to citizens of any foreign state or power.[97] West & Johnston, one of the South's leading publishing houses at that time, accused the 'Yankee swindlers' of robbing foreign authors of the fruits of their labour, and added that fortunately such disgraceful proceedings were not part of Southern practice or legislation.[98]

Using piracy in order to build a domestic publishing industry proved not only detrimental to the group of British authors led by Harriet Martineau, who in 1837 co-wrote a petition entitled 'Address of Certain Authors of Great Britain' and brought the issue of international copyright to the attention of the U.S. Congress for the first time, but to American authors as well, who saw their own interests broadsided by

competition from cheap British imports. In all fairness, American publishers were not the only ones who disregarded copyright; within weeks
of the U.S. publication of Harriet Beecher Stowe's *Uncle Tom's Cabin* in
1852, a million and a half pirated copies began surfacing in England.[99]

The U.S. policy in regard to copyright demonstrates a strong protectionist slant that relied on the implementation of several complicated
formalities, all of which would effectively bar the United States from
coming into compliance with international copyright conventions. The
1976 Copyright Act prescribed three formalities in order to secure copyright: affixation of notice; deposits of copies, and registration of claims
in the Copyright Office. The most contentious barrier was, however, the
so-called manufacturing clause that remained in place up until U.S.
accession to Berne, and which called for manufacturing in the United
States or Canada in order to qualify for copyright. Not being a signa-
tory to the Berne Convention did not hinder the United States from
using Canada as a convenient loophole (Canada had joined Berne in
1928) to secure protection under the convention by publishing first
editions simultaneously in both countries.[100]

If American authors were worried that the absence of any effective
copyright legislation was ruining the prospects for a national cadre of
authors to support themselves, those in favour of international copyright agreements in the political arena visualized that the United States
would be excluded from the workings of the civilized world by its
failure to protect authorship: 'The United States of America must give
its adhesion to international copyright or stand as the literary Ishmael
of the civilized world,' was only one of the arguments in favour of such
a step.[101] On the other hand, the opposition to any form of protection
for foreign authors was extremely vociferous and primarily launched
on behalf of the publishing industry.[102] The argument was one for free
trade – the implications of which will take quite a different turn for the
American involvement in the issue as we move closer to our own time –
and for the democratic accessibility of cheap books to the American
audience.

The perspective of the United States at this time is that of a developing nation, bent on safeguarding its own industry at any cost. If any
sort of regulation were to be implemented, prices would go up, publishers and booksellers would go bankrupt, and the ongoing process of
democratization in the vast country would be undone. The arguments
against U.S. observance of international agreements and standards were

launched in a rebellious tone that came across indicating a very conscious payback by the ex-colony on its former masters. In a memorial presented to the House and Senate on 13 June 1842, from the Philadelphia law-book publishers T.&J.W. Johnson, English literature is described as a common cultural source, one that the previously oppressed now could use to further their own agenda of independence. Their point was made in no uncertain terms:

> All the riches of English literature are ours. English authorship comes free as the vital air, untaxed, unhindered, even by the necessity of translation, into our country; and the question is, Shall we tax it, and thus interpose a barrier to the circulation of intellectual and moral light? Shall we build up a dam, to obstruct the flow of the rivers of knowledge?' ... Shall we refuse to gather the share of this harvest, which Providence, and our own position, makes our own?[103]

Thus, the publishing industry was an ardent proponent for strong protectionist measures during the nineteenth-century in order to ensure its continued prosperity. Illegal copying was a perfectly valid means to this highly desirable end, and the discourse underpinning the activity reverberated with the same intensity and the same ideology as developing nations have always used: special consideration is needed in order to build an infrastructure that otherwise would be harder to come by and severely crippled without the shortcut of unauthorized use. It is from these early days of U.S. publishing that the corporation takes on the role of the author, materialized most distinctly today in the work-for-hire principle. Content becomes a valuable asset, first to be used in order to achieve a certain goal and later, since the 1980s, to be protected against the uses and abuses of others.

What we have caught sight of in this chapter is the emergence of a knowledge-based economy where information and content become principal products *in themselves*. Although I intend to explore the issue of trade and intellectual property rights more in detail in the next chapter, it is without a doubt during the 1980s that the United States reverses its previous, century-old withdrawal from international conventions and agreements, and instead begins to use the emerging global knowledge-based economy with its elaborate trade system in order to secure increased and continued international protection for its valuable resources.

III

Since the 1960s, one of the major incentives behind the conglomeratization of the TNMCs – both horizontally and vertically – has been the continued amassment of one particularly valuable resource: content. Whether we know it as information, knowledge, or entertainment, the largest media conglomerates are by now fully integrated and they continue to seek further consolidation, exercising control not only over content, but over all possible channels used in order to distribute that resource. And this is the point where the third element considered in this chapter enters the picture.

Both the two megamergers discussed previously – AOL Time Warner and Vivendi Universal – came about because of a fundamental expectation in the benefits of *convergence*. Representing a potential for content owners to draw on any number of new technological platforms in order to exploit their resources to the fullest, telecommunications, cable, and Internet *convergence* suggests that the traditional functions of telephones, television sets, and personal computers are merging. Ideally, old and new media would find a home together in this dream of synergy heaven and the Internet would provide the bits to make it all come true. Despite the importance of the media industry, it was still a David compared to the Goliath the International Telecommunication Union (ITU) refers to as the 'info-communications sector' with output valued at almost $1.5 trillion in 1994. Divided between telecommunication (46 per cent), computers (33 per cent) and media (21 per cent), it is a sector that has been growing at twice the rate of the balance of the global economy in the 1990s with, or so it seemed at the time, no indication of a let-up. As in media, telecommunications are becoming global, through alliances and cross-national mergers, partnerships and acquisitions; even more than in the former area, deregulation is central to the expansion of this sector.[104] The example of Mannesman shows just how intense cross-border M&As in telecommunications can be: acquired by Vodafone AirTouch at the price of $200 billion in 2000, Mannesman had previously bought Orange PLC (UK) and Ing C Olivetti-Telecom Int (Italy) in 1999.[105] But the TNMCs are not the only ones who consider convergence the future: in the WIPO Copyright Treaty (WCT) the relationship between content and convergence is made explicit in the preamble, where the reasons for the treaty's existence are laid out; *'Recognizing the profound impact of the development and convergence of information and communication technologies on the creation and use of literary works ...'*

While the promise of a golden hinterland may have set off the AOL Time Warner and Vivendi mergers, both conglomerates fell on hard times in 2002. The combination of a brutal stock market backlash and the 11 September terrorist attacks in New York and Washington in 2001 swiftly turned technological over-optimism into a splitting hangover. Almost within hours of one another in December 2001, Gerald Levin, CEO of AOL Time Warner, surprisingly announced his departure from the company for 'personal reasons,' and Edgar Bronfman Jr, who brought Seagram into the conglomerate merger with Vivendi, announced that he would resign as executive vice-chairman.[106] Their departures were only harbingers of worse things to come. In May 2002, *Fortune* reported that AOL Time Warner's shares had plummeted 60 per cent since the merger in January 2001, wiping out a shareholder value of more than $117 billion.[107] During the same approximate time period, Vivendi Universal stocks collapsed from €120 to €39.[108] For the 2002 first quarter AOL Time Warner reported a loss of $54 billion.[109] Vivendi Universal fared no better when it announced minus €17 billion for the same quarter.[110]

To boot, Vivendi Universal had severe managerial problems to contend with. CEO Jean-Marie Messier was fighting off criticism during the spring of 2002, primarily for firing Pierre Lescure, founder and head of embattled French TV channel Canal+. Suffering from a debt of €5 billion and losses of €700 million a year, Canal+ has a statutory duty to fund French films, and many feared that removing Lescure signalled that the nation's prestigious film industry was in jeopardy and would be drowned in the maelstrom of shallow U.S. corporate culture.[111] At the Vivendi Universal annual meeting, Messier was beleaguered by angry protesters, forced to plow back his €1.5 million bonus into company shares, and pledge not to claim his portion of a controversial option package if share prices did not reach €60 during 2002.[112]

Troubles would escalate even further and throughout the summer of 2002 it became clear that the house that the media moguls had built was falling apart as if its walls were made of cards, not bricks. Bigger had not meant better and very little, if anything, of the hopes of synergy and convergence had been realized in an economy that showed no signs of recovery. Heads began to roll at the beginning of July, and the first to be shown the door was Jean-Marie Messier. Under increasing fire from within the company's board, one of his severest critics turned out to be former ally Edgar Bronfman Jr, a man who since the merger between Seagram and Vivendi had not only seen Vivendi Universal's share take an 85 per cent nose-dive, but who also had to watch $3.6 billion of his family's fortune evaporate. As Messier went and Jean-René Fourtou took his place, Bronfman, who remains on the board and represents the crumbling conglomerate's largest shareholder, may be in a position to vindicate himself in a new, revamped organization by, as he put it 'helping Universal Vivendi organize its strategy and then implement it.'[113]

On 18 July Bob Pittman, chief operating officer at AOL Time Warner, left the company at a time when the bleeding AOL he was supposed to salvage seemed beyond rescue and basically no positive signs could be spotted on the foggy Internet sky.[114] And then, at the end of that tumultuous month, came perhaps the most spectacular departure of them all: Thomas Middelhoff was fired from Bertelsmann after what the *Guardian* termed 'a blistering row over corporate strategy.'[115] In contrast to the financial turmoil of Vivendi Universal and other media conglomerates, Bertelsmann was the only such company to turn a profit in 2001.[116] However, Middelhoff's seemingly successful tactics appear to have backfired on several counts. As the market tightened and advertising spending sank to an all-time low, Middelhoff's controversial acquisition of Napster, his ambitions to take the company from its traditional emphasis on print into new media, and the increasing reluctance from the board to implement a stock market introduction in 2005, were all factors contributing to his downfall.[117]

While the departure of these well-known chieftains was visible as well as dramatic, they are emblematic of developments beyond personal accountability. The days of the media-shopping spree are over, at least for the conceivable future. As 2002 drew to a close, nobody was heard promoting convergence, the Internet hype was long gone, flamboyant executives were replaced by more conservative ones, and selling instead of buying became a favoured corporate activity. At Vivendi Universal Publishing's purchase of Houghton Mifflin in 2001, Jean-Marie Messier talked of a strategic acquisition and 'another step forward for Vivendi Universal to achieve world leadership in key content segments.'[118] In an unintentionally symbolic announcement, Vivendi Universal issued a press release on New Year's Eve 2002 in which it announced selling off the same U.S. publisher, acquired under such fanfare only the year before.[119]

The chaos surrounding the media conglomerates can be read against *Business Week*'s suggestion that 2002 probably will be remembered as the *annus horribilis* of business.[120] AOL Time Warner became implicated in one of the year's nastiest frauds, which typically enough befell a telecommunications giant, WorldCom, who filed the world's biggest bankruptcy after it became clear that the company had falsified accounts to the tune of $6 billion. It was precisely the search for correspondences between telecommunications and media content that made the alliance between the two seem obvious as well as lucrative.[121] Between accounting scandals, publicized personal departures, and the failure of new technology to deliver unlimited profit potential, an organic media evolution proved illusory. When the AOL Time Warner deal was announced, predictions were that the older media, represented by Time Warner, would quickly be surpassed by the growth of AOL and the Internet. While this is being written, things have gone the other way and instead corporate strategies indicate slimmer, more logical organizations and a 'back to basics' approach.[122]

Whether or not the TNMCs will grow, downsize and divest, or perhaps prove to be a mere footnote in media history, remains to be seen. More certain is that the anticipated marriage between conglomeratization, content, and convergence remains one of the pivotal forces behind the current prominence accorded to intellectual property rights.[123]

Chapter Five

FROM THE 'INTELLECTUAL'
TO THE 'CULTURAL':
CAN THERE BE PROPERTY WITH
A 'DIFFERENCE'?

'Only a challenge to the hierarchy of *sites* of discourse, which usually comes from groups and classes "situated" by the dominant in low or marginal positions,' suggest Peter Stallybrass and Allon White in *The Politics and Poetics of Transgression*, 'carries the promise of politically transformative power.'[1] The following pages will mark a radical departure from the perspective deployed in the previous chapter. There, we witnessed the exhaustive penetration and impact of the media conglomerates, providing, through a demonstration of the alluringly familiar yet strikingly limited schema of relentless corporate domination, sufficient reason to expand the perimeters of this book in a different direction. Clearly, the ideology of authorship has served intellectual property rights well, at least in so far as it has been successful enough to ensure the abstracted object content – and the industries profiting from that asset – into major contenders in the knowledge-based economy. Today, the true test of what will and will not count as intellectual property is, as Christopher May so well puts it, if it can be considered trade related or not.[2] As one of the leading interfaces of nations with others,[3] free trade is the founding principle upon which the current global interplay concerning intellectual property rights today rests.

It is hardly to be marvelled at that the powerful core copyright industries have been successful in establishing the ground rules for the relationship between trade and intellectual property rights. For a more complete picture to emerge, however, we need to consider more carefully the contentious *making* of these rights. By focusing on the ongoing efforts to incorporate traditional knowledge and folklore within the current global regime of intellectual property rights, my aim is to assess whether the ideology of authorship can withstand transfer from its successful appropriation in the domain of the 'intellectual' to a possible use in the domain of the 'cultural.' Such an approach should make it possible to include the experiences of those positioned at a disadvantage by current intellectual property regimes, while also incorporating the perspective of agency from below.

Developed in European nation-states and then exported by way of a colonial apparatus, property rights have always worked in favour of the colonizer, and as the post-colonial world struggles to leave legislation imposed from the centre and to formulate policies sensitive to indigenous traditions and resources while striving for inclusion in the world trade system, a number of tensions are brought to bear on intellectual property rights. If intellectual property is contradictory by default, then the challenges facing holders of traditional knowledge who seek to protect and profit from their assets under the existing system or alternatively under a new *sui generis* regime show that theirs is an even more compounded dilemma. As we can expect the discussion on the uneven distribution of power and wealth in the knowledge-based society to intensify even further, we must be aware of the fact that crucial elements in that debate centres on the struggle for recognition of resources that seek validation as property but that encounter resistance in being accepted as such currency. In their function as indicators of what we might consider protectable in the future, these conflicts are perhaps even more important because they provide us with clues as to why and how such choices are made, and with what consequences. Is it therefore possible that the appropriation of intellectual property rights by those groups generally labelled 'marginalized' or as belonging to the developing nations show a possible redistribution of power? To what extent is there a countermovement to the events we saw in the previous chapter? Moreover, how does it relate to the concept of 'culture'? Can there be cultural property rights? What does it look like? Finally, perhaps the most important question of all: why should anyone claim cultural property rights? In light of the many controversies inherent in the *intellectual versus the cultural*, what might appear a mere exercise in semantics is, I argue, much more like opening a Pandora's Box already left temptingly ajar.

I

There is no way to relay the importance of intellectual property rights – or for that matter entertain the possibility of 'cultural' property rights –

without considering the symbiotic relationship between international business and international politics. At the same time as the TNCs and TNMCs gain a firm foothold on an increasingly transnational market, we see a simultaneous growth of intergovernmental organizations and non-governmental organizations (NGOs) take place: the Union des Associations Internationales notes that in 1909 there were 213 of all types, a number increasing to 50,373 ninety years later.[4] While trade benefits unquestionably were an incentive for intellectual property rights as early as in the days of Victor Hugo, in order to comprehend how trade has become such a decisive vehicle for structural power within the knowledge-based economy, we need to backtrack more precisely to the Second World War.

In 1946, plans were made for an international trade organization (ITO) to be set up under the auspices of the United Nations Economic and Social Council (ECOSOC). It has been estimated that the four preparatory meetings leading up to the final ITO charter in Havana, Cuba, in 1948 produced more than twenty-seven thousand pages in over one hundred volumes.[5] Together with the International Monetary Fund (IMF), and the International Bank for Reconstruction and Development (IBRD, better known as the World Bank) – both results of the 1944 Bretton Woods Conference – ITO was envisioned as one in a trio of post–Second World War multinational organizations dedicated to the furthering of economic development.[6]

Intended only as an interim measure awaiting the finalization of ITO, the same twenty-three countries drafting the ITO charter signed the General Agreement on Tariffs and Trade (GATT) in Geneva on 30 October 1947. However, because the United States Congress suspected that U.S. membership would result in the loss of autonomy in trade policy, it voted against ratification of the charter. In 1950 President Truman announced that he would refrain from continuing to seek the support of the Congress for ITO membership, and the organization never came into being.[7] Instead, GATT continued as a 'nonorganization' de facto organizing international trade in a number of 'rounds' up until it emerged as the World Trade Organization (WTO) on 1 January 1995.[8]

Of particular interest in this context is the eighth and final round, the Uruguay round (1986–94). The Uruguay round represents a turning point in GATT trade agreements because for the first time intellectual property becomes an official issue on the agenda. As the discussion in the previous chapter shows, this was in large part thanks to intense efforts from the United States, whose own trade policy in respect to intellectual property rights at the same time underwent momentous changes due to close industry-government cooperation. The first five GATT rounds had exclusively dealt with reductions in tariffs, and it was not until the Tokyo round (1973–9) that GATT began to shift its emphasis of approach in subject matter.[9]

The concerns of the Uruguay round confirm that a decisive reconfiguration of the world economy had taken place – from industrial to informational production – and that prosperity in this new codependent matrix was primarily an issue of access to and participation in global trade flows. Those who for whatever reason did not or could not trade were almost certain to be left behind in a world increasingly favouring the owning of and access to content as the basis for continued prosperity. This development has not abated, but rather accelerated with increased global interconnection. In 2001, the forty-nine nations designated Least Developed Countries (LDCs) by UNCTAD – thirty of whom are members of WTO – represented 10.7 per cent of the world population, but only accounted for 0.5 per cent of the world GNP.[10] There are indications that their contribution to world trade is shrinking, both in general terms and as it relates to their capacity to produce cultural exports.[11] 1.1 billion people survive on less than $1 a day.[12] On the other hand, the world's twenty-four developed nations are finding themselves in a very different situation, where their labour force is substantially and increasingly employed by companies either producing or using highly advanced information technology and/or services.[13]

Inserting intellectual property on the GATT agenda was consequently not an uncontested move.[14] During the 1970s, the position of the developing nations vis-à-vis intellectual property rights could be described as sceptical, if not downright hostile. The South had at that time successfully managed to establish questions relating to North–South inequality primarily on the UN agenda, where the 'one vote, one nation' system provided LDCs with a far more sympathetic venue in which to launch their concerns than the weighted vote in IMF or the World Bank allowed for. Decolonization meant strengths in numbers, and led by the Group of 77 (G77) there was a general call for more, not less, state intervention.[15] Developing nations were boosted in their efforts to accomplish a New International Economic Order (NIEO) by the apparent success of the Organization of the Petroleum Exporting Countries (OPEC), whose commodity leverage during the oil crisis of the 1970s raised hopes in some quarters and fear in others that power of this kind could spawn equally successful constellations elsewhere.[16]

During the Uruguay round it became clear that the negotiating arenas for intellectual property rights were becoming increasingly polarized: the United States was profoundly dissatisfied with UN organizations such as UNCTAD and favoured GATT and walked out of UNESCO in 1984 because of controversies surrounding the work of the International Commission for the Study of Communication Problems.[17] Many LDCs, on the other hand, argued that talks on intellectual property should be carried out within WIPO rather than GATT, disputing the adequacy of the latter to provide a broad forum for debate.[18] It is interesting to note that the position of the United States appears to be much more positive in respect to WIPO than to either UNESCO or the United Nations, partly perhaps due to the fact that WIPO is largely self-financed and consequently operates along market rules, but also due to what some see as its position closer to the Organization for Economic Co-Operation and Development (OECD) than to that of UNCTAD.[19] Even those in basic support of the U.S. policy in intellectual property rights have, however, launched critiques against the U.S. failure to contribute voluntary funds to WIPO's budget.[20]

A combination of internal and external factors – failure to rally a unified front paired with an unstoppable and accelerated transnational flows of an increasingly immaterial and informational, rather than commodity-based nature – made it clear that the New International Economic Order and the New World Information and Communication Order (NWICO) promoted by the Group of 77 and the developing nations in UNCTAD and UNESCO would fail. At the core of their suggestions was a wish to secure both information and more tangible riches as common heritage, refuting and arguing against the privatization of both. The conclusions of the International Commission for the Study of Communication Problems, documented in the so-called MacBride Report, made it emphatically clear that economy and information were two concepts of equal standing, deeply enmeshed and interdependent, and the Report stressed therefore that the two major programs of NIEO and NWICO had to be considered together, and that concrete plans of action linking both processes should be implemented within the United Nations system.[21]

Diane Otto argues that from a subaltern studies perspective, the failure of the G77 can be understood against the complicated position of the LDCs, a position that made it possible to launch these two programs to begin with but which also required them to uncritically embrace a European framework.[22] While it is difficult to conceive of a viable alternative that would secure a more powerful subaltern position in respect to a govermentality built on a colonial system, the combination of self-projection, coercion, less investment, huge debt, direct threats of trade sanctions, and the conditions of a new global economy led developing nations gradually to shift their course of action from a state interventionist politics towards a more market-driven one.[23] As the Uruguay round drew to a close, anxious voices were heard for the fate of developing nations, arguing that they should do their utmost to ensure that intellectual property rights were not inserted and institutionalized into formalized trade regimes.[24] Of concern was, of course, the possibility that such steps would only further cement the division between those who were 'information rich' and those who were 'information poor.'

The Final Act of the GATT agreement was signed in Marrakech, on 15 April 1994. In January that same year, the North American Free Trade Agreement (NAFTA) between the United States, Canada, and Mexico entered into force. However, these two major trade agreements came into fruition with significant exceptions relating to the cultural industries. The issue of whether or not culture could be treated – and hence traded – as any other commodity was central to these controversies. Not only were intellectual property rights now a critical feature of international trade, but culture and trade were also seen as joined at the hip. As figures from UNESCO demonstrate, trade in cultural goods has skyrocketed during the last twenty years. Even if some of these statistics seem questionable, for instance, for the simple reasons outlined previously in terms of conglomeratization and transnationalization (what does it mean to elaborate with national categories such as 'German' when Bertelsmann owns Random House? To which country does the book 'belong'? Is it defined by UNESCO as German or American?), some general observations can still be made. Trade in cultural goods remains concentrated in a few countries. There have been structural changes in the types of goods traded, with the levelling off of traditional forms such as printed matter and a huge expansion of sporting goods, music, and games. The last category makes China's contribution to world cultural exports rise from 0.2 per cent in 1985 to 8.9 per cent in 1998, accounting for more than one-third of world exports in games that year.[25]

Canada had successfully managed to exempt cultural industries from the earlier Free Trade Agreement (FTA) and maintained this provision in NAFTA due to an express wish to safeguard control over both domestic content production and distribution. Mexico managed also to include a form of protectionist measure in Annex 1 of the treaty, where it is stipulated that on an annual basis, 30 per cent of the screen time of every theatre may be reserved for films produced by Mexican enterprises.[26] Because of the precedent set primarily by Canada in the NAFTA negotiations, the European Union – led by the French – successfully excluded television shows and films from the GATT agreement, this despite the fact that the United States considered the practice of channelling income from U.S. movies distributed and shown in Europe back into French and European film production as unfair and therefore actionable.[27]

Signatories to GATT were known as 'Contracting Parties,' and in WTO 'Members,' terms indicating that the latter is an organization, headquartered in Geneva, whereas the former never became one. More significantly still, WTO operates based on an all-inclusive plan: you sign up to comply in all areas, or you are not allowed to join. Another major difference from GATT is the existence of a formal Dispute Settlement Body (DSB) within WTO to solve potential conflicts between members. The Final Act integrated GATT together with TRIPS and the General Agreement on Trade in Services (GATS) into WTO. The TRIPS agreement, which is Annex 1C of the Final Act, has a unique position within the WTO context because it imposes obligations upon governments to adhere to specific policies. This is different from both GATT and GATS, consisting instead of agreements *not to* use specific policies.[28] With the long-awaited 2001 accession of China – the world's third largest economy and the fifth largest trader,[29] whose piracy infringements almost caused a full-scale trade war with the United States in 1996[30] – WTO membership as of 1 January 2002 stands at 144 member states who all have, as Director General Mike Moore put it in a 1999 speech, '*a seat at the table.*'[31]

Notwithstanding the impressive scope of the organization, TRIPS is important for two main reasons. Like no other treaty on intellectual property it has unequivocally strengthened the connection between trade and intellectual property rights, and it has done so on a truly global scale, making it, according to one critic 'one of the most effective vehicles of Western imperialism in history.'[32] Second, TRIPS has helped expand the perimeters of what can be considered intellectual property to begin with. The consequences of both these factors in regard to traditional knowledge and folklore will be discussed in the next section.

II

In November 1997, WIPO established its Global Intellectual Property Issues Division.[33] The close proximity in timing with the formation of WTO and above all, with the implementation of TRIPS, suggests that WIPO now proactively intended to meet a number of new challenges brought on by increased integration and co-dependency of nations in the expansion of the WTO framework. Furthermore, under articles 65 and 66 of TRIPS, Developing Countries and Least Developed Countries were given a grace period of four and ten years respectively during which they were bound to update their intellectual property laws to conform to TRIPS. Thus, they needed to come into compliance with TRIPS either on 1 January 2000 or 1 January 2006 (with a possibility for extension). Before the 1999 Ministerial meeting in Seattle, WTO signalled that several developing countries had asked for more time in order to deal with the 'substantial legislative and administrative burden of complying.'[34] The reasons why WIPO defined holders of traditional knowledge – often found in Developing Countries – as a key target for their efforts included the need for these countries to modernize and update their intellectual property policies to synchronize with what had been agreed on in TRIPS or face possible action under the WTO Dispute Settlement Body; they also reflected the fact that a door had opened for the enlargement of intellectual property itself. The expansionist logic at play, which stretches out the limits of what is allowed to count as intellectual property, could be beneficial to developing nations as it at least in theory meant that their resources, while previously considered neither trade-related, nor intellectual property, now stood a chance of being included in the global intellectual property regime.[35]

Both TRIPS article 10, and articles 4 and 5 of the WIPO Copyright Treaty of 1996 state that computer programs and compilations of data can be protected as intellectual creations. There is nothing remarkable about this. Agreements on intellectual property must be flexible enough to provide for new technology and innovations. The Berne Convention has been revised five times – 1908, 1928, 1948, 1967, and 1971 – partly to accommodate the impact of new technology, but also to provide for an expansion of representation. The need for increased participation from developing countries was explicitly noted in the 1964 Study Group report leading up to the 1967 Stockholm Diplomatic Conference, which read: 'It is also necessary to promote the general development of copyright by reforms intended to make the rules relating to it more simple to apply, as well as to adapt them to the social, technical and economic conditions of the contemporary community.'[36] Decolonization ensured that the needs and expectations of developing nations became a key question at the Stockholm Conference, which would also prove to be a highly conflicted forum placing developing nations and developed nations on a collision course. Developing nations felt that not enough was done to address the needs of countries for whom the higher standards of protection constituted   barriers for development, and developed nations – led by the United Kingdom – opposed any changes that would prove detrimental to either individual authors or to the copyright industries. When the United States in 1967 stated that the adopted Stockholm Protocol containing some of these amended pro-visions for developing countries would prove an insurmountable bar-rier to the predicted and long-awaited accession of the United States to the Berne Convention, the result was an historic impasse. A new Revision Conference intended to solve the problems that had sur-faced in Stockholm therefore took place only a few year later in Paris in 1971.[37]

The recognition in TRIPS of software on a par with literary works, is of course a victory for a powerful industry, but not a move necessarily advocated by the creators of the programs themselves. Few rallying cries are as well known as the 'information wants to be free' doctrine and some of its promoters have been vehemently and vocally opposed to what they perceive as an absurd stance on the part of the United States in respect to the digital environment, especially as it has come to take form in the Digital Millennium Copyright Act (DMCA). Their counterclaim is that software is a tool, the Internet a vast space of free speech, and that both should be used freely, even bettered by those who use them. In its utopian form, the Internet becomes a guarantee for social cohesion and community building on an unprecedented level, at least if it is not further circumscribed by proprietary corporate/govern-mental interests.[38]

The examples of what fall under the heading of intellectual property include any number of far more questionable claims, some of which border on the ludicrous: in the *San Francisco Arts & Athletics, Inc. v. U.S. Olympic Committee* (1987), the word OLYMPIC as well as the signs and symbols of the Olympic Games are the property of the U.S. Olympic Committee;[39] the Dutch ABN/Amro Bank holds the exclusive rights to the combination of the words The and Bank; and author's rights on techno dance were in 1997 claimed by the Zurich-based company

Techno Tanz Veranstaltungsverwertung Zurich GbR, who subsequently demanded that a Berlin disco pay copyright.[40]

There can hardly be any doubt that between them, the traditional Western knee-jerk response to what constitutes an act of creation in terms of individualism and originality favours the first type of property (intellectual) over the second (cultural). Structural power wielded in the system therefore tends to prioritize the 'intellectual' of the major TNMCs, not the 'cultural' customs, patterns, oral traditions, and ancient medicinal treatments of native or indigenous peoples. James Boyle eloquently argues: 'Curare, batik, myths, and the dance "lambada" flow out of developing countries, unprotected by intellectual property rights, while Prozac, Levis, Grisham, and the movie *Lambada!* flow in – protected by a suite of intellectual property laws, which in turn are backed by the threat of trade sanctions.'[41] A succinct commentary setting curare against Prozac and myths against Grisham, the irony of this ordering is much more insidious than witty. Behind the exemplifications lurks a duplicitous trade-off: the artefacts and practices that constitute part of a heritage and/or represent significant trade benefits have a tendency to be sucked into a Western machinery that swiftly turns the same artefacts and practices into intellectual property, and a highly policed one at that, without recognizing or acknowledging the original source. Boyle's illustration of this propensity is only one of many possible examples that all point to one decisive imbalance under scrutiny in this chapter, namely the uneven allocation of wealth stemming from resources that are or can be designated intellectual property. The transfer of lambada into *Lambada!*, placing the word 'Cherokee' on a special brand of car, using the image of the Wandjina spirit as a logo for an Australian surfboard company,[42] or traditional American Indian imagery to promote motorcycles[43] are examples of a usage mostly met with silence. Seen as belonging in the public domain, these resources are considered free for the taking.[44]

If Jane Gaines is correct, however, in claiming that copyright law is a great cultural leveller,[45] one could certainly expect this expansionist logic to be potentially as beneficial to those Stallybrass and White referred to as 'situated' by the dominant discourse, as it would be tailor-made to the wishes of the software industry or the copyright lobby. WIPO, too, argued that one of the reasons behind their proposed strategy was that since databases and software now could be included in intellectual property regimes, there was nothing per se in the system that prevented a similarly effective protection for traditional knowledge.[46]

To pursue these questions and test the validity of their hypothesis, WIPO engaged in a number of activities in 1998–9, including regional consultations in cooperation with UNESCO, two roundtables in Geneva, and perhaps most importantly, nine so-called fact-finding missions (FFM) in order to collect data and information regarding the needs of the traditional knowledge holders. All in all WIPO visited twenty-eight countries in the South Pacific, Southern and Eastern Africa, South Asia, North America, Central America, West Africa, the Arab countries, South America, and the Caribbean.[47] Such a vast geographical area, covering a number of countries placed very differently within the global matrix of economic, social, and cultural resources and needs, suggests that the possible recommendations on what should be considered protectable and what can be inferred by the expression 'traditional knowledge' in the first place, would be equally culture-specific and diverse. The extensive documentation of WIPO's work during this period also substantiates the fact that although there is overwhelming consensus on the validity of the project itself on the part of those participating in the survey, there is also considerable debate on what the terms used to denote the subject matter at hand should be taken to mean.

According to WIPO's definition, 'traditional knowledge' falls under the even broader concept of 'heritage.'[48] Expressions of folklore and indigenous knowledge are both subsets under traditional knowledge, which would make the first category positioned in the same way to traditional knowledge as copyright to intellectual property. Traditional knowledge includes tradition-based literary, artistic, or scientific works; performances; inventions; scientific discoveries; designs; marks, names and symbols; undisclosed information; and all other tradition-based innovations and creations resulting from intellectual activity in the industrial, scientific, literary, or artistic fields.[49] In fact, the only major conceptual difference from the Berne Convention is the provision of 'tradition-based' placed in front of the definition. As many TK holders pointed out to WIPO during the FFM, 'traditional' should not be taken to mean ancient/static/outdated, but rather should be considered a form of knowledge conditioned upon the living community where it is created and used while at the same time being flexible enough to stay attuned to rapidly changing surrounding conditions.[50]

What this means in practice is that a vast range of subject matter will qualify for inclusion. All FFMs mentioned the more or less obvious – patterns, designs on carpets and dresses, songs, music, dances, and so on – but the FFM to Eastern and Southern Africa included traditional methods of hairstyling and preparing foods as well as denotation of numbers by finger language,[51] the FFM to the South Pacific listed indigenous 'styles' and immovable cultural property,[52] and the FFM to Central America mentioned the use of traditional fragrances, for example, incense.[53] In order to understand the mechanisms allowing WIPO and us to even begin to conceptualize these expressions as protectable – as they in many ways represent absolute opposites to what we know would be necessary for something to be considered intellectual property at all – we need to look more closely at the specific problematic posed by cultural expressions in respect to intellectual property rights.

Reflecting directly on the themes of this book, folklore will be at the centre of the following discussion. Article 15(4) of the Berne Convention Stockholm Act, which refers to the protection of 'unpublished works where the identity of the author is unknown,' did not explicitly single out folklore, but since it was clear that this was the intended field of application,[54] it represented an important step in the recognition of authorship without author, or at least without the umbilical cord to either material object or individual/legal person. While folklore has been scrutinized by UNESCO and WIPO for a longer period of time than TK, scholars have concluded that it might be ill-suited to be conceptualized within the domain of copyright.[55] Yet, most developing nations who have special provisions regarding folklore in their national legislation have generally done so under the rubric of copyright.[56] In recapitulating the many joint incentives launched by UNESCO and WIPO in this field since the early 1970s, UNESCO specifically makes it clear that the need to protect folklore is linked to its content,[57] and the WIPO-UNESCO Model Provisions for National Laws on the Protection of Expressions of Folklore Against Illicit Exploitation and other Prejudicial Actions (1982), often mentioned as a standard setting mechanism for the national legislations that exist in the area, refer to people who are the 'authors of their folklore.'[58] The totality of activities undertaken by WIPO shows that this term was perhaps the most problematic of all used, as it has been considered both detrimental in nature as well as profoundly Eurocentric in outlook.[59] In its Recommendation on the Safeguarding of Traditional Culture and Folklore (1989), UNESCO makes the following definition of folklore:

Folklore (or traditional and popular culture) is the totality of tradition-based creations of a cultural community, expressed by a group or individuals and recognized as reflecting the expectations of a community in so far as they reflect its cultural and social identity; its standards and values are transmitted orally, by imitation or by other means.[60]

The four categories of expressions included in the WIPO-UNESCO Model Provisions are the following: verbal (folk tales, folk poetry, riddles); musical sounds (folk songs and instrumental music); by action (folk dances, plays, and artistic forms of rituals); and finally tangible expressions (pottery, sculpture, carvings, woodwork, etc.).[61] Thus, the conflict between the material and the immaterial is downplayed in this instance, since there is no material prerequisite for protection in the Model Provisions. Songs and music need not be written down, dances not choreographed.

As the number of meetings, conferences, and other fora regarding folklore has intensified, so has the apparent need for a reformulated terminology. While the Action Plan for the Safeguarding of the Intangible Cultural Heritage (2001) stresses the need for a study of a more appropriate terminology,[62] and alternatives have been suggested, such as 'cultural and intellectual property of indigenous peoples,'[63] as of the present moment, there is no obvious replacement and despite the negative connotation it might imply, I will continue to use the term in this chapter. It needs to be said that in this maze of variations on a single theme, the 'indigenous' poses yet another, since as WIPO correctly points out, while all indigenous peoples are TK holders, not all TK holders are indigenous.[64] It would be dangerous for this to detract from the main problem at hand: namely if, why, and how folklore can be made into either intellectual or cultural property.[65]

Therefore, if there is an expansionary logic in intellectual property rights then it show us not only that the very items sought for protection can be new (OLYMPIC, software, hairstyles, databases, techno, or incense) but also that those who seek to protect these 'new' assets are represented by a much broader base than previously, including the obvious corporate alliances and lobby groups but also global and highly interconnected grass-roots movements.

In sum, WIPO's mission was twofold: to ensure and secure developing countries' compliance with TRIPS, but also to investigate the possibility of traditional knowledge holders' assets being brought into the orbit of trade-related intellectual property rights. At the WIPO General Assembly in 2000, an Intergovernmental Committee on Intellectual Property and Genetic Resources, Traditional Knowledge, and Folklore was established with the mandate to create a forum in which these questions would be further debated. As of 2002, the Intergovernmental Committee has met four times to engage in three main fields of inquiry: 1) access to genetic resources and benefit sharing; 2) protection of traditional knowledge, innovations, and creativity, whether or not associated with these resources; and 3) the protection of folklore, including handicrafts.[66] While technically all three categories are equally important, in practice the first two have come to somewhat overshadow the third. It is increasingly the case that the biodiversity of developing nations and the question of patents has been the most significant issue of contention in TRIPS, and the reason for this is that it is both more pressing in humanitarian terms and potentially more lucrative than folklore. While the loss of language and culture may be even more acute than the depletion of biological resources, it is equally true that the conceptualization of exactly how culture and language should be safeguarded remains more difficult to identify than the strategies for securing biological diversity.[67] In addition, biodiversity represents serious money: in 1995 it was estimated that the market value of pharmaceutical derivatives from indigenous people's traditional medicine was $43 billion worldwide. In their bioprospecting, together with pharmaceutical giant Merck, the nonprofit Costa Rican Instituto Nacional de Biodiversidad (INBio) stands to gain royalties from its 10,000 collected samples that could generate more than $100 million for Costa Rica per annum.[68]

At the time of the 3rd WTO Ministerial Meeting in Seattle in 1999, the TRIPS agreement was up for review. There is no provision for 'traditional knowledge' in the present wording, and many developing nations saw their chance to insert the question of traditional knowledge on the program. Dreading the imminent loss of traditional medicinal knowledge, the unfair exploitation of developing nations natural resources, and the problematic issue of how to secure patents based on knowledge that by definition could not live up to the novelty demand of patent claims, representative interventions focused on the revision of Article 27(b), considered by many to legitimize private property rights over life forms in the shape of intellectual property rights, while excluding indigenous peoples and communities from the possibility of benefitting from their resources and knowledge.[69] Clearly, as far as the relation between trade and traditional knowledge goes, much attention centres on patents, but it is also true that several of the problems that present stumbling blocks when it comes to patents do so also in respect to folklore.

One of the communications sent in to WTO jointly by Cuba, Honduras, Paraguay, and Venezuela not only wanted to secure traditional knowledge on the agenda at Seattle, but proposed that a mandate be given at the conference to initiate negotiations that would seek to include traditional knowledge in the TRIPS agreement, according 'effective moral and economic intellectual property rights to traditional knowledge.'[70] Because of riots and disagreements the Seattle Conference could not be concluded, and it is not without a certain irony that Mike Moore's opening address was entitled 'Seattle Conference Doomed to Succeed.' A few days after delivering his speech the failure he considered unthinkable, was a fact.[71] In the Ministerial Declaration from the 4th WTO Ministerial Meeting in 2001, hosted by Qatar, the only country willing to accommodate the meeting after the Seattle ruckus, the TRIPS council was however explicitly instructed to pursue the relationship between TRIPS and traditional knowledge and folklore.[72]

III

The very first question that needs to be asked before we proceed is of course: can traditional knowledge be considered intellectual property at all? Is it even property? If we are to believe the reply from the FFM, the answer is ambiguous – yes *and* no.

On the one hand, there is increasing concern for the continued and accelerated looting of indigenous cultural assets precisely according to those lines I have outlined, whereby the 'West' makes intellectual property of the resources of the 'rest.' Since it is more difficult to procure numbers regarding crafts than it is for the more conventionally designated cultural goods UNESCO tracks, it is also far more problematic to contrast the highly publicized losses claimed by the core copyright industries against those that befall holders of traditional knowledge.[73] While we know that biodiversity is of substantial economic importance to developed and developing nations alike, we can be fairly sure that the global market for handicrafts and art produced by indigenous/native peoples is considerable in its own right, and that it too falls victim to counterfeiting and piracy. Although global trade in crafts has been estimated at $30 billion annually, statistics are hard to come by.[74] A few examples will suffice: the market for Native American crafts in the U.S. is estimated at $1 billion a year, half of which is believed to be accounted for by fakes,[75] and in 1999, the Australia Council estimated the indigenous art market at $A 200 million a year.[76] Crafts are useful for my argument for two reasons; it is the most apparently 'material' of the various expressions listed by the Model Provisions, and second, it represents a sector largely employing women.

In the global economy, women are in fact doubly displaced by intellectual property rights, a question that begs a separate volume but is seldom, if ever, analytically problematized in books concerned with the subject. I have already referred to this theoretical lacuna in the introductory chapter, and think it suggests a perspective that should hold any number of interesting possibilities for further analysis in the field.

According to the United Nations, 90 per cent of all women in the developing world are engaged in some kind of craft activity,[77] and with an estimated 90 per cent of Native American Indian families depending on crafts as a primary or secondary source of income,[78] crafts may in effect constitute the bulk of a family's income. When I refer to women as dislodged twice, I am thinking of two main causes for this predicament: first, the Eurocentric notion of copyright has depended on a construction of authorship according to a certain value system that effectively obstructs the contribution of women because it takes for granted that the author in question is always a 'he'; second, these women are affected by the interdependency of trade and intellectual property rights in the shape of expensive filing applications, complex trade agreements, and bureaucratic red tape. This legal framework disallows certain resources and imposes an administrative straightjacket, where microbusinesses in Mexico or Indian collective patent applicants face much steeper thresholds into the global economy then do their Western counterparts. Women, who find themselves further at a disadvantage through lack of education, financial dependency on husbands and/or male relatives, and the struggles of childbirth/rearing, will therefore have to labour harder to exercise control over the legal structure that disqualifies them in the first place. Mexican women who, when their men move across the northern border in droves to seek work, start collectives and begin to use old craft techniques as the basis for new microbusinesses in silver jewellery are also victims of piracy.[79] These Mexican women compete with cheap labour by other women in Thailand, China, and other parts of South-East Asia. *Crafts News* reports that Romania now manufactures and sells knockoffs of Taiwanese knockoffs of [Native American] Indian jewellery.[80] It is indicative of the intertwined global economy that the Tecalpulco women who manufacture the candleholders or the intricate silver jewellery, find themselves struggling not only with NAFTA, but with the sweatshop labour of *other women*.

Australia, a country that did not grant citizenship to its Aboriginal population until 1967, and where unauthorized Aboriginal artwork has appeared on towels and carpets as well as on boxer shorts, is perhaps where the question of indigenous intellectual and cultural property rights has been most tested in courts of law.[81] In the landmark 'Carpet Case,' *Milpurrurru v. Indofurn Pty Ltd.*, three Aboriginal artists and the Public Trustee for the Northern Territory, acting for the estate of five deceased Aboriginal artists, sued Indofurn Pty Ltd., claiming that they had manufactured and sold carpets that reproduced or substantially copied artwork without licence from the artists in question. On a visit to a Hanoi carpet factory, the company owner Mr Bethune sees the work of the applicants on portfolios and calendars issued by the Australian National Gallery and the Australian Information Service. Finding the artwork attractive, he orders several carpets, some obviously based on the reproductions in full and some with a less 'busy pattern.' Cautioned by business partners not to reproduce Aboriginal art without procuring adequate copyright, the company continues production all the same and the full extent of the infringement was not discovered until the carpets were put on exhibition in October 1992. Because its minute rendering of the events behind the case so effectively highlights many of the conflicts between competing regimes of intellectual property rights and systems of traditional knowledge, the verdict is fascinating reading. Judge Von Doussa called the refusal on the part of the defendants to admit the artists' rightful copyright ownership unreasonable and referred to Mr Bethune as having 'emotional and wrongheaded ideas about the issues in the case.'[82] The applicants were awarded a total of $A188,640.52 in damages.[83]

Even if the outcome of the Carpet Case unequivocally favoured the applicants, the problems concerning the issue of communal intellectual property rights remained. Not limited to the Australian context, this question also turned up in the WIPO FFMs and points to one of the major stumbling blocks when trying to fuse traditional knowledge with intellectual property rights. It had surfaced in another Australian case a few years earlier, *Yumbulul v. Reserve Bank of Australia*. At the time of Australia's bicentennial in 1988, the Reserve Bank of Australia issued a commemorative $A10 banknote. Featured on the note was a reproduction of a design of a Morning Star Pole by Terry Yumbulul, a member of the Warimiri clan. Yumbulul, who was in a financial crisis at the time, had signed a contract sublicensing his design through the Aboriginal Artists Agency Limited. His claim against the Reserve Bank and the Agency rested on the assertion that although he had signed the contract, he had not fully understood what it authorized the agency to use his design for. In a sense, Terry Yumbulul's case can be read against the backdrop of Article *6bis* of the Berne Convention, the so-called moral rights clause, which is called upon by several of those whom WIPO met during their FFMs as a possible instrument with which the rights of traditional knowledge holders may be asserted. Based on the idea that moral rights entitle you to claim authorship and object to modifications and other derogatory actions, the first paragraph reads:

> Independently of the author's economic rights, and *even after the transfer of said rights*, the author shall have the right to claim authorship of the work and to object to any distortion, mutilation or other modification of, or other derogatory action in relation to, the said work, which would be prejudicial to his honour or reputation (emphasis mine).

The crucial point here is that the three dimensions of moral rights – the right to disclose or divulge; the right to claim authorship (paternity); and the right to protect against unauthorized alterations (integrity) – *supersede* economic rights, and that the rights of traditional knowledge holders are a question of ethics *and* authorship.[84] Of course, the reproduction of the Morning Star Pole on a banknote – according to traditional belief it has the power to take the spirits of the dead to the Morning Star, which will return them to their ancestral home – represented the ultimate commodification of a sacred piece of art. Yumbulul's own economic predicament, which prompted him to sign the contract, confirmed in no uncertain terms both the cultural *and* the economic quandary of the Aboriginals. It hardly mattered that the judge insisted that the image of the Morning Star Pole on the banknote should be seen as belated homage to the contributions of the Aboriginal community.[85]

Yumbulul's authority to portray the Morning Star Pole came from his mother's clan group and was given to him through a number of ceremonies and initiation rites. Because there is no major conceptual difference between the 'useful' and the 'artistic' in this matrix, there is no possibility of superimposing on traditional knowledge a legal framework based on such a separation, because that would only constitute an artificial differentiation.[86] While the right to perform a certain song or dance or execute a specific design or painting is a question of concern to the clan or group in its entirety, it must be underscored that such a right may be vested in or transferred to an individual. As the *Yumbulul v. Reserve Bank of Australia* case demonstrated, when the song, dance, design, or painting is unlawfully tampered with and removed from its context, it is not necessarily the infringer who is seen as the prime transgressor, but quite possibly the person in whom the right to interpret these images lies. The diffusion and availability of objects and practices depend, therefore, on highly intricate and developed modes of conduct which should be seen as regulatory frameworks to better control and protect the access to these resources. Some objects can be sold to museums and put on display because their meaning is not fully understood by those who see them, or the educational value is deemed more important, but some artefacts should not be detached from their context. Terry Yumbulul did not mind that his Morning Star Pole was put in a museum, but he did mind that it landed on a banknote.

Many of those interviewed by WIPO during the FFMs, pointed out that holders of traditional knowledge often see themselves as operating within both a formal and an informal, or customary regulative framework for intellectual property.[87] One elder of the Blood tribe in Canada explains:

> If I have a tipi design and Dorothy wants my design, she can send a messenger and ask for it to be transferred. If I agree she has to transfer it through a ceremony. Once I give my rights to the design over to her, I transfer her the right to use it. I can't even use it: I cannot make a replica, it is simply not mine anymore, it's hers. She is only allowed to make replica if the first one is destroyed, but she can't pitch two or ten tipis with the same design. There is only one.[88]

There are consequently highly elaborated forms of control and regulation used to ensure that specific knowledge does not fall into the wrong hands. In *Yumbulul v. Reserve Bank of Australia* it was acknowledged that Terry Yumbulul had 'come under considerable criticism' from within the Aboriginal community for the reproduction of the Morning Star Pole and the judge acceded that Australian copyright law did not provide adequate recognition of Aboriginal community claims for works which are essentially communal in origin.[89] Nonetheless, he dismissed the application, arguing that Terry Yumbulul understood the general meaning of the licence he signed, and that he did not in any way indicate any limitations to that licence.[90] While the collective nature of

Aboriginal intellectual property was not recognized in *Yumbulul v. Reserve Bank of Australia* nor in *Milpurrurru v. Indofurn Pty Ltd.*, in the latter suit Judge Von Doussa considered the infringement a case of personal and cultural hurt.[91]

A more recent Australian case putting communal ownership to the test is *John Bulun Bulun v. R & T Textiles Pty Ltd.*, concerning the importation of printed fabric infringing the copyright of the Aboriginal artist John Bulun Bulun in his work 'Magpie Geese and Water Lilies at the Waterhole.' John Bulun Bulun himself sued under the Australian Copyright Act of 1968, but so also did George Milipurrurru, like John Bulun Bulun a member of the Ganalbingu clan. After the respondents admitted to their wrongdoing and consented to permanent injunctions against future infringements of the designs, George Milipurrurru nonetheless continued the action as a test case on the communal intellectual property rights of Aboriginal peoples. As in *Yumbulul v. Reserve Bank of Australia*, the argument was based on the artwork being held in trust and that the Ganalbingu as a group had suffered from the infringement against John Bulun Bulun. However, since the court had already found in favour of John Bulun Bulun, the rights of the Ganalbingu were dismissed. Instead the court stressed that in this specific relationship between an individual and the collective, where both have an interest in the protection of the design, John Bulun Bulun had a responsibility to enforce his property rights against infringers in order to attend to the interests of the clan.[92]

Something now needs to be said about what might be behind the conceptualization of the assets that have been discussed in this chapter as intellectual property, both on the part of WIPO and in reference to the three Australian cases. While the collective aspirations of the Aboriginal applicants may have been suppressed, one thing is uncontested, and that is the affirmation of the artists as the rightful copyright holders, and therefore also the recognition of their work as original, as belonging to them and expressing their artistry.[93] I would, however, disagree with Anne Barron, who seems to locate the willingness to accord legal recognition to these artists to the modernist aesthetic,[94] since it would seem to me that as a measuring device, modernism only reinforces and validates the same ideology that once erected authorship on the basis of romanticism. Ironically enough, Brad Sherman notes that the fact that Aboriginal art was displayed in museums rather than in art galleries worked against its acceptance as art, a status that was not granted until the time of commodification through art galleries.[95]

In his always useful *Keywords: A Vocabulary of Culture and Society* (1976), Raymond Williams describes 'culture' as being one of the most complicated words in the English language. Encompassing horti*culture* as well as the fashion of the French *couture* – now of course denoting a culture industry of its own with significant political, economic, and social implications – there is no doubt that even historically, we are faced with a wider concept than what is usually inferred by the more narrow 'art,' and the even more limited 'high art' with all its lineage of intellectual property regimes.[96] Two specific aspects of this all-encompassing term especially should be noted. First its transformation into a phenomenon that leaves things, if not all together then at least sufficiently enough, to be increasingly seen as a process, a set of *practices*.[97] These practices, which would include spectator sports, cooking, rituals, and almost all forms of human activity, need not be linked to any insistence on the complex notion of authenticity. They can be, and often are, mediated through mass culture. What we can be more certain of is that it appears to be – thanks in no small degree to mass culture – an increasingly simultaneous process in both spatial and temporal terms. From the culture of corporations, via that of the elite or migrant communities, to the culture of travel, style, fashion, shopping, the insertion of 'culture' as a keyword in the vernacular reads like a story of endless expansion of both things and practices.[98] A second important feature which distinguishes culture from its often quoted opposite of 'art,' is that it is both possible and common to think of culture and speak of it in the plural. Implicit is a shift from the 'high' to the 'everyday,' a change that will prove to impact substantially on the notion of intellectual property. In fact, it is in large part due to popular culture, media, tourism, travel, and mass culture as a whole that we have familiarized ourselves with practices and artefacts that are *different* from those that have served to build the European legal framework in this field. Increased tourism and increased cultural exchange have made Aboriginal art into a major asset for Australia. Thus, the transformation that takes Aboriginal art from first being treated as ethnographic objects into being art,[99] from being anonymous, collective, and non-original to being recognized legally as attributable and individual, reflects on the widening realm of culture as a whole, within which the many elements in traditional knowledge may find it easier to secure protection.

To say this is not to state that there are no problems with either the production or consumption that comes out of this interconnectedness, nor does it predict that it will only become easier to insert traditional knowledge into intellectual property regimes. It merely notes that elite culture is not alone responsible for raising the barrier of what can and cannot count as intellectual property. Much of what we think of when we think of culture valorizes production and consumption from groups that previously did not exist, and that had no way of formulating themselves culturally, or translating their practices into experiences that mattered, or producing products that could be sold (much less considered property) with a price tag. Thus, what makes it possible to think of the hairstyles, incense, and numbers by finger language as intellectual property is, I believe, the broadening notion of 'culture.' In that respect, we can argue that despite the resilience of the ideology of the author, the changes incurred by the so-called cultural turn are every bit as significant on the current and future status of intellectual property rights as was once the arrival of the self-contained romantic author.

IV

One of the main obstacles in finding traditional knowledge to be intellectual property is that it constitutes an indelible part of a holistic world view. From a more practical standpoint, much of this knowledge remains undocumented, and to prove ownership, you need records. The immaterial nature of, for instance, oral traditions – constantly reworked and altered in interplay with performativity – works against the requirement of 'fixity.'[100] Undoubtedly, the incorporation of databases into intellectual property regimes can, on the one hand, be seen as deeply problematic and indicative of the hold of the Western TNCs, but another way of looking at them is to view them as a possible tool by which traditional knowledge holders may document their heritage or property.

The second problematic stance in communal rights is linked to space. Cultural and intellectual property of indigenous peoples or traditional knowledge holders cannot be understood outside their right to land and territory. This emphasis on the land as a prerequisite for intellectual property rights and the damage caused by unauthorized copying is described by John Bulun Bulun in his affidavit evidence in *John Bulun Bulun v. R & T Textiles Pty Ltd.* as something which 'interferes with the relationship between people, their creator ancestors and the land given to the people by the creator ancestor.'[101] It stands in stark contrast to the standard image of globalization as something which is increasingly 'place-less,' that is, where advanced technology enables mobility on a global scale, where flexible capital has immediate effects on markets, investments, and labour, and where corporations are constructed as international or global enterprises rather than as national ones. The rapid deterritorialization enabled by global technology and the territorial claims by indigenous peoples should hardly be regarded as absolute polarities, nor are they a question of the ascendancy of the new over the old. While territory is one of the founding principles for traditional knowledge holders' claims to their heritage, this territory need not be in any way related to the nation-state. It expresses one of the geopolitical features of globalization in that it emphasizes regional and local alliances as well as liaisons that can be formal as well as informal while spanning vast distances. It is not something alien to the movements of globalization generally, since this issue of the nation-state versus other configurations of place and space is equally visible in developed nations. Because knowledge or cultural practices and artefacts may be shared across space and among several groups or clans, the issue of how to 'own' that kind of diffused knowledge remains an unresolved dilemma.

However, the central crux of the matter is not that the holders of traditional knowledge WIPO met, or the Aboriginal artists whose claims were addressed in Australian courts, do not consider their heritage and folklore – be it immaterial or material – property. They do. They do not, however, consider it *commodifiable*, and that is the one major reason why traditional knowledge brings to the fore some of the more complex issues of intellectual property rights in relation to trade and to ethics. For traditional knowledge, biodiversity, folklore, and crafts to be seen as intellectual property and protected as such is one thing. The more problematic follow-up question is: can they only be granted that designation under the current trade-based regime of WTO and TRIPS?

While some would certainly claim that all grand narratives are dead, it would not be difficult to counterclaim that the *grand narrative* of the modern knowledge-based society is free trade, and that this has come to weigh particularly heavily on intellectual property rights. As any grand narrative, it is a deeply contested one. Some represent the world trade system after the Second World War as inherently neutral, an almost divine entity that is good in and of itself but whose gleaming and well-oiled machinery unfortunately can be disrupted by the careless intervention of both governments and corporations.[102] Activists opposing this basically rosy view have, as they did in Seattle, taken to the streets to prove their point, but there are also examples of a number of ways in which what is perceived as the hegemonic message of free trade is being countered more peacefully and by using some of the means of globalization itself.[103]

The problem is compounded by the increasing interdependency of features like convergence, communication, information, and the right to own these and other forms of valuable property in the knowledge-based economy. One of the most far-reaching consequences of the free trade doctrine – regardless of whether or not we can make it apply to property as 'cultural' or 'intellectual' – is that it tends to subsume *everything*. It is ironic that the questions that were posed in the initial pages of this chapter now are answered by posing new ones. What are the consequences of making everything into trade? Will it benefit developing nations if folklore and traditional knowledge prove to fit within intellectual property rights? Is doing so the only foreseeable way to correct some of the current imbalances and injustices of the global system?

As we have seen, moral rights are sometimes used in order to promote traditional knowledge holders' rights. However, there are no moral rights in TRIPS. In article 9, after having stated that members shall comply with the Berne Convention, the text continues: 'Members shall not have rights or obligations under this Agreement in respect of the rights conferred under Article 6bis of that Convention or of the rights derived therefrom.' Although moral rights do not constitute the only strategy for traditional knowledge holders to ensure that their resources get adequate treatment in existing intellectual property regimes, the absence of this right is not without possible ramifications. If the only way to hinder further looting is to make folklore into trade, or to take trade as the guarantee for why folklore should be subsumed under TRIPS, and the only way to protection is by way of moral rights, rights that are not recognized in TRIPS, then we at least appear to have on our hands a zero-sum game of the highest order. Add to this that article 1705 in NAFTA has implemented an even clearer definition of copyrights as 'economic rights' and the magnitude of the free trade ideology becomes even more apparent. Will it make any difference if alternative intellectual property rights are elaborated, and can they possibly be made functional outside the free trade regime and make fair trade possible? Or will that too simply contribute to the increasing *tradefication* of everything? In searching for an adequate sui generis system, WIPO has identified seven questions that need to be answered in order for such a system to become effective, and it is telling how the first underlines the distinct *policy objective* of the protection, stressing that any such legal framework needs to consider an active public policy.[104]

The four most contentious components of intellectual property rights and traditional knowledge that have been covered in this chapter are the notion of property as heritage versus the commodification of trade-based intellectual property; the conflicts that arise from claiming communal rights under a system only recognizing private property; the clash as a holistic world view which does not distinguish between the land and/or between the artistic and the useful in terms of intellectual property meets a Western machinery that compartmentalizes; and finally, the problem of a geopolitical space based on other alliances than those frequently represented by the nation-state versus the nationally grounded principles of intellectual property rights. Summing up, the need for *protection* against what the Model Provisions calls 'illicit exploitation' is consequently one of the reasons the traditional knowledge holder may want to use intellectual property rights. The second is the need for *preservation* (as traditional knowledge often constitutes part of a heritage).[105] As we have seen, these two major categories are not necessarily in constant conflict with one another, nor can they be said to cohabit peacefully. Instead, they are indicative of a subset of stumbling blocks that will continue to face WIPO, the TRIPS council, and the many NGOs involved in this issue.

Therefore, while the previous pages may have demonstrated that there now is a presence of traditional knowledge in intellectual property rights discussions within WIPO and even TRIPS, as everybody knows, presence does not automatically mean power. The expansion that allowed for this to happen has also brought with it a concomitant enclosure, something I will discuss in the next, and last, chapter.

Chapter Six

GENIES IN BOTTLES AND BOTTLED-UP GENIUSES: TWO CASES OF UPSET RELATIVES AND A PUBLIC DOMAIN

This book began with Victor Hugo's keynote address at the Congrès Littéraire International in Paris, 17 June 1878. Having now reached the final chapter, I would once more like to revisit that speech and event, not in order to recapitulate its basic tenets, but to introduce an element of Hugo's discourse that I have so far largely avoided and that I believe needs to be considered in order to complete more fully the overall ambitions of this project. Rhetorically, Hugo remained on an abstractly grandiose level that day, setting the stage for the author as a chosen individual searching for the greater good of mankind by pursuing intellectual property rights internationally. However, he also introduced another question on the agenda of the Congrès when he said: 'Let us acknowledge literary property but, at the same time, let us found the public domain.' As if to lend even more force to his words, he continued immediately to say: 'Let us go even further. Let us expand it.'[1]

The public domain is the focus of this last chapter for one overarching reason: it represents the OTHER of intellectual property rights, 'the realm of publications, inventions, and processes that are *not* protected by copyright or patent' (my emphasis).[2] Something usually 'falls into' – the expression denotes loss of control or direction, a vertigo of unbelonging – the 'wilderness'[3] of the public domain because it is not protectable to begin with (ideas, facts), because the monopoly granted has expired (normally seventy years after the death of the author), or because it has been forfeited due to failure to comply with a statutory condition for copyright.[4] The public domain is therefore made up of things that can be used or appropriated by us all without risking infringement. It is free, as the legendary cyber-analogy goes, not as in beer, but as in free speech.[5]

Hugo's preoccupation with the public domain is firmly rooted in his identity as a public intellectual and it rests on a tradition that goes back to the early years of the French Revolution.[6] A more private reason for his emphasis on literary legacy and heritage is perhaps that he is aging rapidly. After his final appearance at the Congrès Hugo suffers a stroke, making him if not incapacitated, then at least putting a stop to his frenzied production for the rest of his life. Intellectual mentor to a nation, he is ironically a patriarch without descendants: four of his five children precede him in death. Only Adèle, who withers away at a lunatic asylum until 1915 and whose fate inspired François Truffaut's film *L'Histoire d'Adèle H* (1975), will outlive her father. There are grandchildren, of course, and relatives, but those closest to him are either dead or locked·up.

Only very briefly, almost accidentally, does Hugo suggest in his opening speech how he views the contours of a public domain. The general idea is this: after the death of the author, his/her works should immediately fall into the hands of his/her (perhaps) many publishers, but only on the condition that a modest sum of no more than 10 per cent of the net profits be set aside for the benefit of the author's heirs.[7] A few days later, on 21 and 25 June, he has occasion to return to the question of the public domain, and to expand on his views. If there are no immediate surviving heirs, he argues then, the money should instead be used, not by governments, but by the force that is French literature. Imagine, he continues, if the leading intellectual movement in Europe, the Société des gens de lettres, were to be put in charge of these funds. Can there be anything more beautiful, he exalts, than using the works of the illustrious dead to encourage the souls of the young![8]

Hugo made it abundantly clear during the Congrès that he considered literature a living entity over which absolute control was in some sense futile. Articulating a modern outlook predating Barthes's argument on the demise of the author a century later, he stated that after a book was published, the author ceased to be its master.[9] As far as whom the principles of literary property concerned, Hugo was convinced that only two categories were invested in literature: the author and society. On the role of the third possible party – the author's heirs – Hugo is unequivocal: 'The heir does not make the book: he cannot have the rights of the author.'[10]

The practical feasibility of Victor Hugo's idea of a public domain can of course be debated. On the one hand, he is at the Congrès promoting the basic soundness of intellectual property rights. On the other hand, he wants all his works to fall into the public domain after his death, and is therefore not advocating a lengthy term of protection post-mortem, even suggesting that there should be a 'domaine public payant,' a form of collective administration and redistribution of funds to the general benefit of new authors.[11] But the one crucial remark that must be made on the basis of his intervention on intellectual property rights during the Congrès, is that from the very outset, he pays as much attention, if not more, to the importance of the public domain as to the question of how literary property can be and should be protected. The interests of authors should be synchronized with the needs of the reading public, and Hugo was very clear about who should benefit the most from this relationship when he declared: 'If I have to choose between the rights of the author and the rights of the public domain, I will choose the rights of the public domain.'[12]

I

Appropriately enough, I am in Paris doing research for the purposes of this book on 15 May 2001, the day that Lauretta Hugo signs a long and incendiary article in *Libération*. Back in 1997, members of the Hugo family had published an open letter in *Libération* to launch their critique against what they saw as unbridled pillage of Hugo's work, especially by Disney.[13] Married to a great-grandchild of the poet, Lauretta Hugo is outraged at the recent publication by Plon – part of the Vivendi Universal conglomerate – of François Cérésa's book, *Cosette ou le temps des illusions*. *Cosette* is, in her mind, a general effrontery to the author's legacy, but more importantly, Lauretta Hugo is appalled at the commercial exploitation of what she refers to as 'works of global artistic heritage,' criticizing the 'Money King' of globalization, which threatens to engulf everything under its rampant market liberalism.[14]

Plon had approached Cérésa – a journalist at *Le Nouvel Observateur* and author of nine previous novels – several years earlier to inquire if he would consider undertaking the project of writing a sequel to Hugo's *Les Misérables*.[15] At the time of its publication in 2001, *Cosette* had not only rendered its author the usual high advance for a predicted bestseller (Fr 300,000), been printed in an impressive number of copies (65,000), and been made the subject of negotiations for the prerequisite movie deals and publicized in advertising campaigns (to the amount of Fr 1.5 million), it had also caused a minor riot in French media and press.[16] Critics called the whole thing distasteful, sacrilegious, and blasphemous; in an incredulous tone Pierre Assouline questioned what the world was coming to, would a sequel to *À la Recherche du temps perdue* be next? Max Gallo, about to finish his own biography of Victor Hugo, would have been happier if the money spent on advertising *Cosette* was used instead to promote *Les Misérables* anew.[17] But the media critique would not turn into legal action until Pierre Hugo, a 43-year-old great-great-grandchild of the author working as a goldsmith in Aix-en-Provence, filed an injunction against *Cosette* the day before its scheduled release, on 2 May 2001, seeking the withdrawal of the book, Fr 4.5 million in damages, and a fine of Fr 50,000 for each day the book remained on the shelves. As if to excuse the presence of such large sums of money, *Le Figaro* reported on the same day that the financial damages were not intended for Pierre Hugo's own pocket, but among other things, they would sponsor a fund for the preservation of France's literary heritage.[18] On 22 June Pierre Hugo explained his action in *Le Figaro*, asking indignantly if the word 'respect' has evaporated from dictionaries of the French language?[19]

Les Misérables had already enjoyed a relatively rich existence in the public domain: the first film made of the novel came in 1935, the most recent version by Bille August in 1998, and there was the successful Broadway musical with the same name. Feeling obligated to protest against what he sees as a defamation of his ancestor's reputation, Pierre Hugo's anger is especially directed at Cérésa's resurrection of Javert, whom Hugo had commit suicide by jumping in the Seine at the end of the story and whose reappearance in *Cosette Le Figaro* compared to having J.R. return from the dead as Bobby in *Dallas*.[20] Pierre Hugo relied on Hugo's own words: 'If this ending does not move, I will give up writing forever,'[21] and secured the backing of both Les Amis de Victor Hugo and the Société des gens de lettres – the organization Victor Hugo helped establish and which sponsored the Congrès in 1878 – in support of his cause. The latter group was, however, very careful not to issue any judgment on the literary qualities of *Cosette*, the work of a man they referred to as 'a fellow writer.'[22] Lauretta Hugo on her part had already called the whole affair tainted by dirty money.[23]

Those who rallied to the defence of *Cosette* included Maurice Druon of l'Académie Française, who on the subject of Javert's new lease on life questioned in *Le Figaro* if it was more serious to prolong the life of a fictional character than to remake and transform it? Should Euripides' descendants seek an injunction against Racine for his *Phèdre*?[24] Dominique Noguez joined him in *Le Monde* on 27 June, arguing that

Hugo's relatives had misunderstood the very nature of literature; that it is always feeding off other literatures, and cannot escape this interweaving with the past. Noguez's argument on the place of Victor Hugo in the public domain is interesting and well articulated:

> The moral rights of an author, especially when, as in the case of Victor Hugo, he incarnates a moment in the history of a people, should belong to that people in its entirety and, in a more general sense to all those who, all over the world, love his works. It is up to them to protect it: collectively, as in the case of the Hunchback of Notre-Dame, by protesting and boycotting, or, if decisions are to be made for a publication of unpublished material, correspondence, or drafts, in the most liberal sense by the intermediaries of competent associations, specialists, critics, or literary institutions.[25]

When the Tribunal de Grande Instance in Paris issued its ruling on 12 September 2001, it declared Pierre Hugo's claim invalid. The opinion of the court draws substantially on Victor Hugo's own statements made during the Congrès Littéraire International. Word for word his many concerns on the proper role of the heir and the importance of the public domain are conjured up and used as weaponry in the case: the claim that the descendant should live by the part of the heritage given to him, because 'the work itself does not concern him,' is complemented by referring to Hugo's irritation over legislators, who had confounded the 'successor in blood' with the 'successor of the mind.'[26] In essence, the court stated that in launching his claim Pierre Hugo did not respect the 'brilliantly' formulated wishes of his forefather, who was referred to as 'an ardent champion of the public domain,' and the case was summarily dismissed.[27]

Almost simultaneously in the United States, Suntrust Bank, the trustee of the Margaret Mitchell estate, took the publisher Houghton Mifflin to court in *Suntrust Bank v. Houghton Mifflin Co.* Owned at that time, just as Plon, by Vivendi Universal, the case concerned Houghton Mifflin's publication of *The Wind Done Gone*, a book by Alice Randall. Suntrust – who claimed that Randall had copied substantial parts of the book, inclusive of characters and plot – asked for an injunction and for damages of $10 million.[28] *The Wind Done Gone* is the story of Cynara, Scarlett's mulatto half-sister, and it retells the story of *Gone With the Wind* (1936) from the perspective of those who were effaced, written out, or stereotyped in the original: the African-American characters.

Gone With the Wind was not immune to remakes. Licensed by the Mitchell estate, *Scarlett: The Sequel to Margaret Mitchell's Gone with the Wind*, by Alexandra Ripley, was published simultaneously in forty countries in 1991.[29] At the time of *The Wind Done Gone*, the Mitchell estate was in the process of licensing a second sequel, under contract to St Martin's Press.[30] Hope Dellon, executive editor in the Trade Division of St Martin's Press, testified for the plaintiff, saying that the financial potential of such sequels – based on the further adventures of characters readers are familiar with and want to learn more of – was regarded as especially valuable property.[31] The Mitchell estate was consequently claiming that Randall's book substituted for such a licensed derivative work and the court concurred, 'that by killing two core characters from *Gone With the Wind* and marrying off another, *The Wind Done Gone* has the immediate effect of damaging or even precluding the Mitchell's Trust's ability to continue to tell the love story of Scarlett and Rhett.'[32] Authors interested in writing a licensed sequel were under strict contractual obligations not to kill Scarlett and not to include any homosexuality or miscegenation scenes.[33] In Randall's book, Rhett Butler leaves Scarlett for Cynara and Ashley Wilkes is portrayed as gay.

Since there was no doubt that *Gone With the Wind* was protected by copyright, Houghton Mifflin had to base their defence on article 107 of the U.S. Copyright Act, which states that 'fair use ... for purposes such as criticism, comment, news reporting, teaching (including multiple copies for classroom use), scholarship, or research, is not an infringement of copyright.' As we saw earlier, fair use was not codified until 1976 and was an issue in all the cases concerning the photocopier in chapter 3. To be able to acknowledge fair use and thus in effect circumvent the copyright owner, each case must be considered in light of four factors: the purpose and character of the use (if for commercial or nonprofit reasons); the nature of the copyrighted work (factual or nonfactual with more leniency for the factual); the amount of the work copied in relation to the whole work (less or more); and the effect of the use upon the potential market for or the value of the copyrighted work. When a parody or comment is considered under the purpose and character of use, the question of the 'transformative' nature of the new work becomes essential, that is, how much it can be said to rework the older text into something new. An important precedent was set in

Campbell v. Acuff-Rose Music, Inc. where the group 2 Live Crew's version of Roy Orbison's 'Pretty Woman' was considered parody within the limits of fair use.

In weighing these four factors concerning *The Wind Done Gone*, United States District Court Judge Charles A. Pannell Jr. overwhelmingly came down on the side of the plaintiff. Calling the book 'unabated piracy,'[34] Suntrust was granted a preliminary injunction on 19 April 2001.[35] On 25 May 2001, the injunction was lifted by the Eleventh Circuit Court of Appeals, which concluded that the district court's ruling was in violation of the First Amendment.[36] When the court of appeals issued its long opinion in October 2001, it showed a completely different interpretation of the case. *The Wind Done Gone had* proven substantial transformative use, it was therefore a parody, and hence applicable to the 'fair use' defence. While Randall had borrowed substantially from *Gone With the Wind*, primarily in the first part of her book, the second part 'flips GWTW's traditional race roles, portrays powerful whites as stupid or feckless and generally sets out to demystify GWTW and strip the romanticism from Mitchell's specific account of this period of our history.'[37] Because the court of appeals concluded there was a lack of injury to Suntrust the judgment of the district court was reversed. In his opinion, Judge Birch stressed that 'the public interest is always served in promoting First Amendment values and in preserving the public domain from encroachment.'[38] In a separate concurring opinion, Judge Marcus seconded Birch's opinion, but stressed that in all likelihood Randall's book did not compete with any sequel the Mitchell estate could license and that the two books acted as complements rather than substitutes.[39] Randall's book was subsequently published and spent six weeks on the *New York Times's* best-seller list.[40] On 9 May 2002, a joint press release by the two parties announced that they would end their litigation and that a confidential settlement agreement had been arranged, whereby *The Wind Done Gone* would continue to be sold as 'an unauthorized parody.'[41]

On the face of it, these two cases appear to have much in common. Here are two groups of relatives who, almost at exactly the same time, try to stop the publication of a new book they consider detrimental to a previous one: in the case of Pierre Hugo, *Les Misérables* by Victor Hugo was to be protected from François Cérésa's *Cosette ou le temps des illu-*

sions, and in the case of the Mitchell estate, *Gone With the Wind* by Margaret Mitchell from Alice Randall's *The Wind Done Gone*. But there the superficial similarities end.

Nobody questioned that *Les Misérables* was in the public domain. Pierre Hugo's *only* possible claim against *Cosette* rests therefore on exercising moral rights, rights that are not necessarily only a matter for relatives, but for all who, as Dominique Nogez wrote in *Le Monde*, feel that they have a stake in the posthumous fate of Victor Hugo. In an interesting comment on the case, Christophe Caron stresses the importance of not letting moral rights be used in such a way as to paralyse creativity and insidiously reinstate a monopoly after the work in question has fallen into the public domain.[42] Since French law recognizes moral rights as *perpetual*,[43] the right to protect against defamation overrides the loss of copyright protection itself, a provision also set down in article 6*bis* of the Berne Convention. However, the Tribunal de la grande instance did not grant Pierre Hugo the injunction he sought; they drew their argument almost exclusively from Victor Hugo's own words in the matter: first, as someone who defended and promoted a vital public domain; second, and perhaps more damaging, as someone who was deeply sceptical of the appropriateness of family heirs to safeguard his heritage; and third, although Pierre Hugo's ancestry was never in doubt, his claim that this fact alone entitled him to act in the name of moral rights was fallacious. This was so because Victor Hugo had, in fact, bequeathed his literary estate to his friend Paul Maurice and so, while Pierre Hugo was undeniably a direct heir to Victor Hugo the person, he could not in strict terms be viewed the direct heir to the *works* of Victor Hugo.[44]

The Wind Done Gone, on the other hand, provided an innovative commentary on one of the most well known of American novels. Just as it was blatantly obvious that *Les Miserables* was in the public domain, it was also clear that Suntrust did own the copyright to *Gone With the Wind*. However, this fact rested solely on the implementation in 1998 of the Sonny Bono Copyright Term Extension Act, which granted the book a safe haven from the public domain until 2031. If the length of copyright in place at the time of Mitchell's death had still been applicable, *Gone With the Wind* would have entered the public domain in 1993.

Despite their differences, both cases may act as a sounding-board for a more elaborate discussion on the public domain, and especially challenge us to rethink why we need such a discussion in the first place.

II

One of the main themes running through the previous chapters is the widening realm of intellectual property rights.[45] This expansion – visible in the scope of what is deemed intellectual property, in the length for which protection is granted, and in its geopolitical reach and impact – has taken place at the expense of instituting higher proprietory fences. Thinking of the enclosure movement in England during the industrial revolution, when common lands were seized and turned into private property, James Boyle refers to the current situation as the 'second enclosure movement.'[46] Innate to cultural/intellectual production per se, intellectual property rights and the public domain are intended to strike a balance between private interests in the form of incentives, remuneration, and control on the one hand, and public good in the shape of society's larger advancement on the other. When this equilibrium is challenged, the results can be measured in highly tangible social/cultural/economic/political inequalities in global relations as well as within the nation-state itself.[47] Rosemary Coombe argues:

> The public domain is inadequately considered and rarely conceptually developed in juridical contexts; no one represents the public domain in intellectual property litigation or acts as its guardian, and rules of civil procedure currently prohibit the participation of third parties who will ultimately be affected (other artists, writers, and performers of current and future generations).[48]

The paramount importance accorded to intellectual properties in the knowledge-based economy has led to tremendous investments by corporations as well as individuals in their protection, and detracted from an equally forceful commitment to the role and importance of the public domain.[49] Defining the public domain becomes therefore almost an inadvertent act, which only takes place *after* considerable time is devoted to the description of the private property rights that we prefer to think of as 'of the mind.' The same reflex designates intellectual property rights as a solution to the current imbalances in the global economy, presenting them as a universally applicable set of rules that will ensure future prosperity for developed and developing nations alike.[50] The far more important societal and cultural ambitions of intellectual property rights are eclipsed by the allure of economic profit.[51]

Rather than beginning by asking what we think should be regarded as a common resource and why, the developments I have outlined facilitate the fencing in of resources as intellectual property, and leave largely unexplored the uncertain rights and obligations lodged in the public domain.[52] In terms of private versus public ownership, private intellectual property rights have steadily encroached on the less easily defined rights of the public, a tendency which can be read in light of a much broader and longer process of increased social and economic privatization.[53]

Every society, says Lawrence Lessig, has resources that are free and resources that are controlled.[54] The public domain, or the cultural commons, is usually thought of as having rivalrous or nonrivalrous resources. Whereas I am just as free to occupy a bench in a park as you are, my doing that may effectively hinder or preclude your use of that bench. What is so unique about information and knowledge is that it is nonrivalrous, it cannot be depleted.[55] My use of the information found in the databases, books, journals, and newspapers that has helped me write this book, does not hinder your use of exactly *the same* resources for the construction of another book. In that sense, all efforts that seek to minimize the public domain of information and knowledge and maximize that of intellectual properties will contribute to the foreclosure of new knowledge-production.

The most important feature of the public domain is to be a prominent producer of authors, because it is 'a device that permits the rest of the system to work,' by, as Jessica Litman writes, 'leaving the raw material of authorship available for authors to use.'[56] However, this very apt description also shows why the public domain takes on this nebulous identity: while it produces authors, no one is the author of the public domain. The ultimate irony of the public domain is that its resources do not really come into being until they are authored, and to be authored, intellectual property rights must protect the resource. This is what happens when Disney uses a work in the public domain – such as *Notre-Dame de Paris* – and makes it into intellectual property – *The Hunchback of Notre Dame* – jealously protected from entering the public domain where others in turn can freely appropriate it.

One of the more obvious ways in which the public domain is being deprived of its resources is by prolonging copyright. While the reasons for determining exactly how long such a monopoly should be appear somewhat arbitrary, certainly the length of protection has steadily grown longer.[57] But time is a multifaceted thing. In some cases we might want to consider *perpetual protection* of resources that otherwise risk extinction, such as Aboriginal ancestral designs.[58] In contrast, the extension of copyright made by the European Union in 1995 was predicated on three main arguments: (1) the expected life span of authors was now longer, (2) the extension would amend the effects of the world wars, and (3) harmonizing at a higher level was desirable considering the importance of these rights to creativity. Despite such good intentions, negative consequences in research and education have resulted from the extension.[59] The 1998 Sonny Bono Copyright Term Extension Act was in turn launched on the premise that the United States could not deviate from the new European norm.[60]

One person directly affected by CTEA was Eric Eldred, who a few years previously had set up a web site offering electronic editions of public domain books. Now he was forced to witness how texts by Sherwood Anderson and Robert Frost that he had intended to publish, as they were about to enter the public domain, become off-limits for an additional twenty years. Eldred decided to act, and his case caught the eye of Stanford Law School professor Lawrence Lessig, who agreed to take the case pro bono.[61] Four years and two dismissals later – in the district court in Washington D.C. and the U.S. Court of Appeals for the D.C. Circuit – the Supreme Court decided on 19 February 2002 to grant certiorari and hear the arguments in *Eldred v. Ashcroft*; some see this as potentially the most important copyright case in decades.[62] Eldred's case rests on one crucial premise; since the Constitution clearly defines the monopoly of copyright as 'for limited times,' the extension of copyright, and especially a *retroactive* one, is unconstitutional. On 9 October 2002 Lawrence Lessig presented the plaintiff's oral argument before the Supreme Court, arguing that the continuous extension of copyrights was not something the framers of the law had intended, and on that the case in question 'is about limits to an enumerated power.'[63] The Supreme Court did not concur, and on 15 January 2003 handed down their 7–2 opinion affirming the lower court's ruling and the right of Congress to prescribe the duration of copyrights. The court argued that the 'CTEA is a rational enactment; we are not at liberty to second-guess congressional determinations and policy judgements of this order, however debatable or arguably unwise they may be.'[64]

When Congress renewed the Mitchell's estate's ownership of *Gone With the Wind*, they achieved no incentive effect in increased creation since the author in question had been dead since 1949, and instead sentenced critical comments such as *The Wind Done Gone* to tedious and

expensive lawsuits in order to prove that their use of the original novel
was 'fair.' But parody is no joke, as maverick music collective
Negativland would learn from its protracted fray with rock group U2.
In 1991 Negativland released a single called U2, featuring the letters
U2, the spy plane with the same name, and Negativland's name on the
cover, and consisting of, among other things, a few seconds of a U2
song. Island Records immediately sued, and the story dragged on for
years until settled out of court.[65] Obtaining permission, perhaps? Well,
that assumes a prior state of unfreedom, as Yochai Benkler correctly
observes, and whereas adding to the ownership of the Mitchell estate
or Island Records only benefits the Mitchell estate or Island Records, an
increase in the public domain generally increases the freedom of a
society's constituents to communicate.[66]

The circular construction of authorship allows some to draw on the
public domain for the purposes of commodification and economic
benefit, as in the case of Disney. This is as it should be. We can hardly
grant access to the public domain to some, and withhold it from others.
However, traditional knowledge holders or indigenous people come
up against great ethical and legal obstacles when they seek protection
for property considered either in the public domain or as collectively
produced and therefore unprotectable. Here, the use of the public
domain is conditioned on the uneven allocation of power in the
knowledge-based society, and the fact that oral traditions, incense, and
hairstyles do not fit the mould of intellectual proprietorship as it has
evolved since the author came into being during the eighteenth century. That the informational resources of the public domain cannot be
used up is obviously true, but traditional knowledge holders and indigenous peoples have intangible *and* tangible property that in many cases
must be controlled, or authored, for the resource *to continue to exist.*
Carol Rose has argued that there is a great need to conceptualize 'limited common property,' what she describes as commons on the inside
and property on the outside,[67] a form of protection that may be quite
elaborate and sophisticated but that in many cases will not be considered as having anything to do with property at all. For the reasons
outlined in the previous chapter, certain property claims – from
biodiversity to folklore – do not make it onto what Rose refers to as 'our
property radar screen.'[68]

The issue of communal ownership – if and how moral rights can be
applied in order to safeguard the resources of indigenous peoples,
which was touched upon in the previous chapter, and above all, if

intellectual property rights (today almost indistinguishable from trade policy) is the answer to this conundrum to begin with – remains one of the most acutely important questions the international community needs to consider in the upcoming years. Certain countries have instituted control mechanisms such as the system of 'le domaine public payant' to ensure that works in the public domain are not inappropriately exploited.[69] Some things in the public domain might be better served if propertized, some should remain a free resource, and certain things are just detritus to begin with and hence negligable.[70] Because the public domain means different things in different cultural contexts, how the free and controlled are managed is a question of cultural contexts, but ultimately a profoundly political issue.

The major backdrop for the 'second enclosure movement' is the increasingly interconnected global economy. Although globalization operates both differently and on a larger and more all-encompassing scale than did the internationalization taking place at the end of the nineteenth century, some of the fundamental tendencies that drive the logic of this contemporary regulatory framework were set in place at the Congrès Littéraire International. At the time of the intense efforts on the part of ALAI and others to secure the Berne Convention in 1886, literature and translations were the prime assets for which protection was sought. New technology, travel, international cooperation, and communication networks had created markets beyond the nation-state and a wider constituency of consumers. France was at the forefront of the initiatives to secure international property rights both in industrial and intellectual production, and its leading role in the latter field was made possible partly by the enduring popularity of French literature, but also because of a cultural leadership Hugo took for granted, while others regarded it a brazen expression of cultural imperialism. ALAI was accused of catering only to French interests when it came to the question of translations, a critique that underscored the extent to which intellectual property rights are seen as primarily of interest to those who have an upper hand in the circulation of cultural commodities.

An intrinsic feature of this basic propensity to benefit exporters rather than importers is the perhaps paradoxical fact that international intellectual property rights fundamentally serve *domestic* or *national* agendas. In his speech at the Congrès Victor Hugo was promoting the superiority of France much as he was endorsing intellectual property rights on the international scene. The Scandinavian countries disputing the assimilation of translation into the Berne Convention a few years later based their opposition on what they saw as an acute need for access to literature in order to bring about internal and external competitiveness in strategic fields such as education. As we witnessed in chapter 4, during that same time the United States legitimized the use of piracy by arguing that it had a basic right to steal from its former colonizer, now symbolically materialized in English novels. As the United States embarked on its aggressive trade policy in intellectual property rights in the 1980s, this strategy relied in no small part on statistics reporting the financial relevance of the 'core copyright industries' to the U.S. domestic economy. It was a clear sign of what these companies, together with policy makers, had come to realize; whereas producers were largely domestic companies and their employees, consumers increasingly translated into foreign citizens.[71] It is one of the major paradoxes of the U.S. position that the promotion of free trade *always* comes accompanied by its Siamese twin: the active pursuit of *stronger* interventionist politics on the part of, for instance, Congress and government.

After the Second World War and decolonialization, developing countries have tried to evoke the same arguments of national interest in order to argue for lower standards of protection, but found it considerably more difficult to gain acceptance for such ideas. Instead, from the viewpoint of WTO, trade is seen as a necessary component for developing countries, without which 'the dream of development will be out of reach.'[72] Organizations profoundly critical of the present world trade system, such as *Oxfam*, acknowledge that history makes a mockery of the claim that trade cannot work for the poor, but concludes that the current system is built on 'rigged rules and double standards,' both of which favours developed nations.[73] Therefore is it quite possible, as Ruth Gana Okediji claims, that weaknesses of the free trade model are negatively reinforced by weaknesses in the intellectual property model, and that this will hit developing countries especially hard.[74] All these various examples point to the fact that domestic and/or nation-state interests tend to influence the development of the international context, and vice versa.

Today, French supremacy is replaced by an Anglo-American – or, perhaps more correctly, an English-language – control of a media culture that includes print, but also spans the Internet, film, music, software, tourism, and academic research. Several overlapping and contributing factors made this reversal of roles possible, and for the purposes of this book, they can be traced back to the 1960s. During that decade, we saw the first steps towards the gradual immersion of publishing into larger media conglomerates; the explosion of technological innovations that both challenged and made the owning of content more lucrative than ever – from teaching machines to photocopiers – the increased use of English as the *lingua franca* of the same areas – entertainment, information, knowledge – where intellectual properties become crucial assets; and of course in more recent years, the synthesis of intellectual property rights and trade policy, led by the United States and culminating in the TRIPS agreement and the formation of WTO.

As Smilla says in *Miss Smilla's Feeling for Snow*: 'There's nothing "local" left any more ... If something happens in Greenland, it's connected to something else in Singapore' (218). Smilla could be talking about the power of global corporations to move manufacturing lines across space. She could be talking about banking, finances, capital, investments, made by a push on a button here, transforming there in a millisecond. But she is talking about Isaiah's murder and how it is connected to another one by the same man. A boy chased from one roof in Copenhagen, a girl pushed off another in Singapore. Only time and distance separate the two crimes, the reasons behind the wrongdoings are one and the same. And the roofs in Copenhagen and Singapore – covered in snow or bathing in sunshine – form one pair in a set of strange intersections across time and space explored by Høeg. There are the icebergs and seaweed that come to mind as Smilla indulges in a soup prepared for her by The Mechanic; there is the impossible relationship between Smilla's Danish father and Greenlandic mother; there is the materiality of the revolver she picks up on the *Kronos*: a Ballester Molina Inûnángitsoq, 'Manufactured in Nuuk under an Argentine licence' (383); and of course there is the eerie correspondence between Southeast-Asian poppy fields and prehistoric worms contained in the icy waters of Gela Alta. When Høeg describes Smilla's world as one of 'compressed juxtapositions' (340), he captures very well how intricately globalization works to create these unexpected yet codependent connections.

TRIPS and WTO organizes the world according to the relationship between national governments; the many NGOs concerned with intellectual property rights may choose to emphasize other spatial alliances; the Mexican women whose silver jewellery is copied by other women in Southeast Asian sweat-shops may choose other issues; all are involved in global flows that are national, regional, supranational, and global at the same time. As correspondences go, they exist independent of nation-states, and yet are heavily indebted to national incentives and motivations. Globalization involves tensions and contradictions: openness, mobility, transgression, hybridity, but also territoriality, nationality, borders, regulation – all tenets that influence the construction of intellectual property rights. New forms of legality arise as these changes affect the nation-state.[75] Multi-layered, extensive, and sophisticated geopolitical connections, these tendencies are not laid out in a random pattern. Doreen Massey keeps us on track when she concludes that flows do not operate haphazardly; she notes that they rather allow some to be on the receiving end while they imprison others.[76] As if to substantiate Massey's claim and place it in the context of intellectual property rights, Carol Rose echoes consent when she concludes: 'Some things get treated as property, some things do not; some persons get treated as owners, some do not.'[77]

III

One of the more concrete challenges intellectual property rights have had to contend with during the time period discussed in this book is the emergence and impact of new technology. From music recordings and photography to the photocopier and the Internet, new ways to distribute and reproduce intellectual properties have consistently spurred changes in cultural consumption as well as in national legislation and international conventions, corroborating the suggestion that copyright and technology have always been at war with one another.[78]

In chapter 3, we saw how the photocopier proved its impact on both these levels: it permitted a radical increase in the dissemination of information, and did so under the auspices of being a machine anybody – even women and animals – could master. Even more important was in fact that the machine challenged the traditional role of the author when it brought home the message of just how easy and quickly the entire bedrock of what it meant to be a producer and consumer in print culture could be called into question. 'Sampling' texts and recombining information from many sources into new 'books' would lead to added provisions in law – for instance, the codification of 'fair use' in the U.S. Copyright Act of 1976 – as well as to the emergence of new organizations whose sole purpose was to license the use of this new machine.

All of these features – the ease with which copying occurs, the realignment of production and consumption, the increase of surveillance, and the subsequent arrival of legislative measures – have earmarked the relationship between intellectual property rights and the most advanced copier to date: the Internet. As Marshal McLuhan so succinctly stated, technology relies on technology for its protection.[79] In the present situation, this translates into a shift from public to private enforcement through technological means.[80] Digitization, which makes copying not only tremendously easier than before, but provides copies just as good, if not better than the original, has prompted enormous efforts in order to ensure that control keep pace with access.[81] On the part of industries heavily invested in intellectual properties, this means increased attempts to develop protective measures such as the previously mentioned Digital Rights Language, XrML (eXtensible rights Markup Language) developed by Xerox and Microsoft through ContentGuard, Inc., or the Secure Digital Music Initiative (SMDI), which promised the music industry to stomp out Napsterism by digitally watermarking audio files but became publicly humiliated and discredited when Princeton professor Edward Felten and his colleagues cracked the code in three weeks.[82] New ways to circumvent and dodge the most elaborate of protective measures will, or so it seems, always be a step ahead of the copyright enforcers.

Governments and international bodies such as WTO and WIPO have responded with new acts and treaties that attempt to adapt intellectual property regimes to this new digital environment. The most important include the EU Directive 2001-29-EC on the Harmonisation of Certain Aspects of Copyright and Related Rights in the Information Society, the adoption of which is a prerequisite for ratification of the WIPO Copyright Treaty from 1996, and The Digital Millennium Copyright Act from 1998. One of the most criticized features of the DMCA also figures in the WIPO Copyright Treaty. Under article 11, legal protection and legal remedies shall be provided against the circumvention of effective technological measures. This clause makes it illegal to bypass any built-in code that protects digital intellectual property, EVEN if the use for which such circumvention occurs is legal, such as fair use. It also forbids the creation of any code that cracks codes that protect copyrighted material.[83] The first test of the legitimacy of this DMCA provision came in July 2001, when Russian computer programmer Dimitry Sklyarov and his Moscow-based employer ElcomSoft were charged with circumventing the protection on the Adobe Acrobat eBook Reader.

Facing five charges, $2.25 million in fines, and up to twenty-five years in prison, Sklyarov's arrest following an appearance at the DefCon hacking convention in Las Vegas caused a public outcry and even demonstrations among cyber-rights activists. Led by the Electronic Frontier Foundation, the protests eventually forced Adobe to drop their charges. Sklyarov, who was released in December 2001, was allowed to return to Moscow, but would remain under supervision of the U.S. government for a year.[84] Although Skylarov was released, there will still be a criminal case under the DCMA, this time solely against his employer, ElcomSoft.[85]

How then should the Internet be viewed on the evolutionary chart of intellectual property rights? Two major interpretations exist. First, since intellectual property rights have been able to accommodate innovations before, the Internet should prove no different in this respect. Most treaties mentioned in this book build on previously established norms going back to the Berne Convention. Those who disagree argue instead that the Internet offers a radically new medium, providing property completely detached from the physical world. If the bottle was protected before and not the wine, the Digital Age must find forms to protect the wine and not the bottle.[86]

Arguably, the most challenging feature raised by the explosion of the Internet when it comes to access and control – as opposed to the problems posed by the copier – is brought on by the spatial mutability of the former. Digital infringements of intellectual property rights might be almost impossible to settle, for the reasons Charles Oppenheim underlines:

> What if I, in the United Kingdom, send instructions to a computer in the United States to copy a large body of machine-readable data to a computer in Argentina? Let us imagine that by all reasonable tests in British and American law, I have infringed, but there is no infringement in Argentinean law. Whose law applies? The data neither start nor end in the United Kingdom. Only my instructions came from there. Yet the owners of the Argentinean computer knew nothing of my instructions to add data to their computer. This may be significant because, say, the law in the United States may allow for far higher damages than British law, and, by the look of it, a copyright owner going to an Argentinean court would be foolish as there was no infringement under Argentina's law.[87]

Therefore, if we accept the premise outlined so far – that the rise of transnational corporations and the prevalent trade system have made intellectual properties and their rights global (in no small part due to technology) – then the follow-up question must be: does such an increase in spatial presence bring with it a concomitant public domain? That is, is there a global public domain?

Before attempting to answer that question, we need to consider an important feature of the public domain, namely that it – think of the parks, town squares, fields, and the resources that can be drawn from nature as a whole – tends to be conceptualized as simultaneously place and space, even as a territory or nation-state. When David Lange once argued that the contemporary public domain in intellectual property rights could be compared to 'the public grazing lands on the Western plains of a century ago,'[88] he was probably not only visualizing the wide-open, virginal pastures where the buffalo roamed, but a specific geographical place in the United States: the 'West.' It is perfectly natural that the retired cattle rancher John Perry Barlow, one of the founding fathers of the 'information wants to be free' movement and lyricist to the Grateful Dead, drew inspiration from the nineteenth-century frontier of the American West when cofounding the Electronic Frontier Foundation with Mitch Kapor. Clearly, there is a romantic allure to the West that is promoted as a place of ingenuity where, as opposed to the lawyer-infested present, 'understandings were preferred over laws.'[89]

It might appear strictly anecdotal, but I believe there is a very important key here that might unlock the door not only to how the powerful construction of the Internet as a giant photocopier without a passport, seemingly operating regardless of place, occurs, but also to the fact that it has become – through a negotiation of place and space – the ultimate contemporary metaphor for the public domain. Let me try and explain what I mean in more detail.

In the ongoing discussion on how cyberspace should or should not be regulated, the many prominent scholars – primarily from the United States and in law – who criticize the expansion of intellectual property rights and lament the concomitant enclosure of the public domain, view the Internet as an 'innovation commons,' the result of fortuitous connections between the U.S. government and individual creativity and genius.[90] This representation resonates profoundly with a built-in appreciation of the same virtues that are conjured up when Lange and Barlow speak of the West: freedom from constraints; innovation and ingenuity; individual creativity; and the law of the land instead of incomprehensible rules no one obeys anyway. Many of these features – individualism, a cult of genius, originality – are part and parcel of the established imagery of authorship and are easily adapted to technological innovations. The storybook chronicle of Chester Carlson and the Xerox copier is antecedent to the mythical history of PARC, surpassed only by legendary mavericks such as John Perry Barlow and Richard Stallman, whose texts on digital matters can best be described as poetic excursions verging on the megalomaniac. In the Digital Age, programmers have become authors, and if put in updated Hugospeak, they prefer a healthy open source to a closed-off and fenced-in code. Ultimately, the battle between free vs control is a battle over the Internet as a 'final frontier,' because it is perceived as a commons that has yet to be circumscribed by either corporate or governmental interests which have succeeded in closing off almost all other American public spaces. I think that this partly accounts for the current U.S. interest in the public domain, but it does not explain why the European discussion on these issues appears to be largely silent. From a European perspective, the historic construction of a public sphere in Jürgen Habermas's terms relates not so much to nature as it depends on a social milieu that is urban, even metropolitan in its contours. It is at a very specific historic moment and in the *Öffentlichkeit* of European coffeehouses and literary salons where the bourgeois public sphere emerges, a public sphere 'critically reflecting on its culture' rather than, as has become the norm in contemporary societies, merely consuming it.[91] This Ur-public sphere does seem to presuppose a completely different society from the knowledge-based, a completely different public from the hybrid and multicultural, and above all, a completely different place from the one offered by globalization and transnationalization. Nonetheless, the basic premise of what a public sphere needs in order to survive can easily be reframed in the perspective of today's concerns: active citizens. The public and the private are intrinsically interconnected, but to equate wealth with property and propertylessness with poverty is, as Hanna Arendt wrote, a misunderstanding, and one of the misapprehensions that work against the interest in the public domain.[92]

I would agree with Graeme B. Dinwoodie that the cyber-revolution merely highlights problems that are endemic to internationalization, which should be confronted more generally.[93] Innovation is a poor excuse for democracy, and the ultimate test of whether or not the Internet truly offers the possibility of a global public domain lies perhaps not in its capacity to stimulate further technological breakthroughs on the part of a privileged elite, but in its capacity to ensure increased public and hence democratic participation. If the innovation challenges of digitization are taken as a *universal* it may effectively obscure and undermine interest for the very different dilemmas facing other concurrent public domains.[94] Juxtapose cyberspace with the environment – both viewed as public domains where the first might be of more interest to the developed nations and the second is of paramount importance to developing nations rich in biodiversity – and you will see how they have prompted two very different responses; on the part of the Internet a vocal espousal of maximum freedom, and on the part of the environment just the opposite, a more distinct call for control and regulation.[95] Environmentalism has also been suggested as a means of providing a framework by which both the public domain and intellectual property can be managed, because as Eric Eldred suggests: 'Protecting the public domain isn't much different than protecting the environment.'[96]

IV

The most pressing question in light of the many complex issues that emerge when discussing the public domain is this: How should it be managed, by whom, and can it be done in such a way as to ensure a democratic participation which seeks to limit and ultimately eradicate the imbalances of the global knowledge-based society? Posing the question to begin with implies that we need, not so much a continued preoccupation with intellectual property rights, but an active intellectual property *policy*.[97] Scholars have argued that the same reversed reasoning that obfuscates the public domain on the expense of intellectual property rights, allows copyright to set the perimeters of policy, rather than ensure that policy as an instrument by which the vicissitudes of copyright can be harnessed.[98] Others have instead suggested that intellectual property rights should be viewed as part of a law of culture more generally, implying a broader cultural approach.[99]

If we agree that a global arena alternative to the one provided by WTO and TRIPS is necessary in order to provide for an alternative outlook on intellectual property rights, let us experiment with the idea that cultural policy answers to that call. However, just as intellectual property laws are enforced and generally also interpreted within a national framework – as for instance *Eldred v. Ashcroft*, with its emphasis on constitutionality, illustrates – does national culture still set the perimeters of cultural policy? While intellectual property rights are increasingly global, the analysis of this fact tends to relapse into an interpretation based on national or domestic experience.[100]

Perhaps it is indicative that the common-law 'copyright' countries, the United Kingdom and the United States, are those who either have integrated culture into a ministry or Department for Culture, Media, and Sport (as in the United Kingdom), or who have no cultural policy at all and no Ministry of Culture (as in the United States). To suggest that some sort of cultural policy would be in order to safeguard the public domain is anathema in the United States where any suggestion of governmental intervention is seen as equally suspect, if not more so, as corporate Disneyfication, and where culture is viewed as something intrinsically meant for private tastes rather than government regulation.[101] This does not imply, of course, that there has been no cultural policy on the part of the United States; quite the reverse.

In fact, the success with which the United States has designated *cultural industries* either a question of foreign policy, trade policy, or more likely both, might be the result of the *absence* of a national or domestic cultural policy. Countries such as France and Sweden, where there is a stronger emphasis on the rights of the author – the *Droit d'auteur* and *Upphovsmannarätt* – differ in any number of aspects in regard to their cultural policies but take them largely for granted, even as necessary and basically beneficial.[102] To this situation must be added the reality that if cultural policy can be applied in order to remedy some of the current imbalances of intellectual property rights, then one of the more intricate dilemmas is that it, too, is an instrument of control to a substantial degree built on *much the same value system* that has been used to legitimize intellectual property rights, namely the ideology of authorship, uniqueness, and individualism.[103]

However, there is no homogenous cultural policy that could simply be lifted out of its present context and be put to work on a global scale. The continued gap between the information 'rich' and the information 'poor' may prove that there are no international regulatory bodies efficient enough to oversee a democratic redistribution of this wealth, and that cultural policies tend to remain an instrument limited to nation-states.[104] In the present situation, the products that are protected by intellectual property rights and the conventions that lay down the ground rules of these rights are global, and when it comes to trade and intellectual property rights, domestic interests have, in the case of developed countries, been transformed into global truths. As the knowledge-based economy continues to forge the relationship between cultural policies and trade policies, the balance between them remains deeply ambiguous and uncertain.

TNCs and governments that have managed to move intellectual property rights onto the global agenda through trade organizations such as the WTO have been quick to utilize this situation to their advantage, whereas there is less evidence of a critical alternative established on a matching scale. The opposition against free trade has certainly not – with the exception perhaps of patents and biodiversity – focused on intellectual property rights, and perhaps understandably so. Shortages in water and food and global imblalances in agriculture must take centre stage; and yet it is crucial to remember that the resources of the knowledge-based society *also* must be disseminated more equally. UNESCO and WIPO are arenas where important work is being done, but as the most influential player in intellectual property rights during the last twenty years, the United States is not a member of UNESCO, and the organization is bogged down by similar problems that face the UN as a whole: financial instability and a bloated bureaucracy. While culture has seeped in everywhere, its policy still remains geopolitically tied to domestic and national interests.

Intellectual property rights are rights granting tremendous power. Historically as well as today they tend to serve those best that occupy positions of structural power. At present, such power is increasingly bestowed on those who produce and control the informational resources needed by the knowledge-based economy. Whether or not developing countries and marginalized groups stand to benefit from the potential conversion of other resources previously considered non-assets into protectable intellectual property remains an open question. More certain is the fact that few areas today are safe havens from the influence of intellectual property rights. From DNA sequences to e-books, from totem poles to traditional medicine, from *Gone With the Wind* to *The Wind Done Gone*, the question of immaterial ownership may never touch us directly and yet it permeates our everyday existence.

Pamela Samuelson has argued that the opaque, obscure, and illogical nature of intellectual property rights makes it almost impossible to rally any interest from the general public in its layout and impact at the time when such interest is needed the most.[105] And yet, intellectual property rights touch the lives of everybody who reads, listens to music, surfs the Web, rents videos, or goes to the movies; who travels and partakes in the global tourism industry; who uses databases and borrows books from the local library; who goes to university or any other educational facility; in fact, it reaches down into the innermost core of the human genome. If we are interested in how any or all of these resources are managed, ours would seem like the perfect time to look beyond the complexities of legalese, since few have such a large stake in what happens to culture and the public domain in the future as the public does.[106]

NOTES

All translations of French quotations are my own. The original is placed in the corresponding note.

Preface

1 Stallybrass and White, *The Politics and Poetics of Transgression*, 196.

Introduction

1 Any claim of this kind can be backed only by examples of an idiosyncratic nature, since such issues have been and continue to be at the forefront of discussion within a number of academic disciplines. Exemplifying by literature studies, one can list on the side of those promoting enduring values Bloom, *The Western Canon*, and on the opposite side, Herrnstein Smith, *Contingencies of Value*.
2 Foucault, 'What Is an Author?' 101.
3 On privileges, see, for instance, Feather, 'From Rights in Copies to Copyright,' and Hesse, 'Enlightenment Epistemology.'
4 Rose, 'The Author as Proprietor,' 75.
5 There appears to be a striking lack of feminist analysis of intellectual property rights, especially in relationship to print culture. The only example I have been able to find exploring the tremendously interesting aspect of gender and literary property is Melissa J. Homestead's dissertation 'Imperfect Title: Nineteenth-Century American Women Authors and Literary Property.'
6 See Woodmansee, 'The Genius and the Copyright'; Jaszi, 'Towards a Theory of Copyright'; and Rose, 'The Author as Proprietor.'

7 Ricketson, *Berne Convention*, is an indispensable goldmine of information on the history of the Berne Convention.

8 Foucault, 'What Is an Author?' 113.

9 The last category refers to the beliefs of certain Aboriginal clans in Australia. See Blakeney, 'What Is Traditional Knowledge?' 3.

10 One of the best introductions to this increased emphasis put on ownership of information is Wells Branscomb, *Who Owns Information?* A more recent but similarly accessible book framed within the public/private discussion is Bollier, *Silent Theft*.

11 For a good introduction to some of these differences, see Goldstein, *Copyright's Highway*, esp. the chapter, 'The Two Cultures of Copyright,' 165–96.

12 Geller, 'Must Copyright Be For Ever Caught Between Marketplace and Authorship Norms?' 159.

13 For an introduction to the history of *droit moral*, see Strömholm, 'Droit Moral – The International and Comparative Scene from a Scandinavian Viewpoint.'

14 According to Peter Jaszi, the 'work for hire' doctrine nonetheless often draws on the principle of the romantic authorship ideal ('Towards a Theory of Copyright,' 486).

15 As suggested by Strowel, 'Droit d'auteur and Copyright,' 248. Pointing out that 'the first framers of copyright laws, both in France and in the United States, sought primarily to encourage the creation of, and investment in, works furthering national social goals,' Jane C. Ginsburg underlines important historical similarities between the two systems ('A Tale of Two Copyrights,' 135).

16 This definition is taken from the WIPO *Intellectual Property Handbook: Policy, Law and Use*, 3. *Black's Law Dictionary* adds 'commercially viable' into their definition ('Intellectual property,' *Black's Law Dictionary*, 7th ed. [St. Paul–West Group] 1999).

17 In the following, any reference to the Berne Convention refers to the Paris Act of 24 July 1971, amended on 28 September 1979.

18 Jones, 'Mass Communication, Intellectual Property Rights, International Trade, and the Popular Music Industry,' 340.

19 On this last point of view, consider the interesting analysis of copyright in China by Alford, *To Steal a Book Is an Elegant Offense*.

20 Held et al., *Global Transformations*, 1.

21 Nonetheless, the spatial dimension is one that has not been explored to its full potential either in book history or in scholarship on intellectual property rights. While I think Franco Moretti in his *Atlas of the European Novel, 1800–1900* is one of the few who have given serious thought to the possi-

bilities this approach opens up in the first field, and I find his analysis both challenging and inspiring, I also consider his separation between the material and the textual somewhat unfortunate. His own book proves that the material and the textual tend to overlap both methodologically and theoretically. As far as intellectual property rights are concerned, I will discuss the analytical tendency to remain in the domain of the nation-state in face of essentially global changes in more detail in chapter 6. For sheer joy of texts and pictures, see also Bradbury, *The Atlas of Literature*. A concrete proposal on how to use spatial analysis primarily in book history research with the aid of Geographical Information Systems is suggested by Black, MacDonald, and Black, 'Geographical Information Systems.' Scholars who have incorporated the dimensions of space and place in their work on intellectual property rights include Aoki, '(Intellectual) Property and Sovereignty,' 'Space Invaders,' and Coombe, 'Authorial Cartographies.'

22 This is certainly the underlying premise in some of the most important contributions to our understanding of globalization, including the works of, for instance, Massey, *Space, Place and Gender*; Castells, *The Information Age*; and Sassen, *Globalization and Its Discontents*.

23 Morley, 'EurAm, Modernity, Reason and Alterity,' 327. Mike Featherstone and Scott Lash suggest in *Global Modernities* that what we see is an overall 'spatialization of social theory' ('Globalization, Modernity and the Spatialization of Social Theory,' 1).

24 For an argument to a similar effect, see Feltes, 'International Copyright.'

25 The EU Directive is 'Council Directive 93/98/EEC of 29 October 1993 harmonizing the term of protection of copyright and certain related rights.' For a useful introduction to some of the directive's consequences see Parrinder and Chernaik, *Textual Monopolies*. The Copyright Term Extension Act (Act. S 505, P.L. 105–298, 11 Stat. 2827) was passed by both the U.S. House and Senate on 7 October 1998, and signed by President Clinton on 21 October 1998. For a detailed description of the Act's consequences, see The University of North Carolina Task Force on Intellectual Property http://www.unc.edu/~unclng/public-d.htm

26 See, for instance, the general comparisons between different nations made by Goldstein in *International Copyright*.

27 Boyle, *Shamans, Software, and Spleens*, 13.

28 The crucial observation that this new economy has led to a form of bargaining that used to be known as 'industrial diplomacy' but is now more a form of 'knowledge diplomacy' has been made by Ryan, *Knowledge Diplomacy*, 1.

29 The three main pillars of the Berne Convention are: national treatment, automatic protection, and independence of protection. WIPO, *Intellectual Property Handbook: Policy Law, and Use*, 263.

30 Altbach, 'Book Publishing,' 320. Since the 1970s, Altbach has published several books concerned with publishing and education in the Third World. See his *Publishing and Development in the Third World*, Altbach and Teferra, *Publishing and Development*, and Altbach, *Copyright and Development*.

31 See May, *A Global Political Economy of Intellectual Property Rights*, 60.

32 Strange, *States and Markets*, 119, 21, 25. Susan Strange is clearly influenced by Foucault and his emphasis on the spatial as expressed in, for instance, 'The Eye of Power.'

33 See Hall, 'The Local and the Global,' 34.

34 Rather than attempt a futile bibliography from a sea of possibilities, I prefer to list a few books that have been important for the overall direction of this book, both in terms of theory and method. Gaines, *Contested Culture*, combines theoretical depth, an interdisciplinary approach and vivid case studies in an excellent example of a scholarly work drawing on cultural studies as well as law. Boyle's *Shamans, Software, and Spleens* is one of the most influential examples of a critical investigation of intellectual property in the Information Age, while Coombe's important *The Cultural Life of Intellectual Properties* touches on a number of fascinating cases in both trademark and copyright law. Woodmansee, *The Author, Art, and the Market*, is by now requisite reading in the field. From within the tradition of political economy I have found Bettig, *Copyrighting Culture*, useful in its emphasis on the international scene, an approach also shared by May in *A Global Political Economy of Intellectual Property Rights*. A number of representative anthologies include Sarat and Kearns, *Law in the Domains of Culture*; Woodmansee and Jaszi, *The Construction of Authorship*; and Sherman and Strowel, *Of Authors and Origins*. One of the best general introductions to the questions raised in this book is Mann, 'Who Will Own Your Next Good Idea?'

35 Strange, *States and Markets*, 66.

36 Felman, 'A Ghost in the House of Justice,' 277. For a minute reconstruction of another trial reverberating with Second World War experiences, but based on archival work and interviews, see Kaplan, *The Collaborator*.

37 Gaines, *Contested Culture*, xv.

38 I am drawing here on Roland Barthes's definition, *'a work conceived, perceived, and received in its integrally symbolic nature is a text'* ('From Work to Text,' 159).

39 That law and literature are two domains that may have much in common is, for instance, apparent in the work of Stanley Fish. See *Doing What Comes Naturally*. An example of the law and literature movement (mostly drawing on what we might refer to as 'high' literature for its purposes) is Posner, *Law and Literature*. On the reading of judicial opinions drawing on literary criticism, see Boyd White, *Justice As Translation*. For a comprehensive introduction to the centrality of law in American culture in general, see Porsdam, *Legally Speaking*.
40 Massey, 'Imagining Globalization,' 35.

1 Wearing the Parisian Hat

1 La Société des Gens des Lettres was founded by Hugo, Honoré de Balzac, Alexandre Dumas, and George Sand in 1838 in order to safeguard the interests of authors, for instance concerning literary property. For more information, see the organization's website www.sgdl.org
2 Robb, *Victor Hugo*, 219.
3 Casanova, *La Republique Mondiale des Lettres*, 184.
4 Charles Hugo quoted in Robb, *Victor Hugo*, 406.
5 In October 1859, the abolitionist John Brown and his Provisional Army of the United States took possession of the United States Armory and Arsenal at Harpers Ferry, West Virgina. The uprising, which intended to arm slaves by seizing the arsenal's 100,000 guns failed, and Brown was hanged on 2 December, 1859.
6 Parkhurst Ferguson, *Paris As Revolution*, 158.
7 John Lough, *Writer and Public in France*, 276.
8 Ibid., 304.
9 Centring on Flaubert, Bourdieu, *Les règles d'art*, must be considered the most substantial contribution concerning this new market as it emerged in France.
10 Moretti, *Atlas*, 17.
11 Mollier, *L'argent et les lettres*, 157.
12 Lough, *Writer and Public in France*, 314.
13 Robb, *Victor Hugo*, 376. For a longer discussion on Hetzel, his publishing career and cooperation with Hugo, see Mollier, *L'argent et les lettres*, 247–61, and Chartier and Martin, *Le temps des éditeurs*, 168–9, 210–13.
14 Balzac, quoted in Lough, *Writer and Public in France*, 299.
15 Lough, *Writer and Public in France*, 298.
16 On early copyright history in England, see Rose, *Authors and Owners*, and

Feather, *Publishing, Piracy and Politics*, esp. chapter 1, 'The Origins of Copyright,' and chapter 2, 'From Custom to Statute,' 10–63.

17 Moretti, *Atlas*, 176–7, 182.

18 Ricketson, *Berne Convention*, 38. For a useful overview of the international development, see Saunders, *Authorship and Copyright*, esp. chapter 7, 'The Internationalization of Copyright and Authorship.'

19 Lough, *Writer and Public in France*, 319–20.

20 Ibid., 331.

21 Ibid., 327.

22 Findling and Pelle, *Historical Dictionary of World Fairs and Expositions*, 63. This volume contains useful information on the 1878 exhibition as well as on subsequent ones.

23 Hugo, 'Discours d'Ouverture, 993.

24 Ibid., 994.

25 Ibid.

26 Homestead, 'Imperfect Title,' 126.

27 Hugo, 'Discours d'Ouverture,' 994.

28 Henry Clay, quoted in Solberg, *International Copyright in the Congress of the United States*, 3.

29 Vaidhyanathan, *Copyrights and Copywrongs*, 55.

30 Wordsworth quoted in Feather, *Publishing, Piracy and Politics*, 126. As his French fellow writer, Wordsworth chose to lobby through political channels, actively engaging himself in legislation through his association with Thomas Noon Talfourd in the House of Commons. Primarily, Wordsworth was concerned with the author's obligation to provide for his family, and for the economic remuneration the family could derive from his work after his death. But this argument encountered strong opposition, raised on the fear that the rights of publishers and readers alike would be threatened. See Feather, *Publishing, Piracy and Politics*, esp. chapter 5, 'The Reform of the Law,' for a detailed discussion on the Wordsworth debate.

31 Feather, *Publishing, Piracy and Politics*, 158–9.

32 'Mais le livre est distinct de la pensée; comme livre, il est saisissable, tellment saisissable qu'il est quelquefois saisi. (*On rit.*)' (Hugo, 'Discours d'Ouverture,' 994).

33 Jane Gaines calls a manoeuver of this kind 'an ideological rescue mission in the evolution of intellectual property doctrine' (*Contested Culture*, 67).

34 'Ah! la lumière! la lumière toujours! la lumière partout!' (Hugo, 'Discours d'Ouverture,' 995).

35 Parkhurst Ferguson, *Paris As Revolution*, 166–7.

36 Ricketson, *Berne Convention*, 21.
37 See Moretti, *Atlas*, 151–8. There are a number of potential fallacies in-volved in making too much of Moretti's line of thought; for instance, that many readers may have read the French books in the original rather than translation. Although I will return to the question of translation in the next chapter, arguments to a similar effect – stressing the dominance of the English language and the possible consequences of this insularity – are launched by Lawrence Venuti in his *The Translator's Invisibility*, and *The Scandals of Translation*.
38 'La France est d'intérêt public. La France s'élève sur l'horizon de tous les peuples. Ah! Disent-ils, il fait jour, la France est là! (*Oui! oui! Bravos répétés*.) Qu'il puisse y avoir des objections à la France, cela étonne; il y en a pourtant; la France a des ennemis. Ce sont les ennemis mêmes de la civilisation, les ennemis du livre, les ennemis de la pensée libre, les ennemis de l'emancipation, de l'examen, de la délivrance; ce qui voient dans le dogme un éternel maître et dans le genre humain un éternel mineur' (Hugo, 'Discours d'Ouverture,' 996).
39 'Rendons-leur coup sur coup. Haine à la haine! Guerre à la guerre!' (Hugo, 'Discours d'Ouverture,' 996).
40 'Plan général et complet de l'Exposition universelle de 1878.'
41 Ekström, *Den utställda världen*, 25, 57.
42 The picture can be found in Kaplan, *Reproductions of Banality*, 127.
43 For the most well-known example of a book underscoring the vital link between literacy, print culture, and the construction of the nation-state, see Anderson, *Imagined Communities*. This propensity is obvious even from an epistemological view; see my discussion on book history in Hemmungs Wirtén, 'Surveying the (Battle)field.'
44 'Je vous défie de porter un autre chapeau que le chapeau de Paris' (Hugo quoted in Casanova, *La République Mondiale Des Lettres*, 128).
45 For a complete list, see Union des Associations Internationales, *Les Congrès Internationaux de 1681 à 1899*, 22–4. There are two congresses in 1878 re-lated to copyright, first the Congrès Littéraire International (17–28 June), and then the Congrès international de la propriété artistique (18–21 September). One could also mention the Congrès de la propriété industrielle (5–17 September). The first Congrès Internationale de la propriété littéraire et artistique takes place in Brussels, 27–30 September 1858.
46 Moretti, *Atlas*, 120.
47 Benjamin, *Passagearbetet*, 9.
48 Ibid., 20.
49 See Hemmungs Wirtén, 'Mat. Betraktelser kring en populär kultur.'

50 Casanova, *La République Mondiale Des Lettres*, 50.
51 'Vous et nous, nous sommes les concitoyens de la cité universelle' (Hugo, 'Discours d'Ouverture,' 994).
52 Bourdieu, 'Deux impérialismes de l'universel,' 151. A personal and highly readable account of the desire for everything French is Kaplan, *French Lessons*.
53 Immanuel Wallerstein, prominent historian and arguably one of the founding fathers of the globalization discourse, puts forward such an approach in his notion of a 'world-system,' basically linking globalization with the onslaught of European-based trade capitalism (see his *The Modern World-System*).
54 Murphy, *International Organization*, 47.
55 Held et al., *Global Transformations*, 43.
56 Initially the organization was named Association Littéraire Internationale, incorporating the 'artistic' five years after its founding (see Ricketson, *Berne Convention*, 48). In the following, I will refer to the organization by its present acronym, ALAI. The International Publishers Association (IPA) established in Paris 1896 and the International Booksellers Federation (IBF, 1950) are later examples of similar bodies.
57 'Les travaux du Congrès touchaient aux questions de l'ordre le plus élevé,' *Bulletin de l'Association Littéraire Internationale*, no. 1 (December 1878), 1.
58 Ibid., 3. This number is augmented to sixty non-French members, none of whom were allowed more than three delegates each, from countries represented at the congress (the French representation remaining at fifteen) in the statutes taken at the conference in London, 29 June 1879. See *Bulletin de l'Association Littéraire Internationale*, no. 7, October–November 1879), 1.
59 *Bulletin de l'Association Littéraire Internationale*, no. 2 (January–February 1879), 1.
60 'L'association littéraire internationale vivra. La race des littérateurs, race rare, marchera devant; les peuples la suivront. La paix universelle sortira de cette immense fraternité spirituelle' (ibid., 2).
61 Murphy, *International Organization*, 60.
62 *Bulletin de l'Association Littéraire Internationale*, no. 6 (August–September, 1879), 4.
63 Ibid., 2.
64 *Bulletin de l'Association Littéraire Internationale*, no. 7 (October–November 1879), 10–12.
65 'Les Dames sont admises.' Advertisement in *Bulletin de l'Association Littéraire Internationale*, no. 10 (October 1880), 69.
66 *Bulletin de l'Association Littéraire Internationale*, no. 14 (April 1882), 1.

67 Giddens, *The Consequences of Modernity*.

68 See also Martha Woodmansee's account of the parliamentary debate in Britain that ended in the Copyright Act of 1842, where the imagery of the 'author' is used precisely in this sphere of representation ('The Cultural Work of Copyright').

69 'Toutes les sciences s'enchaînent,' *Bulletin de l'Association Littéraire Internationale*, no. 10 (October 1880), 3.

70 'Au nom de la patrie de Shakespeare, je suis heureux de saluer la patrie du Dante.' *Bulletin de l'Association Littéraire Internationale*, no. 15 (August 1882), 5.

71 In Berne, 10–17 September 1883. ALAI's conference would be followed by two Diplomatic Conferences in the same city in 1884 and 1885. For more information on the work leading up to the final 1886 Convention, see Ricketson, *Berne Convention*, 49–80.

72 'A mon avis, une convention internationale sur la propriété littéraire et artistique offre beaucoup moins de difficultés que celle sur la propriété industrielle.' *Bulletin de l'Association Littéraire Internationale*, no. 16 (May–June 1883), 11.

73 Parkhurst Ferguson, *Paris As Revolution*, 177.

74 The notion of 'representation' is highly useful in this context, and will be elaborated further in chapter 5 when I discuss 'cultural property.' I draw substantially on Stuart Hall's use of the term as described by him in 'The Work of Representation.'

2 Inventing F. David

1 As Sam Ricketson notes, the question of translation is of course an underlying feature of the Berne Convention itself. The original text was written in French, and the priority rule in case of a disagreement is in favour of the French text, not the English (Ricketson, *Berne Convention*, 132–3).

2 For a notable exception within translation studies, see Venuti, *Scandals*, esp. the chapter 'Copyright,' 47–66. Although Melissa Homestead is one of the few scholars whose work on copyright does include translations – when she considers *Stow v. Thomas* in 1853 – she does not explicitly explore its relationship to authorship (see 'Imperfect Title,' esp. chapter 2, 'When I Can Read My Title Clear': Harriet Beecher Stowe and the *Stowe v. Thomas* Copyright Infringement Suit,' 104–65). Within the analysis of law, translation appears to take on a much broader role as 'interpretation.' For an ex-ample that considers translation both in the way it is used here and in a more encompassing way, see Boyd White, *Justice as Translation*.

3 '... cette sorte de transfusion d'un sang étranger dans les veines d'un pays,

doit être faite avec prudence, savoir et honnêteté),' *Bulletin de l'Association Littéraire Internationale*, no. 10 (October 1880), 29. The first formal report on translations is issued before the second Congrès in London 1879 ('De la Traduction: Rapport au Comité Executif,' *Bulletin de l'Association Littéraire Internationale* no. 3 [March–April 1879], 4–7). Similar reports are published in preparation for the Lisbon conference, recounting the traditions of translations in, for instance, England, France, Denmark, Norway, and Holland (see 'Commission de Traduction,' *Bulletin de l'Association Littéraire Internationale*, no. 9, [September 1880], 26–82).

4 Ricketson, *Berne Convention*, 384.

5 *Bulletin de l'Association Littéraire Internationale*, no. 10 (October 1880), 29.

6 'Comment voulez-vous que je prenne part aux travaux du Congrès? A la fin du compte, l'Association littéraire internationale ne travaille-t-elle pas exclusivement pour le profit des romanciers et des auteurs dramatiques français dont les productions dominent le marché universel, au grand détriment des autres littératures?' *Bulletin de l'Association Littéraire Internationale*, no. 10 (October 1880), 31.

7 UNESCO www.unesco.org/culture/xtrans/html_eng/index4.shtml. Downloaded 16 January 2003.

8 Hence of course the title of his book, *The Translator's Invisibility*.

9 The reason why this chapter relies on the British Harvill Press edition is explored in the main body of the text. All quotes in the text refer to Høeg, *Miss Smilla's Feeling for Snow* (London: Harvill Press, 1996).

10 Møller, 'Peter Høeg or the Sense of Writing,' 30.

11 Westman Tullus, 'Peter Høeg, 38.

12 A representative anthology surveying the various approaches within translation studies, is Venuti, *The Translation Studies Reader*.

13 Westman Tullus, 'Peter Høeg,' 38. According to Westman Tullus, *Smilla* was most successful in Germany, where a third of the total print run had been sold. On the reception in German-speaking nations, see Schou, 'Danmark set nedefra,' 300–3.

14 Dyssegaard quoted in Gloin, 'Danish Mystery.'

15 See, for instance, the interesting contributions on translating the 'Third World' in Dingwaney and Meier, *Between Languages and Cultures*.

16 Lefevere, 'Mother Courage's Cucumbers,' 233. See also Lawrence Venuti's interesting discussion on the publication of Giovanni Guareschi's Don Camillo books in the United States in respect to such transpositions (*Scandals*, chapter 7, 'The Bestseller,' 124–57).

17 Hall, 'The Local and the Global,' 20–1.

18 Review of *Smilla's Sense of Snow*, 56

19 Maryles, 'Behind the Bestseller,' 15.

20 'Uhørt Høeg-succes.'
21 See, for instance, Jansson, 'En postmodern undergångsvision.'
22 These arguments were advanced by one of the book's severest critics, Leif
    Zern; see 'En berättelse med skräddarsydd kostym.'
23 Thorvall, 'Välsvarvad hjältinna.' Peter Høeg became the object of a special
    issue of the Swedish literary magazine *Bonniers Litterära Magasin* 1 (1995),
    where the debate on *Smilla* and his other books can be consulted.
24 Williams, Book review of *Miss Smilla's Feeling for Snow*, 41.
25 Review of *Smilla's Sense of Snow*, 56.
26 Leithauser, 'Thrills and Chills,' 39.
27 Skow, 'A Big Hit, A Small Miss,' 77.
28 McCue, 'Arctic Nights,' 20.
29 Nathan, 'Irritable, Depressed, Spoiled and Terrific,' 12.
30 Peter Høeg quoted in Trolle, *Miss Smilla's Feeling for Snow*, 26. In much the
    same way, Høeg describes the writing process of Smilla as entering into a
    'linguistic state.'
31 For an analysis of Smilla from a postcolonial perspective, see Kruger, 'Luk-
    susgrølænderen, papgrølænderen, fupgrølænderen, pladaskgrølænderen.'
32 Norseng, 'A House of Mourning,' 61.
33 Danius, 'Fröken Smilla skakar om,' and 'Bortom Öresund.' That *Smilla* was
    first of all a postcolonial novel was also noted by Andrews, 'Mystery Takes
    Icy Turns,' and Dolhem, 'Qui a tué l'enfant inuit?'
34 North, 'The Snow Must Go On.'
35 Åhlund, 'Bille Augusts känsla för snö.' See Trolle, *Miss Smilla's Feeling for
    Snow*, for details about the film. Financially, it was referred to as a 'classic
    Europudding,' funded not only with Swedish, Danish, and Norwegian
    money, but also funds from Germany and from the EU-sponsored fund
    Eurimages (Wennö, 'Staten stäms av filmbolag').
36 Johnson, Movie review of *Smilla's Sense of Snow*, 63, and Bacchus, 'Smilla's
    Sense of Silliness.'
37 Ukespeilet Norden, 'Grønland: Likte Frøken Smilla' www.interpost.no/
    aktuelt/ukespeil/norden/norden_1088.html. Downloaded 5 September
    1999.
38 Leithauser, 'Thrills and Chills,' 41.
39 Nathan, 'Irritable, Depressed, Spoiled and Terrific,' 12.
40 See, for instance, Bawer, 'Take My Queen, Please.'
41 Sue Terry, one of the readers in the Book Group List, points out that
    the Australian version was entitled <u>Ms</u> *Smilla's Feeling for Snow*.
    lwhyte@acslink.net.au, 8 January 1997. http://books.rpmdp.com/
    archives/v01.n035. Downloaded 28 May 2002.
42 Satterlee, 'A Case for Smilla,' 14.

43 Guido Waldman quoted in Satterlee, 'A Case for Smilla,' 14.

44 I have explored my argument on 'transediting' in detail in *Global Infatuation*, esp. chapter 5, 'Transediting: The Global Made Local,' 121–53.

45 See, for instance, Sengupta, 'Translation as Manipulation,' and Chatterjee, 'Canon Without Consensus.'

46 Kundera, 'Author's Note.'

47 Stanger, 'In Search of The Joke,' 94.

48 Homestead, 'Imperfect Title,' 135.

49 Gwinn, 'Finding the Right Words.' In his discussion on the English translations of the succesful Don Camillo books, Lawrence Venuti notes that the translator Una Troubridge received a total of $125.20 for her translation of *The Little World of Don Camillo* (1950) (*Scandals*, 151).

50 Ricketson, *Berne Convention*, 286.

51 Satterlee, 'A Case for Smilla,' 17.

52 Waldman, quoted in Malmkjær, 'A Tale of "Two" Smillas,' 5.

53 The complete discussion on *Smilla* can be accessed at http://books.rpmdp.com/rated97/rating97.htm. The Book Group List provides hyperlinks to all books discussed by the list, and a click will immediately transport you to www.amazon.com

54 Suzz, SavvyTen@aol.com 8 January 1997. http://books.rpmdp.com/archives/v01.n035. Downloaded 28 May 2002.

55 Johagan@aol.com 8 January 1997. http://books.rpmdp.com/archives/v01.n035. Downloaded 28 May 2002.

56 Suzz, SavvyTen@aol.com 8 January 1997. http://books.rpmdp.com/archives/v01.n035. Downloaded 28 May 2002.

57 Lawrence Venuti, who mentions *Smilla* as an example of a translated book that does succeed, paradoxically falls into the same trap when, in support of his claims, he lists the F. David translation in his bibliography and not the 'real' translation by Tiina Nunnally (see *Scandals*, 198).

58 Nancy Hudson, giving the book the final rating of 4, Nhallo@alaweb.com 13 May 1997. http://books.rpmdp.com/archives/v01.n153. Downloaded 28 May 2002.

59 Diane Christy, dchristy10@earthlink.net 2 May 1997. http://books.rpmdp.com/archives/v01.n143. Downloaded 28 May 2002.

60 Martin H. Van Houten, martysan@sweden-c.it.earthlink.net 2 May 1997. http://books.rpmdp.com/archives/v01.n143. Downloaded 28 May 2002.

61 peret@geocities.com; www.amazon.com/exec/obidos/ts/book-customer-review ... /002-8999764-548745. Downloaded 31 August 1999.

62 Høeg, *Frøken Smillas fornemmelse for sne*, 301. This page refers to the fifth paperback edition by Rosinante [1999].

63 At the Royal Library in Copenhagen, I consulted three translations that have all retained the commandos: *Smilla et l'amour de la neige* ('commandos anglais' [Paris: Seuil, 1996], 321), *La Señorita Smila y su especial percepción de la nieve* ('soldatos ingleses' [Madrid: Tusquets, 1995], 301), and *Il Senso di Smilla per la neve* ('commandos britannici' [Milan: Mondadori, 1995], 304). Of course, these are books in major European languages, and most likely, they have been translated directly from the Danish original. A comprehensive investigation into this question would need to consider the trajectory into more 'minor' languages, something which of course requires substantial language skills or access to such proficiency as well as a larger sample of translations.

64 UNESCO, http://www.unesco.org/culture/xtrans/html_eng/index6.shtml. Downloaded 29 March 2002.

65 Venuti, *Translator's Invisibility*, 12. For a different take on these statistics and the role of the English language today, see Pym, 'Two Principles.'

66 Venuti, *Scandals*, 160.

67 Lemieux and Saint-Jaques, 'U.S. Best-sellers in French Québec and English Canada,' 285.

68 For obvious linguistic reasons, Sweden is at present as well as historically an 'importing' country. In some periods, the ratio of translations has therefore been higher than 50 per cent (see statistics collated by Johan Svedjedal for translations in different periods between 1866 and 1970 in 'Den svenska bokmarknaden,' 32). In more recent years it is important to note that English-language dominance tends to become more visible in specific segments of the book market – such as that of mass market paperbacks – where it can reach numbers around 80 per cent (see Lindung, 'Den angloamerikanska litteraturens dominans,' 18).

69 Held et al., *Global Transformations*, 346 and 359.

70 Schäffner, 'Introduction: Globalization, Communication, Translation,' 3, citing *Der Spiegel*.

71 For an outline of some of the problems, see Whitney, 'International Book Production Statistics.'

72 See *UNESCO Statistical Yearbook 1999*, 'International Trade in Books and Pamphlets, Newspapers and Periodicals,' IV–134–50.

73 To get a sense of the tremendous geopolitical complexities of publishing and the many various forms of power and agency that have earmarked this business from its inception until today, see the contributions in Michon and Mollier, *Les Mutations du livre et de l'édition dans le monde du XVIII siècle à l'an 2000*.

74 Gloin, 'Danish Mystery.'

75 Ricketson, *Berne Convention*, 64, 74–5.

76 Ibid., 93.

77 Bourdieu, 'Deux impérialismes de l'universel,' 148. The general bent of Eric Hobsbawm's classic *The Age of Revolution, 1789–1848,* also comes to mind.

78 Mary Snell-Hornby makes the interesting, and correct, I think, remark that one of the reasons English has been so successful in this respect is because of 'a general policy of non-puristic openness among the English-speaking cultural institutions.' As she goes on to point out, the French language has taken an opposite track, and instead reinforced a normative linguistic policy aimed at securing the language from outside influences, at the same time as the role of the latter as a world language has been reduced ('Communicating in the Global Village,' 14).

3 The Death of the Author and the Killing of Books

1 Venuti, *Scandals*, 31.

2 Nunberg, *The Future of the Book*, still gives a good introduction to many of these changes as they pertain to print culture.

3 For further accounts of Chester Carlson's early years and his struggles with the invention that was to become known as 'xerography,' see Hall and Hall, 'Chester F. Carlson'; Dinsdale, 'Chester F. Carlson, Inventor of Xerography'; Xerox Corporation, *The Story of Xerography*, available at http://a1851.g.akamaitech.net/f/1851/2996/24h/cache.xerox.com/downloads/usa/en/s/Storyofxerography.pdf; Dessauer, *My Years With Xerox*; and Kearns and Nadler, *Prophets in the Dark.*

4 See Silvio A. Bedini's account of the many futile efforts on the part of Charles Willson Peale – who furnished Jefferson with his polygraphs – to sell his various models in *Thomas Jefferson.*

5 Jefferson, quoted in Bedini, *Thomas Jefferson*, 160.

6 See The Early Office Museum's website www.officemuseum.com/copy_machines.htm for details on the copier in a historical perspective. Downloaded 28 May 2002.

7 'I went to the lab that day and Otto had a freshly-prepared sulfur coating on a zinc plate. We tried to see what we could do toward making a visible image. Otto took a glass microscope slide and printed on it in India ink the notation "10–22–38 ASTORIA." We pulled down the shade to make the room as dark as possible, then he rubbed the sulfur surface vigorously with a handkerchief to apply an electrostatic charge, lay the slide on the surface and placed the combination under a bright incandescent lamp for a few seconds. The slide was then removed and lycopodium powder was

sprinkled on the sulfur surface. By gently blowing on the surface, all the loose powder was removed and there was left on the surface a near-perfect duplicate in powder of the notation which had been printed on the glass slide. Both of us repeated the experiment several times to convince ourselves that it was true, then we made some permanent copies by transferring the powder images to wax paper and heating the sheets to melt the wax. Then we went out to lunch and to celebrate.' Chester Carlson quoted in Xerox Corporation, *The Story of Xerography*, 5–6.

8 Initially, the agreement was set at 25 per cent. However, on the condition that Carlson could reimburse Battelle within five years for its research expenditures, approaching at that time $17,000, the share would go up to 40 per cent. He procured the funds by borrowing money from his wife and her relatives. John Dessauer writes that when Carlson became wealthy, he generously distributed Xerox shares to those who had helped him along the way, for instance, Otto Kornei. See Dessauer, *My Years with Xerox*, 36, 73, 186–7.

9 See Smith and Alexander, *Fumbling the Future*, 37.

10 The manual is quoted in Owen, 'Copies in Seconds,' 68.

11 Details of the agreement are found in Dessauer, *My Years with Xerox*, 92–4.

12 Xerox Corporation, 'Now X Marks the Spot.'

13 Dessauer, *My Years with Xerox*, 186–7.

14 Kearns and Nadler, *Prophets in the Dark*, 30.

15 Dessauer, *My Years with Xerox*, 129–30.

16 John Dessauer refers to a member of the public relations staff, who vehemently protested against the fire extinguisher, arguing that it would cost the company half its potential sales. See Dessauer, *My Years with Xerox*, 127.

17 Jacobson and Hillkirk, *Xerox: American Samurai*, 62.

18 Kearns and Nadler, *Prophets in the Dark*, 77.

19 Owen, 'Copies in Seconds,' 66. See a comparison chart of these various processes and companies in 'Out to Crack Copying Market,' 90.

20 Both commercials are described in Kearns and Nadler, *Prophets in the Dark*, 32–3.

21 Xerox Corporation, 'Now! Office Copying Enters the Age of Automation ... Copying Costs Dramatically Cut!'

22 Brooks, 'Xerox, Xerox, Xerox, Xerox,' 57.

23 Xerox Corporation, 'What Xerox gives you for your nickel.'

24 The quote is attributed to Eddie Miller, who conducted the 1981 Xerox-McKinsey study of the corporation and who is interviewed in Jacobson and Hillkirk, *Xerox, American Samurai*, 178.

25 The ad is regularly listed as one of the 100 best TV commercials; see, for instance, Kanner, *The 100 Best TV Commercials – and Why They Worked*, 169–71.
26 Xerox Corporation, 'Which is the $2,800 Picasso? Which is the 5¢ Xerox 914 Copy?'
27 Kearns and Nadler, *Prophets in the Dark*, 34–5.
28 Hammer, 'There Isn't Any Profit Squeeze at Xerox,' 153.
29 Kearns and Nadler, *Prophets in the Dark*, 36.
30 'Out to Crack Copying Market,' 89.
31 Kearns and Nadler, *Prophets in the Dark*, 43.
32 Xerox Corporation, *The Story of Xerography*, 10.
33 Hammer, 'There Isn't Any Profit Squeeze at Xerox,' 153.
34 Kearns and Nadler, *Prophets in the Dark*, 44–5.
35 Jacobson and Hillkirk, *Xerox, American Samurai*, 63.
36 Ibid., 72.
37 Kearns and Nadler, *Prophets in the Dark*, 134–5.
38 Ibid., 113.
39 Jacobson and Hillkirk, *Xerox: American Samurai*, 179.
40 Jacobson and Hillkirk, *Xerox: American Samurai*, 75–6 and Kearns and Nadler, *Prophets in the Dark*, 83–4.
41 Kearns and Nadler, *Prophets in the Dark*, 121–2.
42 Steve Jobs, quoted in Hiltzik, *Dealers of Lightning*, 389.
43 For a detailed and comprehensive account of PARC, see Hiltzik, *Dealers of Lightning*. Smith and Alexander, *Fumbling the Future*, is particularly focused on the fate of the Alto.
44 'Downfall,' special issue of *Business Week* on Xerox, 5 March 2001.
45 McLuhan, Fiore, and Agel, *The Medium is the Massage*, 123.
46 McLuhan, 'Address at Vision 65,' 202. McLuhan first raised the problematics in *The Gutenberg Galaxy*.
47 On the imperative role of the printing press as such an agent of change, not only in terms of technology, but in respect to the very foundation of the circulation of texts, see Eisenstein, *The Printing Press as an Agent of Change*, and Febvre and Martin, *L'apparition du livre*.
48 Benjamin, 'The Work of Art,' 232.
49 Woodmansee, 'The Genius and the Copyright,' 429.
50 Benjamin, 'The Work of Art,' 221.
51 Brooks, 'Xerox, Xerox, Xerox, Xerox,' 62–3. In his overview of the many possible scenarios that the future had in store for the printed word, Brooks sketched out the possibility of tiny chips of computer film replacing the book.

52 For a detailed discussion of *Williams & Wilkins Co. v. United States*, see Goldstein, *Copyright's Highway*, esp. chapter 3, 'Fifty Dollars to Collect Ten,' 78–128.
53 *Williams & Wilkins Co. v. United States*, 487 F.2d 1345 (Ct. Cl. 1973), at 1345.
54 The verdict was left standing because Justice Blackmun took no part in the decision. For a longer discussion on the possible reasons why, see Goldstein, *Copyright's Highway*, chapter 3, 'Fifty Dollars to Collect Ten,' 78–128.
55 See Litman, 'Copyright Legislation and Technological Change,' for a detailed analysis of some of these changes leading up to the new Copyright Act in 1976.
56 *Williams & Wilkins Co. v. United States*, 487 F.2d 1345 (Ct. Cl. 1973), at 1360.
57 Such change is, of course, the general impetus behind the Information Infrastructure Task Force White Paper: Intellectual Property and the National Information Infrastructure. The Report of the Working Group on Intellectual Property Rights (1995), available from http://www.uspto.gov/web/offices/com/doc/ipnii/, and the Directive 2001/29/EC of the European Parliament and of the Council of 22 May 2001 on the harmonisation of certain aspects of copyright and related rights in the information society, available at http://europa.eu.int/smartapi/cgi/sga_doc?smartapi!celexapi! prod!CELEXnumdoc&lg=EN&numdoc =32001L0029&model=guichett. Downloaded 29 May 2002.
58 For an argument that explores the possibility of fair use in order to ensure a better legal status for translations, see Venuti, *Scandals*, 63–5. For a comprehensive discussion on the U.S. 'fair use' principle in relation to international conventions such as the Berne Convention and TRIPS, see Gana Ɔkediji, 'Toward an International Fair Use Doctrine.'
59 Quoted in original Texaco Brief, March 1993, at 3; see http://fairuse.stanford.edu/primary/cases/texaco/brief.html. Downloaded 16 January 2002. Most legal documents pertaining to *American Geophysical Union v. Texaco, Inc.*, can be accessed through Stanford University Libraries excellent web page 'Copyright and Fair Use,' http://fairuse.stanford.edu/primary/index.html#caselaw
60 *Sony Corp. v. Universal City Studios, Inc.*, 464 U.S. 417 (1984). For an interesting comparison between these cases, especially in relation to file-sharing and the Internet, see Das, 'The Availability of the Fair Use Defense in Music Piracy and Internet Technology.'
61 *American Geophysical Union v. Texaco, Inc.*, 802 F. Supp. 1 (S.N.D.Y).
62 *American Geophysical Union v. Texaco, Inc.*, 60 F.3d 913, Judge Jacobs, dissenting opinion, at 935.
63 Ibid., Jacobs, dissenting opinion, at 939–40. See also Paul Edward Geller's

argument that market incentives in copyright seem only partially successful, not able to 'incite more than incremental creation' ('Must Copyright,'
177).

64 *American Geophysical Union v. Texaco, Inc.*, 60 F.3d 913, Judge Jacobs, dis-
    senting opinion, at 937.
65 See http://fairuse.stanford.edu/primary/cases/texaco/tex.html.
    Downloaded 16 January 2002.
66 *American Geophysical Union v. Texaco, Inc.*, 60 F.3d 913, Judge Jacobs, dis-
    senting opinion, at 940.
67 *Basic Books Inc. v. Kinko's Graphics Corp.*, 758 F. Supp. 1522 (S.D.N.Y. 1991)
    at 1526.
68 For a very interesting discussion problematizing these issues in regard to
    academia and the idea of the university as a public domain, see McSherry,
    Who Owns Academic Work?
69 Barthes, 'The Death of the Author,' 146.
70 Jaszi, 'On the Author Effect,' 49.
71 For an overview of music sampling and the creative and financial conse-
    quences in regard to copyright, see McLeod, *Owning Culture*, 83–108, and
    Sanjek, 'Don't Have to DJ No More.'
72 For a thorough overview of what is also referred to as 'collecting societies,'
    see Sinacore-Guinn, *Collective Administration of Copyrights and Neighboring
    Rights.*
73 Goldstein, *International Copyright*, 249.
74 Sinacore-Guinn, *Collective Administration of Copyright and Neighboring
    Rights*, 807.
75 For further information on this fund, see Sveriges Författarförbund/The
    Swedish Writer's Union website http://www.forfattarforbundet.se
76 'Architecture of information' was to become a lead slogan during the
    turbulent years. The expression is, in most accounts of Xerox, attributed to
    a speech given by then CEO Peter McColough to the New York Society of
    Security Analysts in March of 1970 (see Smith and Alexander, *Fumbling the
    Future*, 48–50).
77 See ContentGuard, Inc. website http://www.contentguard.com/xrml.asp
78 McLuhan, 'Address at Vision 65,' 202.

4 How Content Became King

1 Bagdikian, *The Media Monopoly*, 28–9.
2 Wasserstein, *Big Deal: 2000 and Beyond*, 12. Viacom bought Paramount
    Communications in 1994.

3 When Reed Elsevier acquired Harcourt General for $4.5 billion in 2001 to secure access to the U.S. market, it was a deal that for antitrust clearance required Reed Elsevier to sell off parts of the newly acquired company to the Canadian Thompson Corporation. See 'Reed Elsevier,' Hoover's Company Profile Database. Load date 1 May 2002.

4 UNCTAD, *World Investment Report 2000. Cross-border Mergers and Acquisitions and Development*, 99.

5 On Bertelsmann-EMI, see Drozdiak, 'Big Music Merger Is Called Off.' On GE-Honeywell, see Hargreaves and Hill, 'Brussels Poised to Veto GE Move for Honeywell.'

6 This is by no means unprecedented or unique to contemporary businesses. UNCTAD claims that the creation of U.S. Steel at the beginning of the twentieth century would be worth something like $600 billion in today's prices (*World Investment Report 2000*, 106).

7 One of the best known and vocal of these critics is Andre Schiffrin. See *The Business of Books*. At least two other publishers directly involved in and affected by conglomeratization – both of whom are criticized by Schiffrin – have also written memoirs addressing this turbulent period. See Epstein, *Book Business*, and Korda, *Another Life*. See also Michael Korda's interesting and illuminating review of Schiffrin's and Epstein's respective books, 'Out of Print.'

8 These expressions were used in a presentation by Thomas Middelhoff, Bertelsmann CEO at the time. www.bertelsmann.com/bag/management/bio.cfm?id=113.7 'Content powerhouse,' was used when I first downloaded this page on 9 September 2001, but is absent in the latest update from March 2002. Downloaded 13 May 2002.

9 See Odlyzko, 'Content Is Not King.'

10 See, for instance, the discussion on convergence in the International Telecommunication Union (ITU), European Common Proposals for the Work of the World Telecommunication Development Conference (WTDC–02), Istanbul, Turkey, 18–27 March 2002, available at www.itu.int/itu-d/pdf/2128-018-en.doc

11 Ohman, *Selling Culture*, 22. For a general introduction to the emerging U.S. market, see also Tebbel, *Between Covers*.

12 Thomas Guinzburg quoted in Whiteside, 145.

13 Bourdieu, 'Une révolution conservatrice dans l'édition,' 16.

14 See, for instance, the various country profiles in International Institute of Communications, *Media Ownership and Control in the Age of Convergence*.

15 The standard work on publishing is Coser, Kadushin, and Powell, *Books: The Culture and Commerce of Publishing*. For a more recent update on the

business of publishing, particularly in the U.S., see Greco, *The Book Publishing Industry*. Fouché, *L'Édition Française depuis 1945*, provides an invaluable source of information on post–Second World War French publishing.

16 Daniel Simon, publisher at the Seven Stories publishing house, writes in his review of André Schiffrin's *The Business of Books* that one-third of his company's list is expected to cover losses on the other two-thirds (Simon, 'Keepers of the Word,' 28).

17 Whiteside, *Blockbuster*, 111.

18 Schiffrin, *The Business of Books*, 81.

19 Michon, Introduction to *Édition et Pouvoirs*, vii.

20 See Whiteside, *Blockbuster*, 13–14.

21 Weber, 'Culture or Commerce?' 128 and 141. Wishful thinking, unconscious (or conscious) attempts at justification, and/or embellishment of the current situation by those interviewed are, of course, present in any undertaking such as the one by Weber.

22 Gründ, Opening remarks to the 26th Congress of the International Publishers Association.

23 All documents in *Random House, Inc. v. RosettaBooks LLC* can be consulted at RosettaBooks website http://www.rosettabooks.com/pages/legal.html. Commenting on the district court's decision, RosettaBooks CEO, Arthur Klebanoff, estimated the value of the backlist business for books in the United States at $10 billion (CNN, 'The Biz,' 12 July 2001). The press release announcing the licensing agreement can be read at http://www.rosettabooks.com/pages/RB_RH_Release.html. That publishers have high hopes for their backlists in digital form is also noted by Cohen and Joy, 'A Crisis of Content.'

24 Thomas Whiteside suggests that the arrival of sophisticated inventory control may have helped reinforce what he calls a 'big-book policy' (*Blockbuster*, 110).

25 Jean-Yves Mollier notes that not only had the profession remained fairly unchanged for a long period of time, but from the mid-nineteenth century, when the the modern publishing house begins to materialize, it was in fact an entity marked by a rigid internal organizational structure (see 'Les mutations de l'espace éditorial Français du XVIIIe au XXe siècle,' 36).

26 Greco, *The Book Publishing Industry*, 54. Greco stands for a more positive interpretation of this increase in titles, stressing diversity rather than conglomerate power, whereas André Schiffrin generally emphasizes the aspect of concentrated ownership and thus represents the other camp.

27 Barnet and Cavanagh distinguish four stages in this development (see *Global Dreams*, esp. chapter 4, 'Of the Making of Books,' 90–111). I have,

however, found it more useful to boil these down to three, placing the search for vertical integration together with the tendency towards an increasingly global media market.

28 From a French perspective, Fabrice Piault makes a similar chronology to mine, beginning in the 1940s–1950s with the consolidation of content; then he continues to describe the 1960s–1970s in much the same way as here, as a 'boom period' of education and literacy, and ends by calling the 1980s–1990s a period of 'hyperconcentration' (see 'De la rationalisation à l'hyperconcentration,' 630).

29 Dessauer, *My Years with Xerox*, 199.

30 On Houghton Mifflin, see Whiteside, *Blockbuster*, esp. chapter 11, 'The Boston Resisters,' 123–38. Because of his many interesting interviews Whiteside's book is still one of the best documents of this period.

31 See Vivendi Universal Publishing, Hoover's Company Profile Database, load date 8 May 2002. See also Milliot, 'Vivendi to Acquire HM in $2.2 Billion Deal,' 20.

32 Brooks, 'Xerox, Xerox, Xerox, Xerox,' 52.

33 Hiltzik, *Dealers of Lightning*, 209.

34 Xerox Corporation, *Xerox Online Fact book 2002–2003*. Available at http://www.xerox.com/go/xrx/template/019d.jsp?view=Factbook&id=Historical&Xcntry=USA&Xlang=en_US. Downloaded 8 May 2002.

35 Barnet and Cavanagh, *Global Dreams*, 97.

36 *Mergerstat® Review 2000*, 288. Trumped by the sale of Times Mirror Co. to Tribune Co. in 2000 for $7,302.8 million. *Mergerstat® Review 2001*, 275.

37 Barnet and Cavanagh, *Global Dreams*, 96.

38 See Thomas Whiteside's discussion on Bennett Cerf and Donald Klopfer's choice to go public as a direct result of the IRS putting such a high price on Random House as to effectively bar any surviving partner from owning the publishing house in the case of the other partner's death (*Blockbuster*, 5–6). Ben H. Bagdikian also notes the importance that inheritance taxes played in the restructuring of newspaper ownership in the United States, where the empires of the early twentieth-century could be left in trust for grandchildren, but no longer (*Media Monopoly*, 12). When Si Newhouse, owner of Random House, the largest trade publisher in the United States, sold the company to Bertelsmann on 23 March 1998, he was quoted as saying: 'With a third generation coming up, ... we had to make strategic decisions' (Si Newhouse quoted in Dugan, 'Boldly Going Where Others Are Bailing Out,' 46). Pierre Bourdieu also notes that the business is filled with many heirs and younger family members ('Une révolution conservatrice dans l'édition,' 16).

39 Herman and McChesney describe a 'tiered global media market,' domi-
    nated by a handful of companies (*The Global Media*, 52). At the end of the
    1990s those companies included News Corporation, Time Warner, Disney,
    Bertelsmann, Viacom, and TCI, all fully integrated producers of content
    and owners of distribution networks, supplanted by PolyGram, NBC,
    Universal, and Sony. David Demers talks of a 'global dozen' corporations,
    accounting for more than half of the $250 billion industry. In his *Global
    Media: Menace or Messiah?* Demers lists Time Warner, Disney, Bertelsmann,
    News Corporation, Viacom, Sony, Havas, Universal, TCI, Thomson, NBC,
    and Advance Publications. In his introduction to the fifth edition of *The
    Media Monopoly* (Boston: Beacon Press, 1997), Ben H. Bagdikian speaks of a
    communications cartel (ix). In the sixth edition of his book, published in
    2000, he instead refers to an 'international cartel' (viii). That the sixth
    edition was published before the arrival of AOL Time Warner and Vivendi
    Universal is apparent from Bagdikian's list of six major 'parent firms' that
    dominate American mass media: GE (General Electric), Viacom, Disney,
    Bertelsmann, Time Warner, and News Corp.
40 See AOL Time Warner and Viacom, Hoover's Company Profile Data-
    base. Load date 1 May 2002. Disney's percentage was 86 per cent in the
    U.S. in 2000. Hoover's Company Profile database, load date September
    2001.
41 Barnet and Cavanagh, *Global Dreams*, 105.
42 Gershon, *Transnational*, 9.
43 Ibid., 168. Bertelsmann differs in two ways from most other TNMCs: its
    headquarters are still located in the small German town of Gühtersloh,
    where Carl Bertelsmann once founded his publishing house in 1835; and
    the company is still privately owned and not listed on the stock market.
    See Mikael Löfgren 'Ett medieimperium som luktar jord.'
44 Wolters Kluwer originated in the 1993 merger of two educational publish-
    ers: J.B. Wolters from 1836 and Abele Kluwer from 1889. Albert E. Reed
    and Co. was initially a newsprint manufacturer founded in 1894, and
    Elsevier was founded by five Rotterdam booksellers and publishers in
    1880. Bertelsmann started out as a religious publisher in 1835. Havas –
    now part of the media conglomerate Vivendi Universal – began as a news
    publication in 1832, and became the news agency Agence Havas three
    years later. Although the Lagardère Group offers a strange mix of media,
    auto, and space industry, the corporation also owns the venerable pub-
    lisher Hachette, founded in 1826. See Hoover's Company Profile Database
    for respective companies. Load date 1 May 2002. Even Rupert Murdoch's
    News Corporation – today heavily invested in satellite television more

than in print properties – began when Murdoch inherited two newspapers from his father in 1952. News Corps's strong emphasis on satellites makes it somewhat different in approach than the otherwise fairly unanimous concentration on online and Internet-based services. See Ingrid Carlberg, 'Mediemogulen som siktar mot stjärnorna.'

45 Jeremy Tunstall and David Machin distinguish five various forms of connections between larger U.S. media companies: cross-ownership, revenue sharing, co-production, co-purchasing, and swaps of local outlets between major owners (*The Anglo-American Media Connection*, 64–6).

46 Gershon, *Transnational*, 185.

47 Together with Herman and McChesney, and Herbert Schiller, Ben H. Bagdkian is one of the most outspokenly critical of the U.S. media scholars. In the fifth edition of *The Media Monopoly* (1997), he predicted a single possible mega owner of media, but he modified his position somewhat, noting that the concentration into a dozen or so owners would be more likely (*The Media Monopoly*, 6th ed., [2000], 3).

48 UNCTAD, *World Investment Report 2000*, xix. Due to incompability issues, the list of the 100 largest TNCs published by UNCTAD excludes financial TNCs.

49 The 2000 AOL Time Warner deal is the second largest M&A announcement in history, estimated at $101,002.5 million (*Mergerstat® Review 2001*, 264). It is also the largest M&A in *Mergerstat® Review's* category Leisure and Entertainment as well as the largest statutory merger (*Mergerstat® Review 2001*, 259).

50 Thal Larsen, 'The Year the Giants Chose to Merge.'

51 Vivendi Universal, 'Creation of Vivendi Universal, a Global Communications Giant.'

52 On 19 December 2000, Vivendi Universal announced the sale of the Seagram's spirits and wine business to Diageo and Pernod Richard for $8,150 billion ('Seagram's Spirits and Wines Business Sold to Diageo and Pernod Ricard').

53 Agnes Touraine quoted in Lottman, 'Milia Stresses U.S.–European E-Differences,' 17.

54 Like Vivendi Universal's eclectic mix of environmental services and media, Lagardère combine their media interests with arms and automobile manufacturing. For more on Lagardère, see Pagold, 'Med medier som vapen.'

55 Piault, 'De la rationalisation à l'hyperconcentration,' 633–5. For a detailed analysis of the present state of French publishing, see Rouet, *Le livre*. Established in 1876, Flammarion was owned by Ernest Flammarion's

descendants until it was sold to the Italian Rizzoli Group (Corriere de la Sera, Rizzoli) in October 2000. For more updated information on the ever-changing scene of international publishing, see Schiffrin, 'The Eurocrash on Books,' 38–40.

56 Peter Olson, quoted in Dugan, 'Boldly Going Where Others Are Bailing Out,' 46. Bertelsmann's purchase of Random House meant that nearly 40 per cent of the company's $16 billion in revenues would come from books. Described as one of those persons who cannot imagine life without books, Peter Olson, in his presentation on the Bertelsmann website, also goes to great lengths to underline his 'bookish' interests, noting that he learned Russian in order to read the Russian classics in the original. See the presentation of Peter Olson at http://www.bertelsmann.com/bag/management/bio.cfm?id=2170. Downloaded 8 May 2002.

57 2000 refers here to the fiscal year ending 30 June 2000. All numbers are from Milliot, 'The Land of the Giants,' 62–3.

58 UNCTAD, *World Investment Report 2001. Promoting Linkages*, 90. In 1998, Seagram was placed 34, News Corp. 22, and Vivendi SA was not even listed (see *World Investment Report 2000*, 72). Reflecting the situation in 1999, before the Vivendi-Seagram merger, Vivendi Universal is currently placed 91 on the 2002 *Fortune* Global 500 list. All the various sources that list transnational or global corporations do so according to different parametres. The *World Investment Report* uses foreign assets and TNI, *Fortune* 500 revenues, and the *Financial Times* focuses on market capitalization, or the value of a corporation on the stock market at the time of ranking (see Plimmer, 'A Measure of Financial Muscle'). Obviously, there are companies on the *World Investment Report* list that are not officially designated media corporations but still retain a highly active presence within the field. This holds true for corporations such as the leading General Electric, ranked as the number 1 TNC by the *World Investment Report 2001* in 1998 and 1999, owning, for instance, the NBC television channel, and Sony at place 22 and Matsushita at place 56, both labelled as electronics companies, but with investments in publishing, film, and television. The *Fortune* 2002 Global 500 has Exxon Mobile in the top seat and General Electric at place 8 (see *Fortune*, 23 July 2001, F1–2). AOL Time Warner is not listed in the *World Investment Report 2001* (which refers to 1999), because the merger did not take place until 2001. Nor is AOL Time Warner on the 2002 *Fortune* Global 500 list, which might be more suspect. Ranked 37 in the 2002 *Fortune* 500, AOL Time Warner did not make the Global 500 list because of fiscal technicalities (Murphy, 'Where's AOL? Missing in Action,' 152).

59 UNCTAD, *World Investment Report 2001*, 101.
60 UNCTAD, *World Investment Report 2000*, 79.
61 UNCTAD, *World Investment Report 2001*, 101.
62 UNCTAD, *World Investment Report 2000*, 8.
63 This is still a marked change from 1998, when Petróleos de Venezuela was the *only* TNC from the developing world to appear on the list of the 100 largest TNCs at place 91. UNCTAD, *World Investment Report 2000*, 72.
64 UNCTAD, *World Investment Report 1999*, xvii.
65 Greco, *Book Publishing Industry*, 45.
66 Bertelsmann *Annual Report 1999/2000*, 10.
67 Ibid., 9.
68 Schiffrin, 'The Corporatization of Publishing,' 148.
69 Herman and McChesney, *The Global Media*, 20.
70 Numbers from ibid., 14.
71 Ibid., 39 and 42.
72 See Ryan, *Knowledge Diplomacy*, esp. chapter 4, 'Business Mobilization and U.S. Trade Diplomacy,' 67–89, for a longer account of these events.
73 Drahos, 'Thinking Strategically about Intellectual Property Rights,' 202. The two previous periods were the territorial and the international periods. In respect to the Berne Convention, Sam Ricketson defines three distinct periods: first, what he calls an initial period based on a Eurocentric doctrine of authors' rights (Berne to Berlin, 1886–1908); then the expansion of new technology and new interest groups (Rome to Brussels, 1928–48); and finally, the emergence of the developing nations and their place in international conventions (Stockholm to Paris, 1967–71) (see Ricketson, *Berne Convention*, 125).
74 Siwek, 'Executive Summary,' 3.
75 Ibid., 4.
76 Ibid., 24.
77 Ibid., 5.
78 The International Intellectual Property Alliance, 2002 'Special 301' Recommendations, 2.
79 Business Software Alliance, *Sixth Annual BSA Global Software Piracy Study*, 1.
80 Software and Information Industry Association, Press release, 'Five Years: $59.2 Billion Lost.' 24 May 2000.
81 Herman and McChesney, *The Global Media*, 51.
82 See Tunstall and Machin, *The Anglo-American Media Connection*, esp. chapter 5, 'Washington As Media Policy,' 40–52.
83 Lehman, 'The United States and the Global Intellectual Property System,'

available at http://www.hdf.net/iipi/views/detail.asp?itemID=19.
Downloaded 15 May 2002.

84 Herman and McChesney, *The Global Media*, 41–2.

85 For a longer account of the events surrounding the U.S. accession to
Berne, see Bettig, *Copyrighting Culture*, 222.

86 My account of the role of the USTR in this chapter draws substantially
from Sell, *Power and Ideas*, 133–6. On section 301, see also Hoekman and
Kostecki, *The Political Economy of the World Trading System*, 147.

87 United States Trade Representative, 'Executive Summary,' *Special 301
Report*, 1.

88 For a longer discussion on specific 301 cases and the implementation of
the U.S. trade policy in regard to developing countries, see Sell, *Power and
Ideas*, 182–216.

89 Callan, *Pirates on the High Seas*, 82.

90 See, for instance, the piracy questionnaire at the website of the Business
Software Alliance, http://www.bsa.org/usa/report/report.php

91 Sergio Robleto quoted in Iwata, 'Software Piracy Takes Toll on Global
Scale.'

92 Ibid.

93 See the website of the British Alliance against Counterfeiting and Piracy
at http://www.aacp.org.uk/cost/casestudies.html. Downloaded
16 January 2002.

94 For an overview of the organization's policy, see the Association of
American Publishers, Inc. website on intellectual property at http://
www.publishers.org/antipiracy/index.cfm. For another industry-
representative outlook on AAP's activities in the area, see Kobrak,
'Current Copyright Enforcement.'

95 News Corp. President Peter Chemin, quoted in Milliot, 'Copyright
Protection Stressed at AAP Meeting,' 17.

96 Tebbel, *The Expansion of an Industry, 1865–1919*, 641.

97 Tebbel, *The Creation of an Industry, 1630–1865*, 561.

98 Ibid., 561.

99 Carter, 'A History of International Publishing,' 161.

100 The so-called back door to Berne. See Goldstein, *International Copyright*,
189–96, for a longer discussion regarding the many restrictions in pre-
Berne U.S. copyright.

101 Report of the Hon. W.E. Simonds, of Connecticut, from the house Committee on Patents, 10 June 1890, in Putnam, *The Question of Copyright*, 121.

102 Senate representative William C. Preston, of South Carolina, put it
bluntly: 'Great Britain [...] had two authors to our one, and was, therefore,

more interested in the protection of mental labor; while the United States published three or four times as many books, and therefore, more interested in protecting publishers' (quoted in Solberg, *International Copyright in the Congress of the United States, 1837–1886*, 4).

103 The T.&J.W. Johnson quotation is from Solberg, *International Copyright in the Congress of the United States, 1837–1886*, 10.

104 Herman and McChesney, *The Global Media*, 109–14. Among the 100 largest M&A announcements in history, two major deals in telecommunications are placed 4 and 5 respectively: SBC Communications Inc. buying Ameritech Corp in 1998 for $75,233.5 million and Vodafone Group PLC buying AirTouch Communications Inc. in 1999 for $62,768.0 million. It is worth pointing out that the largest M&A cancellation to date also involved telecommunication firms; MCI World Com Inc. buying Sprint at $115,972.6 million in 1999 (*Mergerstat® Review 2001*, 264, 262).

105 UNCTAD, *World Investment Report 2000*, 110–11.

106 Gerald Levin announced his decision on 5 December, Edgar Bronfman the day after. See Dan Milmo. 'AOL Time Warner Boss Bows Out,' and 'Bronfman Quits Vivendi.'

107 Gunther and Metha, 'Can Steve Case Make Sense of This Beast?'

108 Barker, 'Messier Puts Money Where His Mouth Is.'

109 Grimes, 'AOL Time Warner Reports $54bn Loss.'

110 Vivendi Universal, 'Vivendi Universal reports strong first quarter consolidated financial results.'

111 A number of protests took place in Paris in defence of Lescure and about 400 actors, including Catherine Deneuve and Juliette Binoche, signed a petition demanding that he be reinstated (Verrier, 'Messier Likely to Fend Off Ouster Bid').

112 Barker, 'Messier Puts Money Where His Mouth Is.'

113 Edgar Bronfman Jr quoted in Lenzner and Christopher Helman, 'Edgar's Encore.'

114 Shook, 'Wanted at AOL: Another Bob Pittman.'

115 Casey, 'Middelhoff out of Picture.'

116 Casey, 'Death of the American Dreams.'

117 For a longer discussion on Middelhoff's departure and Bertelsmann, see Casey, 'Death of the American Dreams'; Milmo, 'Bertelsmann: What's up for grabs'; and Milner and Teather, 'Gütersloh Goes Off Line.'

118 Jean-Marie Messier quoted in Milliot, 'Vivendi to Acquire HM in $2.2 Billion Deal,' 20.

119 Vivendi Universal, 'Closing Off Sale of Houghton Mifflin.'

120 'The Best (& Worst) Managers of the Year.'

121 Patsuris, 'Another Black Eye for AOL.'
122 See, for instance, Grover, 'Moguls Who Shopped till They Dropped.'
123 James Boyle has also underscored that it is the 'focus on content that makes intellectual property increasingly important in the information age' ('A Politics of Intellectual Property,' 94).

5 From the 'Intellectual' to the 'Cultural'

1 Stallybrass and White, *Politics and Poetics of Transgression*, 201.
2 May, *Global Political Economy*, 77.
3 Raghavan, *Recolonization*, 59.
4 Union des Associations Internationales, *Yearbook of International Organizations 1998/9*, vol. 1B, 2357.
5 Jackson, *The World Trading System*, 37.
6 Jackson defines six categories of organizations making up the landscape of international economic institutions: the Bretton Woods System, inclusive of WTO, OECD, and UNCTAD; the United Nations Specialized Agencies like ILO; regional organizations like EU and NAFTA; international commodity agreements; specialized agencies such as WIPO; and finally all bilateral agreements governing trade (*World Trading System*, 32–4).
7 Ibid., 38.
8 There is no shortage of books devoted to ITO, GATT, and the WTO. For a good introduction and comprehensive overview of WTO, see Adamantopoulos, *An Anatomy of the World Trade Organization*. For a detailed account of TRIPS, see Maskus, *Intellectual Property Rights In the Global Economy*.
9 Hoekman and Kostecki, *Political Economy of the World Trading System*, 15.
10 UNCTAD, *Statistical Profiles of the Least Developed Countries 2001*, 10, 4. Membership in WTO as of April 2001.
11 UNESCO, *International Flows*, 3.
12 Oxfam, *Rigged Rules and Double Standards*, executive summary of chapter 3. Available at http://www.maketradefair.org stylesheet.asp?file= 03042002154 231&subcat=6&cat=2&select=6. Downloaded 16 January 2002.
13 According to Bruce Lehman, the U.S. Department of Commerce estimates that by 2006 almost half of the U.S. workforce will be employed in information-intensive companies ('International Property As a Means Of Wealth Creation)'. UNESCO defines developed nations as: Australia, Austria, Belgium, Canada, Denmark, Finland, France, Germany, Greece,

Iceland, Ireland, Israel, Italy, Japan, Luxemburg, Netherlands, New Zealand, Norway, Portugal, Spain, Sweden, Switzerland, the United Kingdom, and the United States. UNESCO, *International Flows, 4.*

14 For a good overview of the pros and cons of stronger intellectual property protection on the part of the LCDs, see Primo Braga, 'The Economics of Intellectual Property Rights and the GATT.'

15 Sell, *Power and Ideas*, esp. chapter 1, 'Power and Ideas,' 9–40, provides a comprehensive introduction to the North-South dichotomy in matters of intellectual property rights. For a highly critical account of the role of the United States and previous colonies from the point of view of developing countries, see Raghavan, *Recolonization.*

16 Sell, *Power and Ideas*, 29–31, 73.

17 The U.K. also left at the same time, but later reentered. More on the NWICO debate in Herman and McChesney, *The Global Media*, 22–5. Manuel Castells notes that when the Communist ghost disappeared post-1989, Christian fundamentalists in the United States had to find a new enemy. They did so in 'world government institutions,' such as UN, UNESCO, IMF, and the like (*Power of Identity*, 26). Although many of these organizations are post–Second World War-phenomena, there were important predecessors. For a history of the international organization predating UNESCO, see Renoliet, *L'UNESCO oubliée.*

18 Primo Braga, 'Economics,' 250.

19 Sell, *Power and Ideas*, 116.

20 In the summer of 2001, Bruce Lehman compared the zero voluntary contribution of the United States to WIPO with the $16,736 (mandatory $890) provided by Bhutan, and the $2,101,558 (mandatory $712,172, same as the U.S.) provided by Japan, finding the U.S. position deplorable. See Lehman, 'The United States and the Global Intellectual Property System.'

21 UNESCO, *Many Voices, One World*, 268, at 68.

22 Otto, 'Subalternity and International Law,' 159.

23 Sell, *Power and Ideas*, 34.

24 They insisted 'that any regime that might emerge is not institutionalized in GATT or in any way tied to it and its general trade policy regimes' (Raghavan, *Recolonization*, 306).

25 UNESCO, *International Flows*, 15.

26 NAFTA, Annex 1, Schedule of Mexico, sector Communications, subsector Entertainment Services, available at http://www-tech.mit.edu/Bulletins/Nafta/mexico.1

27 Hoskins, Finn, and McFayden, 'Television and Film in a Freer International Trade Environment,' 65–7.

28 Hoekman and Kostecki, *Political Economy of the World Trading System*, 144.
29 Moore, 'Seattle: What's at Stake?'
30 For an overview of the tactics and arguments used by the West to secure compliance in intellectual property regimes from China, see Burrell, 'A Case Study in Cultural Imperialism.'
31 Moore, 'Address to the Ministerial Meeting of Least-Developed Countries.'
32 Hamilton, 'The TRIPS Agreement,' 243. Among those scholars who share in the critique against TRIPS, few suggest any counter-measures. For an exception, see Drahos, 'Thinking Strategically about Intellectual Property Rights,' 201–11, where he offers seven strategies against TRIPS.
33 For the most recent information and documentation on WIPO's work in the field of intellectual property and genetic resources, traditional knowledge and folklore, consult www.wipo.org/globalissues. In 1998, Rosemary Coombe notes that she has found no evidence of WIPO being engaged in the rights of indigenous peoples vis-à-vis intellectual property ('Intellectual Property, Human Rights and Sovereignty,' *Indiana Global Legal Studies Journal* 6:11 (1998), 76). Since the WIPO Global Division was not institutionalized until late 1997 and the diverse activities listed in this chapter did not occur until 1998–9, her claim that WIPO has been uninterested in anything but 'individual authorship as a prerequisite for protection' is to a certain extent belied by these more recent activities. Unfortunately, when drawing on Coombe's article without examining WIPO's work directly, Kembrew McLeod perpetuates unnecessarily this misconception in his *Owning Culture*, 159.
34 See the WTO Official ministerial website for the 1999 Seattle conference at http://www.wto.org/english/thewto_e/minist_e/min99_e/english/about_e/10trips_e.htm. Developed nations were given a grace period of one year in order to comply, and thus the four- and ten-year extensions are calculated based on the date 1 January 1996, which was the date when developed nations needed to come into compliance with TRIPS.
35 WIPO wanted 'to identify and explore the intellectual property needs and expectations of new beneficiaries, including the holders of indigenous knowledge and innovations, in order to promote the contribution of the IP system to their social, cultural and economic development' (WIPO Main program 11, Program and budget 1998/1999, quoted in WIPO, *Intellectual Property Needs and Expectations of Traditional Knowledge Holders*, 16 [henceforth WIPO, *FFM Report*]).
36 Quoted in Ricketson, *Berne Convention*, 599.
37 For a detailed history of the Stockholm Diplomatic Conference and devel-

oping nations within the Berne Convention, see Ricketson, *Berne Convention*, 114–25, esp. chapter 11 'Developing Countries,' 590–664.

38 Consider, for instance, Richard Stallman's argument in 'Why Software Should Be Free.'
39 Gaines, *Contested Culture*, 237–8.
40 Smiers, 'Copyrights,' available at www.constantvzw.com/copy.cult/ cjs1.html, at 4, 'The Common Cultural Good and the Future of the Arts.' Downloaded 29 August 2001.
41 Boyle, *Shamans*, 125.
42 Blakeney, 'What Is Traditional Knowledge?' 8.
43 See Shammel and Stephenson, 'Protecting American Indian Intellectual Property,' for a longer discussion on the Indian Motorcycle Company. Rosemary Coombe provides several interesting accounts of how Native Peoples struggle to secure the rights to their own resources in *The Cultural Life of Intellectual Properties*, esp. the section 'Consuming Crazy Horse,' 199–204.
44 This problem is noted in the United Nations Economic and Social Council, 'Discrimination against Indigenous Peoples,' for instance at 81 (henceforth ECOSOC, *Study*).
45 Gaines, *Contested Culture*, 64.
46 WIPO, *FFM Report*, 8.
47 For details on the various activities, see ibid., 16–17.
48 Ibid., 26. In the Stockholm Action Plan on Cultural Policies for Development, UNESCO defines heritage as 'all natural and cultural elements, tangible or intangible, which are inherited or newly created. Through these elements social groups recognize their identity and commit themselves to pass it on to future generations in a better and enriched form.' See http://www.unesco.org/culture/laws/stockholm/html_eng/ actionpl2.shtml. Visited 30 May 2002.
49 WIPO, *FFM Report*, 25.
50 Ibid., 212.
51 Ibid., 86.
52 Ibid. 70.
53 Ibid., 134.
54 Ricketson, *Berne Convention*, 314.
55 See, for instance, Berryman, 'Toward More Universal Protection of Intangible Cultural Property,' 315–16; Puri, 'Preservation and Conservation of Expressions of Folklore,' 7; and Jordan, 'Square Pegs and Round Holes,' 113.

56 WIPO, 'The Attempts to Protect Expressions of Folklore and Traditional Knowledge,' 2.
57 See UNESCO, 'Protection of Folklore,' available at www.unesco.org/culture/copyright/folklore/html_eng/pretoria.shtml
58 WIPO-UNESCO Model Provisions for National Laws, 3.
59 For an interesting overview of the debate on folklore, see Blakeney, 'What Is Traditional Knowledge?' 2–3.
60 UNESCO, Recommendation on the Safeguarding of Traditional Culture and Folklore, adopted by the General Conference at its twenty fifth session, Paris, 15 November 1989, at A. Available at www.unesco.org/culture/laws/paris/html_eng/page1.shtml.
61 WIPO-UNESCO, Model Provisions for National Laws, 9–10.
62 UNESCO, Action Plan for the Safeguarding of Intangible Cultural Heritage, Annex, page 1 at 7.
63 As in the title of ECOSOC, Study.
64 WIPO, FFM Report, 26. Therefore, while the problems under discussion may hit indigenous peoples harder, they are by now means exclusive to them.
65 The most comprehensive WIPO document to date on folklore is WIPO, 'Preliminary Systematic Analysis of National Experiences.'
66 WIPO, 'Matters Concerning Intellectual Property and Genetic Resources,' 5.
67 Brush, 'Whose Knowledge, Whose Genes, Whose Rights?' 3–4.
68 Blakeney, 'What Is Traditional Knowledge?' 9. For a longer account of the many implications for traditional knowledge holders in regard to medicine and bio-prospecting, see ECOSOC, Study, 90–102.
69 See, for instance, the Indigenous Peoples' Seattle Declaration, available at http://www.itpcentre.org/legislation/english/wto99.htm.
70 WTO, Proposal on Protection of the Intellectual Rights of the Traditional Knowledge of Local and Indigenous Communities. All member proposals can be found on the official website for the Seattle Ministerial Conference at http://www.wto.org/english/thewto_e/minist_e/min99_e/min99_e.htm
71 Moore, 'Seattle Conference Doomed to Succeed,' opening address to the WTO's 3rd Ministerial Conference, Seattle, 30 November 1999.
72 World Trade Organization, Doha Ministerial Declaration, 19.
73 The delegation from Iran states that in 1993, the total value of carpet and handicrafts exports amounted to $1.7 billion, but that this had fallen in recent years (see WIPO, FFM Report, 168).

74 Smith and White, 'Freedom to Craft a Future?' available at http://
www.womensedge.org/trade/craftwomen.htm. Downloaded 16 January
2003.

75 Fowler, 'Intellectual Property Rights and the Native American Experience,'
1.

76 The Australia Council, 'Conference Aims for a Better Future for Aboriginal
and Torres Strait Islander Artists.' Brad Sherman notes that 'some $A 418.4
million was generated by the Aboriginal crafts "industry" in retail sales in
the 1987 financial year, with an expectation of a 33% increase in the following year' ('From the Non-Original to the Ab-Original,' 113).

77 Smith and White, 'Freedom to Craft a Future?'

78 Fowler, 'Intellectual Property Rights and the Native American Experience,'
7.

79 'Artcamp: Resilience in a Time of Poverty,' 8.

80 Fowler, 'Intellectual Property Rights and the Native American Experience,'
1.

81 For a useful introduction to the Australian context, see Puri, 'Preservation
and Conservation of Expressions of Folklore.' The House of Aboriginality
website is an excellent starting point for those who would like to learn
more about intellectual property rights in the context of Australian Aboriginal culture. See http://www.mq.edu.au/house_of_aboriginality/. For a
longer discussion on some of these Australian cases and the question of
folkore, see Janke, *Minding Culture.*

82 *Milipurrurru v. Indofurn Pty Ltd.*, at 62 and 102. All cited Australian cases
have been accessed via the database of the Federal Court of Australia,
available at http://www.austlii.edu.au/au/cases/cth/federal_ct/
index.html. References are to subsections in the documents.

83 Ibid., at 166.

84 For more on moral rights within the framework of the Berne Convention,
see Ricketson, *Berne Convention,* 455–76.

85 *Yumbulul v. Reserve Bank of Australia,* at 24.

86 ECOSOC, *Study,* 31.

87 See WIPO, *FFM Report,* esp. the section 'Customary Laws and Protocols,'
57–65.

88 Elders of the Blood tribe during a meeting at the Glenbow Museum,
Calgary, 24 November 1998. WIPO, *FFM Report,* 125.

89 *Yumbulul v. Reserve Bank of Australia,* at 21.

90 Ibid., at 19.

91 *Milipurrurru v. Indofurn Pty Ltd.*, at 146.

92 *John Bulun Bulun v. R & T Textiles Pty Ltd.*, [1998] 1082 FCA (3 September 1998).

93 There was, argues Brad Sherman, considerable consensus on protecting Aboriginal art under copyright (see 'From the Non-Original to the Ab-original,' 113).

94 Barron, 'No Other Law?' 73.

95 Sherman, 'From the Non-Original to the Ab-Original,' 124.

96 Williams, *Keywords*, 76–82.

97 Hall, introduction to *Representation*, 2.

98 Of course, culture also spurred the arrival of 'Cultural Studies' as an increasingly institutionalized field of inquiry. From the writings of Raymond Williams and his 'culture as a way of life,' Stuart Hall relied on structuralism and French high theory to distinguish Williams's 'cultur-alist' approach from his 'structuralist' one. Hall stressed culture as 'ways of struggle,' using Gramsci's theory of hegemony on contemporary conditions of rupture, conflict, race, and ethnicity. For Hall's take on Gramsci, see his 'Gramsci's Relevance for the Study of Race and Ethnicity.' Hall's own version of his experience at the Centre for Contemporary Cultural Studies in Birmingham (CCCS) and the ensuing 'institutionaliza-tion' of Cultural Studies are addressed in several accounts. See, for instance, Hall, 'The Emergence of Cultural Studies and the Crisis of the Humanities,' and 'Cultural Studies and Its Theoretical Legacies.' The arrival of Cultural Studies beginning in the late 1950s only confirms this development, and with its gradual institutionalization we have come to witness a broadening of the 'cultural' objects being studied and analysed in academia.

99 Sherman, 'From the Non-Original to the Ab-Original,' 112.

100 See Collins, 'The Problem of Oral Copyright.' The many problematic aspects of orality are largely found outside the scope of this present book. However, I think it is deeply problematic to use oral traditions as a scapegoat to explain plagiarism, which seems to be the case when Kembrew McLeod discusses the story of the plagiarism found in Martin Luther King's dissertation (see McLeod, *Owning Culture*, esp. chapter 3, 'Copyright, Authorship and African-American Culture,' 71–108). For a more detailed analysis of the King case and others similar to it as well as a historic discussion, see Randall, *Pragmatic Plagiarism*.

101 John Bulun Bulun quoted in *John Bulun Bulun v. R & T Textiles Pty Ltd.*

102 This is unmistakably the tone of John H. Jackson, when he writes: 'This is why one of the most important problems facing the world today is institutional – the question of whether national and international govern-

mental institutions (such as the WTO/GATT) have the capacity to meet the challenges of private and governmental behavior that *could undermine the world trading system and the prosperity it brings*' (emphasis mine) (Jackson, *World Trading System*, 49).

103 See the many examples to this effect in Klein, *No Logo*.

104 These eight questions are as follows: 1) what is the policy objective of the protection? 2) what subject matter? 3) what criteria should this subject matter meet to be protected? 4) who owns the rights? 5) what rights? 6) how are the rights acquired? 7) how to administer and enforce the rights? 8) how are the rights lost or how do they expire? (WIPO, 'Elements of a *Sui Generis* System for the Protection of Traditional Knowledge,' 16).

105 WIPO, *FFM Report*, 193.

6 Genies in Bottles and Bottled-up Geniuses

1 'Constatons la propriété littéraire, mais, en même temps, fondons le domaine public. Allons plus loin. Agrandissons-le' (Hugo, 'Discours d'Ouverture,' 995).

2 'Public domain,' *Black's Law Dictionary*, 7th ed., 1999.

3 The expression is Berryman's, 'Toward More Universal Protection,' 324.

4 Litman, *Digital Copyright*, 202.

5 See the discussion on 'free' at the Free Software Foundation (FSF) website www.gnu.org/philosophy/free-sw.html

6 As both Jane Ginsburg and Carla Hesse point out, the 1791 French law of 13 January abolished past 'privileges' and was primarily concerned with, not author's rights, but those of the public domain (see Ginsburg, 'A Tale of Two Copyrights,' 144, and Hesse, 'Enlightenment Epistemology,' 125–7).

7 Hugo, 'Discours d'Ouverture,' 995.

8 Victor Hugo, 'Séance du 25 juin,' 1005.

9 'Mais dès que l'œuvre est publiée l'auteur n'en est plus le maître' (Hugo, 'Discours d'Ouverture,' 999).

10 'L'heritier ne fait pas le livre: il ne peut avoir le droit de l'auteur' (Hugo, 'Le Domaine Public Payant,' 998).

11 Sam Ricketson also notes that the Congrès did pass a motion recommending the adoption, in present national laws, of a transitional system of 'domaine public payant' (*Berne Convention*, 47). Although Adolf Dietz prefers the expression 'right of the community of authors,' to 'domaine public payant,' the same basic idea whereby 'dead generations serve living ones,' remains, and is clearly reminiscent of Hugo's sentiment. See

Dietz, 'A Modern Concept for the Right of the Community of Authors,' 14. As Dietz correctly points out, some of this redistribution of funds is achieved through collecting societies (15).

12 'Je déclare que s'il me fallait choisir entre le droit de l'écrivain et le droit du domaine public, je choisirais le droit du domaine public' (Hugo 'Le Domaine Public Payant,' 1000).

13 Charles Hugo et al., 'Halte au pillage Disney.' See also 'Les raisons de notre colère.'

14 Lauretta Hugo, 'Victor Hugo,' 6.

15 Le Fol, Palou, and d'Estienne D'Orves, 'Les Misérables II.'

16 Salles, 'Les descendants de Victor Hugo.'

17 Le Fol et al., 'Les Misérables II.'

18 Delacroix, 'La suite des "Misérables" sera-t-elle interdite?'

19 Pierre Hugo, 'L'affaire "Cosette."'

20 Le Fol et al., 'Les Misérables II.'

21 'Si cette fin n'emeut pas, je renonce a ecrire jamais' ('Les héritiers de Hugo demandent l'interdiction de la suite des "Misérables"').

22 Lamy and Delacroix, 'Pourquoi Clavel a refusé d'écrire la suite des "Miserables."'

23 Lauretta Hugo, 'Victor Hugo,' 6.

24 Druon, 'Vous avez dit: droit moral?'

25 'Le droit moral d'un écrivain, surtout lorsque, comme Hugo, il a incarné un moment de l'historie d'un peuple, devrait appartenir a ce peuple tout entier et, d'une façon générale, a tous ceux qui, a travers le monde, aiment son œuvre. A eux de la protéger: collectivement, dans le cas d'affaires comme celle du Bossu de Notre-Dame, en protestant et en boycottant, ou bien, si des décisions sont à prendre pour la publication d'inédits, de letters ou de brouillons, et dans le sens le plus libéral, par l'intermédiaire d'associations compétentes, reunissant spécialistes, critiques et représentants des institutions littéraires' (Noguez, 'Victor Hugo appartient à tous').

26 'Ils on cru entrevoir que l'héritier du sang était l'héritier de l'esprit' (Hugo, 'Séance du 25 juin,' 1003, quoted in *La Semaine Juridique* 49, 5 December 2001, 2254).

27 *Hugo contre SA Plon*, TGI Paris, 1ère chambre, 1ère section, 12 September (2001).

28 For a good introduction to the case, see 'Gone with the Wind Done Gone.' The complete legal history of the case is available at Houghton Mifflin's website http://www.houghtonmifflinbooks.com/features/randall_url/courtpapers.shtml

29 Barnet and Cavanagh, *Global Dreams*, 95.

30 *Suntrust Bank v. Houghton Mifflin Co.*, 136 F. Supp. 2d 1357, at 1363.

31 Hope Dellon, quoted in *Suntrust Bank v. Houghton Mifflin Co.*, 136 F. Supp. 2d 1357, note 12 at 1374.

32 *Suntrust Bank v. Houghton Mifflin Co.*, 136 F. Supp. 2d 1357, at 1382.

33 Testified to by Pat Conroy, who had been approached to write an authorized sequel, but who declined because of the many limitations imposed by the Mitchell estate (*Suntrust Bank v. Houghton Mifflin Co.*, 268 F.3d 1257, at 1282).

34 *Suntrust Bank v. Houghton Mifflin Co.*, 136 F. Supp. 2d 1357, at 1369.

35 Ibid., at 1386.

36 *Suntrust Bank v. Houghton Mifflin Co.*, 252 F.3d 1165, 1166.

37 *Suntrust Bank v. Houghton Mifflin Co.*, 268 F.3d 1257, at 1270.

38 Ibid., at 1276.

39 Judge Marcus, concurring opinion, ibid., at 1277.

40 'Gone with the Wind Done Gone,' 1195.

41 Houghton Mifflin, 'Settlement Reached Regarding *The Wind Done Gone.'*

42 Caron, 'Note,' 2256 at 7.

43 Geller, 'Must Copyright Be Forever Caught,' 193. On moral rights in the art world with special emphasis on France, see John Henry Merryman, 'The Refrigerator of Bernard Buffet,' and 'The Moral Right of Maurice Utrillo,' in *Thinking About the Elgin Marbles*, 316–40, 342–50.

44 *La Semaine Juridique* 49, 5 December 2001, 2254.

45 Noted by, for instance, David Lange, who called it 'uncontrolled to the point of recklessness' ('Recognizing the Public Domain,' 147), and Lawrence Lessig, who thinks the distinctive feature of modern American copyright law is its almost 'limitless bloating' (*Future of Ideas*, 106).

46 Boyle, 'The Second Enclosure Movement,' 1. For a brief introduction the the English enclosure movement, see Bollier, *Silent Theft*, 44–6.

47 Ruth Gana Okediji makes the important comment that the inequalities that exist on a global scale and that place developing nations at a disadvantage in respect to developed nations, may also be understood against a similar widening gap between people within a country ('Copyright and Welfare,' 173).

48 Coombe, *Cultural Life*, 98.

49 David Lange noted in 1981, and many others have agreed since then, that the expansion of intellectual property rights has not been countered by a similar interest in the protection of the public domain ('Recognizing the Public Domain,' 177). See also Lessig, *Future of Ideas*, 86.

50 Gana Okediji, 'Copyright and Welfare,' 122.

51 As Graeme B. Dinwoodie points out, copyright law 'implicates more than trade,' and may effectively be seen as a crucial instrument by which democratic ideals may be achieved ('A New Copyright Order,' 510).

52 Lessig, *Future of Ideas*, 21.

53 Parrinder, 'Introduction: Literary Copyright and the Public Domain,' 2.

54 Lessig, *Future of Ideas*, 11, 14.

55 For a good description of both types, see Lessig, *Future of Ideas*, 95.

56 Litman, 'The Public Domain,' 968.

57 Ricketson, *Berne Convention*, 320. Ricketson notes that a general assumption behind the length of copyright appears to be related to the needs of surviving spouse and children, that is, it is related to the protection of following generations. For a longer discussion on the length of protection in the history of the Berne Convention, see Ricketson, *Berne Convention*, esp. chapter 7, 'Duration of Protection,' 318–63.

58 Puri, 'Preservation and Conservation of Expressions of Folklore,' 19.

59 Harmonizing at a lower level than the seventy years granted in Germany would be impossible, since existing vested rights could not be revoked (Sherman and Bentley, 'Balance and Harmony in the Duration of Copyright,' 24–5).

60 See, for instance, Senator Orrin Hatch's argument to this effect in his Statement Before Congress, 20 March 1997, available at www.copyrightextension.com/page04.html.

61 The legal history of *Eldred v. Ashcroft* is available at www.eldred.cc. The best general introduction to *Eldred v. Ashcroft* (previously *Eldred v. Reno*) is Fonda, 'Copyright Crusader.' See also the more recent interview with Eric Eldred and one of his co-plaintiffs, Laura Bjorklund, by Damien Cave, 'Mickey Mouse v. The People,' available at www.salon.com/tech/feature/2002/02/21/web_copyright/print.html. Downloaded 1 May 2002.

62 Greenhouse, 'Supreme Court to Intervene.'

63 Lessig's oral argument can be accessed at the web site of the U.S. Supreme Court; see transcript 01-618, 3 at 22–3, http://www.supremecourtus.gov/oral_arguments/argument_transcripts.html.

64 *Eldred v. Ashcroft*, 239 F.3d 372, *affirmed*. The majority opinion as well as the two long dissents by Judge Breyer and Stevens, can be accessed at the Legal Information Institute Supreme Court Collection, http://supct.law.cornell.edu/supct/html/01-618.ZO.html.

65 The whole story is documented in Negativland, *Fair Use*. Negativland provides a wealth of information on intellectual property rights, especially questions of fair use and the public domain, on their web site at http://www.negativland.com/intprop.html.

66 Benkler, 'Free As the Air to Common Use,' 393.
67 Rose, 'The Several Futures of Property,' 155.
68 Ibid., 143.
69 For a useful introduction and overview of 'le domain public payant' (also discussing different national implementations), see Harvey, 'The *domaine public payant* in Comparative Law.'
70 Samuelson, 'Digital Information, Digital Networks, and the Public Domain,' 80.
71 Benkler, 'Free As the Air to Common Use,' 425.
72 Moore, 'Seattle: What's at Stake?'
73 Oxfam, *Rigged Rules and Double Standards*, executive summary of chapter 2. See http://www.maketradefair.org/stylesheet.asp?file=03042002154154
74 Gana Okediji, 'Copyright and Welfare,' 134.
75 Sassen, 'The Spatial Organization of Information Industries,' 46.
76 Massey, *Space, Place and Gender*, 149.
77 See Rose, 'The Several Futures of Property,' 152.
78 Lessig, *Code and Other Laws of Cyberspace*, 124.
79 McLuhan, 'Address at Vision 65,' 202.
80 Speaking on the Digital Millennium Copyright Act (DMCA), Gana Okediji, 'Copyright and Welfare,' 178. Note also Lawrence Lessig's argument that 'code can, and increasingly will, displace law as the primary defense of intellectual property in cyberspace' (*Code and Other Laws of Cyberspace*, 126).
81 This is viable even in a historical perspective; see Martha Woodmansee's argument that legislative measures always lag behind technological innovations in 'Genius and the Copyright,' 437.
82 For further information on *Felten v. RIAA*, see the Electronic Frontier Foundation's web site http://www.eff.org/IP/DMCA/Felten_v_RIAA. Felten later filed a lawsuit against the Recording Industry Association of America (RIAA), arguing that they in turn had threatened him with a lawsuit if he made his findings public. The recording industry had, however, backed down from suing Felten, and his case was dismissed on 28 November 2001 (Schwartz, '2 Copyright Cases').
83 Lessig, *Future of Ideas*, 187.
84 See Delio, 'Russian Hacker Charges Dropped,' available at www.wired.com/news/politics/0,1283,49122,00.html, and Benner, 'Russian Hacker Has a Party,' available at www.wired.com/news/politics/0,1283,49272,00.html. Downloaded 17 May 2002. The case was covered in detail in *Wired News*; see http://search.wired.com/news default.asp?query=Sklyarov&first=11&num=10&abs=1. Downloaded 17 May 2002.

85 Manjoo, 'Judge: ElcomSoft Case Can Proceed,' available at www.wired. com/news/politics/0,1283,52404,00.html. Downloaded 17 May 2002.

86 Barlow, 'The Economy of Ideas,' available at www.wired.com/wired/ archive/2.03/economy.ideas_pr.html. Dowloaded 18 April 2002.

87 Oppenheim, 'Copyright in the Electronic Age,' 351. For a useful introduction to many of the complexities involved, see Ginsburg, 'Copyright Without Borders?'

88 Lange, 'Recognizing the Public Domain,' 176. For an interesting discussion on resources that traditionally considered and managed as a commons, see Rose, *Property and Persuasion*, esp. chapter 5, 'The Comedy of the Commons: Custom, Commerce, and Inherently Public Property,' 105–62.

89 Barlow, 'The Economy of Ideas.'

90 See the general inclination of Boyle, Lessig, Liman, and Samuelson.

91 Habermas, *Structural Transformation of the Public Sphere*, 175. Habermas's history of the bourgeois public sphere is one of unremittent decline. Mass culture precludes any form of active participation because it caters to the lowest common denominator in consumers (165). One of the best introductory volumes to Habermas's concept of the public sphere is Calhoun, *Habermas and the Public Sphere*. Hanna Arendt also viewed mass society as a destroyer not only of the public realm, but of the private as well ('The Public and Private Realm,' 205).

92 Arendt, 'The Public and Private Realm,' 207. According to Arendt, it is the public life that allows you to contribute to the 'common world of things,' and achieve something more permanent than life itself (205).

93 Dinwoodie, 'A New Copyright Order,' 542.

94 Recent years have seen an upsurge in books concerned with democracy and the Internet, all of which are focused on the concept of digital democracy. See Alexander and Pal, *Digital Democracy*; Hague and Loader, *Digital Democracy*; and Hacker and Van Dijk, *Digital Democracy*.

95 See Rose, 'The Several Futures of Property,' 132.

96 Eric Eldred, quoted in Fonda, 'Copyright Crusader.' One example of the 'enviromentalist' approach is Boyle, 'Enviromentalism for the Net?'

97 Vaidhyanathan, *Copyrights and Copywrongs*, 12.

98 Litman, *Digital Copyright*, 28.

99 Dietz, 'Modern Concept for the Rights of the Community of Authors,' 13.

100 Dinwoodie, 'A New Copyright Order,' 471.

101 Lessig, *Future of Ideas*, 263. I am also greatful to Jim Lewis, who at a dinner in Chapel Hill once made this position perfectly clear to me when he said that culture in the United States was separated from the state in

the same was as religion was, which I think, is a comment that makes perfect sense of the absence of cultural policy in the United States.

102 The state plays a much more substantial role in both France and Sweden when it comes to cultural policy. This is clearly more elaborated in France than in Sweden, where cultural policy remains both a question for the state, *and* a grass-roots movement. David Loseley, *The Politics of Fun*, gives a comprehensive account of the relationship between the state and culture in France. For a history of Swedish cultural policy, see Nilsson, *Kulturens vägar*.

103 For a longer discussion of this point, see Eva Hemmungs Wirtén, 'Fences and Wide-Open Spaces.'

104 Bennett, 'Cultural Policy-Issues of Culture and Governance,' 26. A similar concern for the scope and power of cultural policies is launched by Garcia Canclini in 'North Americans or Latin Americans?' 152.

105 Samuelson, 'Towards a New Politics of Intellectual Property,' 98.

106 Litman, *Digital Copyright*, 32.

REFERENCES

Adamantopoulos, Konstantinos. *An Anatomy of the World Trade Organization.* London: Kluwer Law International, 1997.

Agreement on Trade-Related Aspects of Intellectual Property Rights (1994) (TRIPS). http://www.wto.org/english/tratop_e/trips_e/t_agm0_e.htm

Alexander, Cynthia J., and Leslie A. Pal, eds. *Digital Democracy: Policy and Politics in a Wired World.* Oxford: Oxford University Press, 1998.

Alford, William P. *To Steal a Book Is an Elegant Offense: Intellectual Property Law in Chinese Civilization.* Stanford: Stanford University Press, 1995.

Altbach, Philip G. 'Book Publishing.' In *World Information Report 1997/98.* Paris: UNESCO, 1997.

Altbach, Philip G., ed. *Copyright and Development: Inequality in the Information Age.* Chestnut Hill, Mass.: Bellagio Publishing, 1995.

– *Publishing and Development in the Third World.* London: Hans Zell, 1992.

Altbach, Philip, and Damtew Teferra. *Publishing and Development: A Book of Readings.* Chestnut Hill, MA: Bellagio Publishing, 1998.

Anderson, Benedict. *Imagined Communities: Reflections on the Origin and Spread of Nationalism.* London: Verso, 1983.

Andrews, Audrey. 'Mystery Takes Icy Turn.' *Calgary Herald,* 15 January 1994.

Aoki, Keith. '(Intellectual) Property and Sovereignty: Notes towards a Cultural Geography of Authorship.' 48 *Stanford Law Review* 1293 (May 1996).

– 'Space Invaders: Critical Geography, The "Third World" in International Law and Critical Race Theory.' 45 *Villanova Law Review* 913 (2000).

Arendt, Hanna. 'The Public and Private Realm.' In *The Portable Hanna Arendt,* ed. Peter Baehr, 182–212. London: Penguin, 2000.

'Artcamp: Resilience in a Time of Poverty.' *Crafts News* 12 no. 48 (summer 2001): 8.

Association Littéraire et Artistique Internationale (ALAI). *Bulletin de l'Association Littéraire Internationale*, nos. 1–3, 6–7, 9–10, 14–16 (December 1878–83).

Australia Council. 'Conference Aims for a Better Future for Aboriginal and Torres Strait Islander Artists.' Media release, 25 October 1999.

Åhlund, Jannike. 'Billie August känsla för snö: Ingen vet hur det slutar när Peter Høegs succéroman blir film...' *Expressen*, 9 February 1997.

Bacchus, Lee. 'Smilla's Sense of Silliness.' *Vancouver Province*, 21 March 1997.

Bagdikian, Ben H. *The Media Monopoly*. 6th ed. Boston: Beacon Press, 2000.

Barker, Sophie. 'Messier Puts Money Where His Mouth Is.' *Daily Telegraph*, 25 April 2002.

Barlow, John Perry. 'The Economy of Ideas: A Framework for Patents and Copyrights in the Digital Age (Everything You Know about Intellectual Property Is Wrong).' *Wired* 2.03 (March 1994). http://www.wired.com/wired/archive/2.03/economy.ideas_pr.html

Barnet, Richard J., and John Cavanagh. *Global Dreams: Imperial Corporations and the New World Order*. New York: Simon and Schuster, 1994.

Barron, Anne. 'No Other Law? Author-ity, Property and Aboriginal Art.' In *Intellectual Property and Ethics*, ed. Lionel Bentley and Spyros M. Maniatis, 37–87. London: Sweet and Maxwell, 1998.

Barthes, Roland. 'The Death of the Author.' In *Image, Music, Text*, ed. Stephen Heath, 142–8. New York: Hill and Wang, 1977.

– 'From Work to Text.' In *Image, Music, Text*, ed. Stephen Heath, 155–64. New York: Hill and Wang, 1977.

Bawer, Bruce. 'Take My Queen Please.' Book review of *The Royal Physician's Visit*, by Per-Olof Enquist. *New York Times*, 18 November 2002.

Bedini, Silvio A. *Thomas Jefferson and His Copying Machines*. Charlottesville: University Press of Virgina, 1984.

Benjamin, Walter. *Paris 1800 – talets huvudstad*. Vol. 1, *Passagearbetet*. Stockholm: Symposium, 1990.

– 'The Work of Art in the Age of Mechanical Reproduction.' In *Illuminations*, ed. Hannah Arendt, 217–51. New York: Schocken Books, 1969.

Benkler, Yochai. 'Free As the Air to Common Use: First Amendment Constraints on Enclosure of the Public Domain.' 74 *New York University Law Review* 354 (May 1999).

Benner, Jeffrey. 'Russian Hacker Has a Party.' *Wired News*, 19 December 2001. http://www.wired.com/news/politics/0,1283,49272,00.html

Bennett, Tony. 'Cultural Policy-Issues of Culture and Governance.' In *Culture, Society and Market*, ed. Folke Snickars, 13–28. Stockholm: Swedish National Council for Cultural Affairs, 2001.

The Berne Convention for the Protection of Literary and Artistic Works (1886).

Paris Act of 24 July 1971, amended on 28 September 1979. http://
www.wipo.int/clea/docs/en/wo/wo001en.htm

Berryman, Cathryn A. 'Toward More Universal Protection of Intangible
Cultural Property.' 1 *Journal of Intellectual Property Law* 293 (spring 1994).

Bertelsmann. *Annual Report 1999/2000*.

'The Best (& Worst) Managers of the Year,' *BusinessWeek online*, 13 January
2003, http://www.businessweek.com/magazine/content/03 02/
b3815601.htm

Bettig, Ronald V. *Copyrighting Culture: The Political Economy of Intellectual
Property*. Boulder: Westview Press, 1996.

'The Biz.' CNN, 12 July 2001.

Black, Fiona A., Bertrum H. MacDonald, and J. Malcolm W. Black. 'Geographical Information Systems: A New Research Method for Book History.' *Book
History* 1 (1998): 11–31.

Blakeney, Michael. 'What Is Traditional Knowledge? Why Should It Be Pro-
tected? Who Should Protect It? From Whom? Understanding the Value
Chain.' Paper presented at the Roundtable on Intellectual Property and
Traditional Knowledge, Geneva, 1–2 November 1999; WIPO Document
WIPO/IPTK/RT/99/3. Geneva: WIPO, 2000.

Bloom, Harold. *The Western Canon: The Books and School of the Ages*. New York:
Harcourt Brace and Company, 1994.

Bollier, David. *Silent Theft: The Private Plunder of Our Common Wealth*. New
York and London: Routledge, 2002.

Bourdieu, Pierre. 'Deux impérialismes de l'universel.' In *L'Amérique des
Français*, ed. Christine Fauré and Tom Bishop, 149–55. Paris: Éditions
Francois Bourin, 1992.

– *Les règles d'art: Genèse et structure du champ littéraire*. Paris: Seuil, 1992.

– 'Une révolution conservatrice dans l'édition.' *Actes de la recherche en sciences
sociales* 126–7 (1999): 3–28.

Boyd White, James. *Justice As Translation: An Essay in Cultural and Legal Criticism*. Chicago: University of Chicago Press, 1990.

Boyle, James. 'A Politics of Intellectual Property: Enviromentalism for the
Net?' 47 *Duke Law Journal* 87 (1997).

– 'The Second Enclosure Movement and the Construction of the Public
Domain.' Paper presented at the Conference on the Public Domain, Duke
University, Durham, NC, 9–11 November 2001.

– *Shamans, Software, and Spleens: Law and the Construction of the Information
Society*. Cambridge, MA: Harvard University Press, 1996.

Bradbury, Malcolm, ed. *The Atlas of Literature*. New York: Stewart, Tabori and
Chang, 1998.

Brooks, John. 'Xerox, Xerox, Xerox, Xerox.' *New Yorker*, 1 April 1967.

Brush, Stephen B. 'Whose Knowledge, Whose Genes, Whose Rights?' In *Valuing Local Knowledge: Indigenous People and Intellectual Property Rights*, ed. Stephen B. Brush and Doreen Stabinsky, 1–21. Washington DC: Island Press, 1996.

Burrell, Robert. 'A Case Study in Cultural Imperialism: The Imposition of Copyright on China by the West.' In *Intellectual Property and Ethics*, ed. Lionel Bentley and Spyros M. Maniatis, 195–224. London: Sweet and Maxwell, 1998.

Business Software Alliance. *Sixth Annual BSA Global Software Piracy Study*. Washington, D.C., 2001.

Calhoun, Craig, ed. *Habermas and the Public Sphere*. Cambridge, MA: Harvard University Press, 1992.

Callan, Bénédicte. *Pirates on the High Seas: The United States and Global Intellectual Property Rights*. New York: Council on Foreign Relations, 1998.

Carlberg, Ingrid. 'Mediemogulen som siktar mot stjärnorna.' *Dagens Nyheter*, 9 September 2001.

Caron, Christophe. 'Note.' *La Semaine Juridique* 49 (December 2001): 2255–6.

Carter, Robert A. 'A History of International Publishing.' In *International Book Publishing: An Encyclopedia*, ed. Philip G. Altbach and Edith S. Hoshino, 156–63. London: Fitzroy Dearborn, 1995.

Casanova, Pascale. *La Republique mondial des lettres*. Paris: Seuil, 1999.

Casey, John. 'Death of the American Dreams.' *The Guardian*, 30 July 2002.

– 'Middelhoff out of Picture.' *The Guardian*, 29 July 2002.

Castells, Manuel. *The Information Age: Economy, Society and Culture*. 3 vols. Malden, MA: Blackwells, 1996.

Cave, Damien. 'Mickey Mouse v. The People.' *Salon*, 21 February 2002. www.salon.com/tech/feature/2002/02/21/web_copyright/print.html

Chartier, Roger, and Henri-Jean Martin. *Histoire de l'édition Française*. Vol 3. *Le temps des éditeurs*. Paris: Promodis, 1990.

Chatterjee, Rimi B. 'Canon without Consensus: Rabindranath Tagore and "The Oxford Book of Bengali Verse."' *Book History* 4 (2001): 303–33.

Cohen, Adam, and Bill Joy. 'A Crisis of Content.' *Time*, 2 October 2000.

Collins, John. 'The Problem of Oral Copyright: The Case of Ghana.' In *Music and Copyright*, ed. Simon Frith, 146–58. Edinburgh: Edinburgh University Press, 1993.

Coombe, Rosemary J. 'Authorial Cartographies: Mapping Proprietary Boundaries in a Less-Than-Brave New World.' 48 *Stanford Law Review* 1357 (1996).

– *The Cultural Life of Intellectual Properties*. Durham: Duke University Press, 1998.

– 'Intellectual Property, Human Rights and Sovereignty: New Dilemmas in International Law Posed by the Recognition of Indigenous Knowledge and the Conservation of Biodiversity.' 6 *Indiana Journal of Global Legal Studies* 59 (1998).

Copyright Law of the United States of America (1976). http://www.loc.gov/copyright/title17/

The Copyright Term Extension Act. S 505, P.L. 105–298, 11 Stat. 2827 (1998) (CTEA). www.loc.gov/copyright

Coser, Louis A., Charles Kadushin, and Walter W. Powell. *Books: The Culture and Commerce of Publishing.* Chicago: University of Chicago Press, 1985.

Danius, Sara. 'Bortom Öresund: Peter Høeg följer en postkolonial karta.' *Dagens Nyheter*, 28 July 1994.

– 'Fröken Smilla skakar om.' *Dagens Nyheter*, 18 June 1994.

Das, Sonia. 'The Availability of the Fair Use Defense in Music Piracy and Internet Technology.' 52 *Federal Communications Law Journal* 727 (2000).

Delacroix, Olivier. 'La suite des "Misérables" sera-t-elle interdite?' *Le Figaro*, 2 May 2001.

Delio, Michelle. 'Russian Hacker Charges Dropped.' *Wired News*, 13 December 2001. http://wwwwired.com/new/politics/0,1283,49122,00

Demers, David. *Global Media: Menace or Messiah?* Cresskill, NJ: Hampton Press, 1999.

Dessauer, John. *My Years with Xerox: The Millions Nobody Wanted.* New York: Doubleday, 1971.

Dietz, Adolf. 'A Modern Concept for the Rights of the Community of Authors (*domaine public payant*).' *Copyright Bulletin* 24, no. 4 (1990): 13–24.

Digital Millennium Copyright Act (1998) (DMCA). http://www.loc.gov/copyright/

Dingwaney, Anuradha, and Carol Meier, eds. *Between Languages and Cultures: Translation and Cross-Cultural Texts.* Pittsburgh: University of Pittsburgh Press, 1995.

Dinsdale, A. 'Chester F. Carlson, Inventor of Xerography – A Biography.' *Photographic Science and Engineering* 7 (1963): 1–4.

Dinwoodie, Graeme B. 'A New Copyright Order: Why National Courts Should Create Global Norms.' 149 *University of Pennsylvania Law Review* 469 (December 2000).

Dolhem, Nancy. 'Qui a tué l'enfant inuit?' *Le Monde Diplomatique*, December 1995, 26.

'Downfall,' *Business Week*, special issue on Xerox. 5 March 2001.

Drahos, Peter. 'Thinking Strategically about Intellectual Property Rights.' *Telecommunications Policy* 21, no. 3 (1997): 201–11.

Drozdiak, William. 'Big Music Merger Is Called Off.' *Washington Post*, 2 May 2001.

Druon, Maurice. 'Vous avez dit: droit moral?' *Le Figaro*, 27 June 2001.

Dugan, Jeanne. 'Boldly Going Where Others Are Bailing Out: Why Does Bertelsmann Think It Can Profit with Random House?' *Business Week*, 6 April 1998.

Eisenstein, Elisabeth. *The Printing Press As an Agent of Change: Communications and Cultural Transformations in Early-Modern Europe*. Cambridge, MA.: Cambridge University Press, 1985.

Ekström, Anders. *Den utställda världen: Stockholmsutställningen 1897 och 1800–talets världsutställningar*. Stockholm: Nordiska Museets samlingar, 1994.

Epstein, Jason. *Book Business: Publishing, Past, Present, and Future*. New York: W.W Norton, 2001.

European Union. Council Directive 93/98/EEC of 29 October 1992 harmonizing the term of protection of copyright and certain related rights. http://europa.eu.int/smartapi/cgi/sga doc?smartapi!celexapi!prod!CELEX numdoc&lg=EN& numdoc+31993L0098&model=quichett

– Directive 2001/29/EC of the European Parliament and of the Council of 22 May 2001 on the harmonisation of certain aspects of copyright and related rights in the information society. http://europa.eu.int smartapic gisgadoc? smartapi!celexapi!prod!CELEXnumdoc&lg=EN&numdoc =32001L0029&model=quichett

Feather, John. 'From Rights in Copies to Copyright: The Recognition of Authors' Rights in English Law and Practice in the Sixteenth and Seventeenth Centuries.' In *The Construction of Authorship*, ed. Woodmansee and Jaszi, 191–209.

– *Publishing, Piracy, and Politics: A Historical Study of Copyright in Britain*. London: Mansell, 1994.

Featherstone, Mike, and Scott Lash. 'Globalization, Modernity and the Spatialization of Social Theory: An Introduction.' In *Global Modernities*, ed. Mike Featherstone, Scott Lash, and Roland Robertson, 1–24. London: Sage, 1995.

Febvre, Lucien, and Henri-Jean Martin. *L'Apparition du livre*. Paris: Albin Michel, 1958.

Felman, Shoshana. 'A Ghost in the House of Justice: Death and the Language of Law.' 13 *Yale Journal of the Law and the Humanities* 241 (2001).

Feltes, N.N. 'International Copyright: Structuring "The Condition of Modernity" in British Publishing.' In *The Construction of Authorship: Textual Appropriation in Law and Literature*, ed. Woodmansee and Jaszi, 271–80.

Findling, John E., and Kimberly D. Pelle. *Historical Dictionary of World Fairs and Expositions, 1851–1988*. New York: Greenwood Press, 1990.

Fish, Stanley. *Doing What Comes Naturally: Change, Rhetoric, and the Practice of Theory in Literary and Legal Studies.* Durham: Duke University Press, 1998.

Fonda, Darren. 'Copyright Crusader.' *Boston Globe Magazine*, 29 August 1999.

'*Fortune* 2002 Gobal 500.' *Fortune*, 23 July 2001.

Foucault, Michel. 'The Eye of Power.' In *Power/Knowledge: Selected Interviews and Other Writings 1972–1977*, ed. Colin Gordon, 146–65. New York: Pantheon, 1980.

– 'What Is an Author?' In *The Foucault Reader*, ed. Paul Rabinow, 101–20. New York: Pantheon, 1984.

Fouché, Pascal, ed. *L'Édition Française depuis 1945.* Paris: Cercle de la Librairie, 1998.

Fowler, Betsy. 'Intellectual Property Rights and the Native American Experience.' *Crafts News* (summer 2001): 1, 7.

Gaines, Jane M. *Contested Culture: The Image, the Voice, and the Law.* Chapel Hill: University of North Carolina Press, 1991.

Gana Okediji, Ruth. 'Copyright and Welfare in Global Perspective.' 7 *Indiana Journal of Global Legal Studies* 117 (fall 1999).

– 'Toward an International Fair Use Doctrine.' 39 *Columbia Journal of Transnational Law* 75 (2000).

Garcia Canclini, Nestor. 'North Americans or Latin Americans? The Redefinition of Mexican Identity and the Free Trade Agreements.' In *Mass Media and Free Trade: NAFTA and the Cultural Industries*, ed. Emile G. McAnahy and Kenton T. Wilkinson, 142–56. Austin: University of Texas Press, 1996.

Geller, Paul Edward. 'Must Copyright Be Forever Caught Between Marketplace and Authorship Norms?' In *Of Authors and Origins: Essays on Copyright Law*, ed. Sherman and Strowel, 159–201.

Gershon, Richard. *The Transnational Media Corporation: Global Messages and Free Market Competition.* Mahwah, NJ: L. Erlbaum, 1997.

Giddens, Anthony. *The Consequences of Modernity.* Stanford: Stanford University Press, 1990.

Gilroy, Paul. *The Black Atlantic: Modernity and Double Consciousness.* London: Verso, 1993.

Ginsburg, Jane C. 'Copyright without Borders? Choice of Forum and Choice of Law for Copyright Infringement in Cyberspace.' 15 *Cardozo Arts and Entertainment Law Journal* 153 (1997).

– 'A Tale of Two Copyrights: Literary Property in Revolutionary France and America.' In *Of Authors and Origins: Essays on Copyright Law*, ed. Sherman and Strowel, 131–58.

Gloin, Lew. 'Danish Mystery Loses Nothing in Translation.' *Toronto Star*, 19 June 1993.

Goldstein, Paul. *Copyright's Highway: From Gutenberg to the Celestial Jukebox.* New York: Hill and Wang, 1994.

– *International Copyright: Principles, Law, and Practice.* Oxford: Oxford University Press, 2001.

'Gone With the Wind Done Gone: Re-Writing and Fair Use.' 115 *Harvard Law Review* 1193 (February 2002).

Greco, Albert. *The Book Publishing Industry.* Boston: Allyn and Bacon, 1997.

Greenhouse, Linda. 'Supreme Court to Intervene in Internet Copyright Dispute.' *New York Times*, 19 February 2002.

Grimes, Christopher. 'AOL Time Warner Reports $54bn Loss.' *Financial Times*, 25 April 2002.

Grover, Ronald. 'Moguls Who Shopped till They Dropped,' *Businessweek*, 5 August 2002.

Gründ, Alain. Opening remarks to the 26th Congress of the International Publishers Association, Buenos Aires, 1–4 May 2000. http://www.ipa–uie.org

Gunther, Marc, and Stephanie N. Metha. 'Can Steve Case Make Sense of This Beast?' *Fortune*, 13 May 2002.

Gwinn, Mary Ann. 'Finding the Right Words.' *Seattle Times*, 9 September 2001.

Habermas, Jürgen. *The Structural Transformation of the Public Sphere: An Inquiry into a Category of Bourgeois Society.* Cambridge, MA.: MIT Press, 1995.

Hacker, Kenneth L., and Jan Van Dijk, eds. *Digital Democracy: Issues of Theory and Practice.* London: Sage, 2000.

Hague, Barry N., and Brian D. Loader, eds. *Digital Democracy: Discourse and Decision Making in the Information Age.* London: Routledge, 1999.

Hall, Dennis G., and Rita M. Hall. 'Chester F. Carlson: A Man to Remember.' *Optics and Photonics News* (September 2000): 14–18.

Hall, Stuart. 'Cultural Studies and Its Theoretical Legacies.' In *Stuart Hall: Critical Dialogues in Cultural Studies*, ed. David Morley and Kuan-Hsing Chen, 262–75. London: Routledge, 1996.

– 'The Emergence of Cultural Studies and the Crisis of the Humanities.' *October* 53 (1990): 11–23.

– 'Gramsci's Relevance for the Study of Race and Ethnicity.' In *Stuart Hall: Critical Dialogues in Cultural Studies*, ed. David Morley and Kuan-Hsing Chen, 411–40. London: Routledge, 1996.

– Introduction. In *Representation: Cultural Representation and Signifying Practices*, ed. Stuart Hall, 1–11. London: Sage, 1997.

– 'The Local and the Global: Globalization and Ethnicity.' In *Culture, Globalization and the World-System: Contemporary Conditions for the Representation of Identity*, ed. Anthony D. King, 19–39. London: Macmillan, 1991.

– 'The Work of Representation.' In *Representation: Cultural Representation and*

Signifying Practices, ed. Stuart Hall, 13–64. Milton Keynes: Open University, 1997.

Hamilton, Marci A. 'The TRIPS Agreement: Imperialistic, Outdated, and Overprotective.' In *Intellectual Property: Moral, Legal, and International Dilemmas*, ed. Adam D. Moore, 273–63. Lanham, MD: Rowman and Littlefield, 1997.

Hammer, Richard. 'There Isn't Any Profit Squeeze at Xerox.' *Fortune*, July 1962.

Hargreaves, Deborah, and Andrew Hill. 'Brussels Poised to Veto GE Move for Honeywell.' *Financial Times*, 3 July 2001.

Harvey, Edwin R. 'The *domaine public payant* in Comparative Law with Special Reference to Argentina.' *Copyright Bulletin* 28 (1994): 29–39.

Hatch, Orrin. Statement before Congress, 20 March 1997. www.copyrightextension.com/page04.html

Held, David, Anthony McGrew, David Goldblatt, and Jonathan Perraton. *Global Transformations: Politics, Economics and Culture*. London: Polity Press, 1999.

Hemmungs Wirtén, Eva. 'Fences and Wide-Open Spaces: Cultural Policy and Globalization.' *Nordisk Kulturpolitisk Tidskrift* 2, no. 2 (1999): 58–80.

– *Global Infatuation: Explorations in Transnational Publishing and Texts*. Publications from the Section for Sociology of Literature 38. Uppsala: Uppsala University, 1998.

– 'Mat. Betraktelser kring en populär kultur.' In *Populära fiktioner*, ed. Anders Öhman and Kjell Jonsson, 129–45. Stockholm: Symposium, 2000.

– 'Surveying the (Battle)field: Book History, SHARP, and the Guerilla Tactics of Research,' *SHARP-News* 12, no. 1 (winter 2003): 3–4.

'Les heritiers de Hugo demandent l'interdiction de la suite des "Miserables."' Agence France Press, 3 May 2001.

Herman, Edward S., and Robert W. McChesney. *The Global Media: The New Missionaries of Corporate Capitalism*. London: Cassell, 1997.

Herrnstein Smith, Barbara. *Contingencies of Value: Alternative Perspectives of Critical Theory*. Cambridge, MA: Harvard University Press, 1988.

Hesse, Carla. 'Enlightenment Epistemology and the Laws of Authorship in Revolutionary France, 1777–1793.' *Representations* 30 (spring 1990): 109–37.

Hiltzik, Michael. *Dealers of Lightning: Xerox PARC and the Dawn of the Computer Age*. New York: HarperCollins, 1999.

Hobsbawm, Eric. *The Age of Revolution 1798–1848*. London: Weidenfeld and Nicholson, 1962.

Hoekman,Bernard M.,and Michel M. Kostecki. *The Political Economy of the World Trading System: From GATT to WTO*. Oxford: Oxford University Press, 1995.

Homestead, Melissa J. 'Imperfect Title: Nineteenth-Century American Women Authors and Literary Property.' PhD diss., University of Pennsylvania, 1998.

Hoskins, Colin, Adam Finn, and Stuart McFayden. 'Television and Film in a Freer International Trade Environment: U.S. Dominance and Canadian Responses.' In *Mass Media and Free Trade: NAFTA and the Cultural Industries*, ed. Emile G. McAnahy and Kenton T. Wilkinson, 63–91. Austin: University of Texas Press, 1996.

Houghton Mifflin. 'Settlement Reached Regarding *The Wind Done Gone*.' Press release, 9 May 2002.

Hugo, Charles, et al. 'Halte au pillage Disney,' *Libération*, 10 March 1997.

– 'Les raisons de notre colère.' *Libération*, 20 March 1997.

Hugo, Lauretta. 'Victor Hugo: La misérable récupération.' *Libération*, 15 May 2001.

Hugo, Pierre. 'L'affaire Cosette: Les raisons de ma colère.' *Le Figaro*, 22 June 2001.

Hugo, Victor. 'Discours d'Ouverture Congrès Littéraire International 17 June 1878.' In *Œuvres Complètes*. Vol. 11, *Politique*, ed. Jean-Claude Fizaine, 993–8. Paris: Laffont, 1985.

– 'Le Domaine Public Payant.' In *Œuvres Complets*. Vol. 11, *Politique*, ed. Jean-Claude Fizaine, 1002–6. Paris: Laffont, 1985.

– 'Séance du 25 juin.' In *Œuvres Complets* Vol. 11, *Politique*, ed. Jean-Claude Fizaine, 998–1002. Paris: Laffont, 1985.

Høeg, Peter. *Frøken Smillas fornemmelse for sne*. Copenhagen: Rosinante, 1992 [1999].

– *Miss Smilla's Feeling for Snow*. Trans. F. David. London: Harvill Press, 1996.

– *Smilla's Sense of Snow*. Trans. Tiina Nunnally. New York: Farrar, Straus and Giroux, 1993.

Indigenous Peoples' Seattle Declaration on the Occasion of the Third Ministerial Meeting of the World Trade Organization, 30 November–3 December, 1999.

The Information Infrastructure Task Force. White Paper: Intellectual Property and the National Information Infrastructure: The Report of the Working Group on Intellectual Property Rights (1995). http://www.uspto.gov/web/offices/com/doc/ipnii/

International Institute of Communications. *Media Ownership and Control in the Age of Convergence*. London: International Institute of Communications, 1996.

International Intellectual Property Alliance (IIPA). 2002 'Special 301' Recommendations.

International Telecommunication Union (ITU). European Common Proposals for the Work of the World Telecommunication Development Conference (WTDC-02). Istanbul, Turkey, 18–27 March 2002.

Iwata, Edward. 'Software Piracy Takes Toll on Global Scale.' *USA Today,* 1 August 2001.

Jackson, John H. *The World Trading System: Law and Policy of International Economic Relations.* Cambridge, MA.: Harvard University Press, 1997.

Jacobson, Gary, and John Hillkirk. *Xerox: American Samurai.* New York: Collier Books, 1986.

Janke, Terri. *Minding Culture: Case-Studies on Intellectual Property and Traditional Cultural Expressions.* Geneva: WIPO, 2002.

Janson, Bo G. 'En postmodern undergångsvision. Eller: från modern detektivroman och till postmodern science fiction. Om Peter Høeg's *Frøken Smillas fornemmelse for sne.*' *Hjärnstorm* 55 (1996): 2–7.

Jaszi, Peter. 'On the Author Effect: Contemporary Copyright and Collective Creativity.' In *The Construction of Authorship: Textual Appropriation in Law and Literature,* ed. Woodmansee and Jaszi, 29–56.

– 'Towards a Theory of Copyright: The Metamorphoses of "Authorship."' 40 *Duke Law Journal* 455 (1991).

Johnson, Brian D. Movie review of *Smilla's Sense of Snow. Maclean's,* 31 March 1997.

Jones, Steve. 'Mass Communication, Intellectual Property Rights, International Trade and the Popular Music Industry.' In *Mass Media and Free Trade: NAFTA and the Cultural Industries,* ed. Emile G. McAnahy and Kenton T. Wilkinson, 331–50. Austin: University of Texas Press, 1996.

Jordan, David B. 'Square Pegs and Round Holes: Domestic Intellectual Property Law and Native American Economic and Cultural Policy: Can It Fit?' 25 *American Indian Law Review* 93 (2000).

Kanner, Beatrice. *The 100 Best TV Commercials – and Why They Worked.* New York: Random House, 1999.

Kaplan, Alice. *The Collaborator: The Trial and Execution of Robert Brassillach.* Chicago: University of Chicago Press, 2000.

– *French Lessons.* Chicago: University of Chicago Press, 1993.

– *Reproductions of Banality: Fascism, Literature, and French Intellectual Life.* Minneapolis: University of Minnesota Press, 1986.

Kearns, David T., and David A. Nadler. *Prophets in the Dark: How Xerox Reinvented Itself and Beat Back the Japanese.* New York: HarperCollins, 1992.

Klein, Naomi. *No Logo.* London: Flamingo, 2000.

Kobrak, Fred. 'Current Copyright Enforcement.' *Publishing Research Quarterly* 8 (summer 1992): 30–4.

Korda, Michael. *Another Life: A Memoir of Other People.* New York: Random House, 1999.

– 'Out of Print: Publishing's Future, Seen from the Inside.' *Harper's Magazine,* April 2001, 82–5.

Krüger, Mechthild. "Luksusgrønlænderen, papgrønlænderen, fupgrøenlænderen, pladaskgrønlænderen' - hvad er jeg?' In *Fragmente einer skandinavischen Poetikgeschichte*, ed. Heiko Uecker, 303–21. Frankfurt: Peter Lang, 1997.

Kundera, Milan. 'Author's Note.' In *The Joke*, vii–xi. London: Faber and Faber, 1992.

Lamy, Jean-Claude, and Olivier Delacroix. 'Pourquoi Clavel a refusé d'écrire la suite des Misérables.' *Le Figaro*, 8 May 2001.

Lange, David. 'Recognizing the Public Domain.' 44 *Law and Contemporary Problems* 147 (autumn 1981).

Lefevere, André. 'Mother Courage's Cucumbers: Text, System and Refraction in a Theory of Literature.' In *The Translation Studies Reader*, ed. Venuti, 233–49.

Le Fol, Sébastien, Anthony Palou, and Nicolas d'Estienne d'Orves. 'Les Misérables II.' *Le Figaro*, 24 April 2001.

Lehman, Bruce. 'Intellectual Property As a Means of Wealth Creation in the Market Economies of Developing Nations.' Speech presented in Dacca, Bangladesh, 22 November 1999.

– 'The United States and the Global Intellectual Property System: Leadership and Responsibilities.' 1 June 2001. http://www.hdf.net/iipi/views/detail.asp?itemID=19

Leithauser, Brad. 'Thrills and Chills.' *New Republic*, 1 November 1993.

Lemieux, Jacques, and Denis Saint-Jacques. 'U.S. Best-sellers in French Quebec and English Canada.' In *Mass Media and Free Trade: NAFTA and the Cultural Industries*, ed. Emile G. McAnahy and Kenton T. Wilkinson, 279–305. Austin: University of Texas Press, 1996.

Lenzner, Robert, and Christopher Helman. 'Edgar's Encore,' *Forbes*, 30 September 2002.

Lessig, Lawrence. *Code and Other Laws of Cyberspace*. New York: Basic Books, 1999.

– *The Future of Ideas: The Fate of the Commons in a Connected World*. New York: Random House, 2001.

Lindung, Yngve. 'Den angloamerikanska litteraturens dominans.' *Kulturrådet: Statens Kulturråd informerar* 5 (1993): 16–31.

Litman, Jessica. 'Copyright Legislation and Technological Change.' 68 *Oregon Law Review* 275 (1989).

– *Digital Copyright*. Amherst, NY: Prometheus Books, 2001.

– 'The Public Domain.' 39 *Emory Law Journal* 965 (fall 1990).

Loseley, David. *The Politics of Fun: Cultural Policy and Debate in Contemporary France*. Oxford: Berg, 1995.

Lotman, Herbert R. 'Milia Stresses U.S.–European E-Differences.' *Publisher's Weekly*, 12 March 2001.

Lough, John. *Writer and Public in France: From the Middle Ages to the Present Day*. Oxford: Clarendon Press, 1978.

Löfgren, Mikael. 'Ett medieimperium som luktar jord.' *Dagens Nyheter*, 23 September 2001.

Malmkjær, Kristen. 'A Tale of "Two" Smillas.' http://www.literarytranslation.com/pdf/smilla.pdf

Manjoo, Farhad. 'Judge: ElcomSoft Case Can Proceed.' *Wired News*, 8 May 2002. http://wired.com/new/politics/0,1283,52404,00.html

Mann, Charles. 'Who Will Own Your Next Good Idea?' *Atlantic Monthly*, September 1998.

Maryles, Daisy. 'Behind the Bestseller: "Think Snow."' *Publisher's Weekly*, 22 August 1994.

Maskus, Keith E. *Intellectual Property Rights in the Global Economy*. Washington: Institute for International Economics, 2000.

Massey, Doreen. 'Imagining Globalization: Power-Geometries of Time-Space.' In *Global Futures: Migration, Environment and Globalization*, ed. Avtar Brah, Mary J. Hickman, and Máirtín Mac an Ghaill, 27–44. Basingstoke: Macmillan, 1999.

– *Space, Place and Gender*. Oxford: Polity Press, 1994.

May, Christopher. *A Global Political Economy of Intellectual Property Rights: The New Enclosures?* London: Routledge, 2000.

McCue, Jim. 'Artic Nights.' *Times Literary Supplement*, 17 September 1993.

McLeod, Kembrew. *Owning Culture: Authorship, Ownership, and Intellectual Property Law*. New York: Peter Lang, 2001.

McLuhan, Marshall. 'Address at Vision 65.' *American Scholar* 35 (spring 1966): 196–205.

– *The Gutenberg Galaxy*. Toronto: University of Toronto Press, 1962.

McLuhan, Marshall, Quentin Fiore, and Jerome Agel. *The Medium Is the Massage*. New York: Random House, 1967.

McSherry, Corynne. *Who Owns Academic Work? Battling for Control of Intellectual Property*. Cambridge, MA: Harvard University Press, 2001.

Merryman, John Henry. *Thinking of the Elgin Marbles: Critical Essays on Cultural Property, Art and Law*. The Hague: Kluwer, 2000.

Michon, Jacques. Introduction. In *Édition et Pouvoirs*, ed. Jacques Michon, vii–xii. Sainte-Foy, QC: Les Presses de L'Université Laval, 1995.

Michon, Jacques, and Jean-Yves, Mollier. *Les Mutations du livre et de l'édition dans le monde du XVIII siècle à l'an 2000*. Sainte-Foy, QC: Les Presses de l'Université Laval, and Paris: L'Harmattan, 2001.

Milliot, Jim. 'Copyright Protection Stressed at AAP Meeting.' *Publisher's Weekly*, 19 February 2001.

- 'The Land of the Giants.' *Publisher's Weekly*, 1 January 2001.
- 'Vivendi to Aquire HM in $2.2 Billion Deal.' *Publisher's Weekly*, 11 June 2001.

Milmo, Dan. 'AOL Time Warner Boss Bows Out.' *The Guardian*, 5 December 2001.

- 'Bertelsmann: What's Up for Grabs.' *The Guardian*, 30 July 2002.
- 'Bronfman Quits Vivendi.' *The Guardian*, 6 December 2001.

Milner, Mark, and David Teather. 'Gütersloh Goes Off line,' *The Guardian*, 3 September 2002.

Mollier, Jean-Yves. *L'argent et les lettres: Histoire du capitalisme d'Édition 1880– 1920*. Paris: Fayard, 1988.

- 'Les mutations de l'espace éditorial français du XVIIIe au Xxe siècle.' *Actes de la recherche en sciences sociales*, 126–7 (1999): 29–38.

Moore, Mike. Address to the Ministerial Meeting of Least Developed Countries. New York, 28 September 1999.

- 'Seattle Conference Doomed to Succeed.' Opening address at the WTO 3rd Ministerial Conference, Seattle, 30 November 1999.
- 'Seattle: What's at Stake?' Speech given at the Transatlantic Business Dialogue, Berlin, 29 October 1999.

Moretti, Franco. *Atlas of the European Novel, 1800–1900*. London: Verso, 1999.

Morley, David. 'EurAm, Modernity, Reason and Alterity: Or, Postmodernism, the Highest Stage of Cultural Imperialism.' In *Stuart Hall: Critical Dialogues in Cultural Studies*, ed. David Morley and Kuan-Hsing Chen, 326–60. London: Routledge, 1996.

Murphy, Cait. 'Where's AOL? Missing in Action.' *Fortune*, 23 July 2001.

Murphy, Craig. *International Organization and Industrial Change: Global Governance since 1850*. Cambridge: Polity Press, 1994.

Møller, Hans Henrik. 'Peter Høeg or the Sense of Writing.' *Scandinavian Studies* 79 (1997): 29–51.

Nathan, Robert. 'Irritable, Depressed, Spoiled and Terrific.' Review of *Smilla's Sense of Snow* in the *New York Times Book Review*, 26 September 1993.

Negativland. *Fair Use: The Story of the Letter U and the Numeral 2*. Concord, CA: Seeland, 1995.

Nilsson, Sven. *Kulturens vägar*. Malmö: Polyvalent, 1999.

Noguez, Dominque. 'Victor Hugo appartient à tous.' *Le Monde*, 27 June 2001.

Norseng, Mary Kay. 'A House of Mourning: Frøken Smillas fornemmelse for sne.' *Scandinavian Studies* 79 (1997): 52–84

North, John. 'The Snow Must Go On.' *Toronto Star*, 16 October 1993.

North American Free Trade Agreement (1992) (NAFTA). http://www-tech.mit.edu/Bulletins/Nafta/

Nunberg, Geoffrey, ed. *The Future of the Book*. Berkeley and Los Angeles: University of California Press, 1996.

Odlyzko, Andrew. 'Content Is Not King.' *First Monday* [online journal], 6, no. 2 (February 2001). www.firstmonday.org/issues/issue6_2/odlyzko/index.html

Ohman, Richard. *Selling Culture: Magazines, Markets, and Class at the Turn of the Century*. London: Verso, 1996.

Oppenheim, Charles. 'Copyright in the Electronic Age.' *World Information Report 1997/98*, 349–60. Paris: UNESCO, 1997.

Otto, Diane. 'Subalternity and International Law: The Problems of Global Community and the Incommensurability of Difference.' In *Laws of the Postcolonial*, ed. Eve Darian-Smith and Peter Fitzpatrick, 145–80. Ann Arbor: University of Michigan Press, 1999.

'Out to Crack Copying Market.' *Business Week*, 19 September 1959.

Owen, David. 'Copies in Seconds.' *Atlantic Monthly*, February 1986.

Oxfam. *Rigged Rules and Double Standards: Trade, Globalization, and the Fight Against Poverty*, 2001. www.maketradefair.org

Pagold, Susanne. 'Med medier som vapen.' *Dagens Nyheter*, 7 October 2001.

Parkhurst Ferguson, Priscilla. *Paris As Revolution: Writing the Nineteenth-Century City*. Berkeley and Los Angeles: University of California Press, 1994.

Parrinder, Patrick. 'Introduction: Literary Copyright and the Public Domain.' In *Textual Monopolies: Literary Copyright and the Public Domain*, ed. Parrinder and Chernaik, 1–12.

Parrinder, Patrick, and Warren Chernaik, eds. *Textual Monopolies: Literary Copyright and the Public Domain*. London: Office for Humanities Communication Publication 80, 1997.

Patsuris, Penelope. 'Another Black Eye for AOL.' *Forbes*, 23 August 2002.

Piault, Fabrice. 'De la rationalisation à l'hyperconcentration.' In *L'Édition Français depuis 1945*, ed. Pascal Fouché, 629–39. Paris: Editions du Cercle de la Librairies, 1998.

'Plan général et complet de l'exposition universelle de 1878.' Paris: Maison Logerot, 1878.

Plimmer, Gill. 'A Measure of Financial Muscle: How to Read the Tables.' *The Financial Times*, 9 May 2001.

Porsdam, Helle. *Legally Speaking: Contemporary American Culture and the Law*. Amherst: University of Massachusetts Press, 1999.

Posner, Richard A. *Law and Literature*. Cambridge, MA: Harvard University Press, 1998.

Primo Braga, Carlos Alberto. 'The Economics of Intellectual Property Rights and the GATT: A View from the South.' 22 *Vanderbilt Journal of Transnational Law* 243 (1989).

Puri, Kamal. 'Preservation and Conservation of Expressions of Folklore.' *Copyright Bulletin* 32, no. 4 (1998): 5–36.

Putnam, George Haven. *The Question of Copyright: A Summary of the Copyright Laws at Present in Force in the Chief Countries of the World*. New York: G.P. Putnam's Sons, 1891.

Pym, Anthony. 'Two Principles, One Probable Paradox and a Humble Suggestion, All Concerning Percentages of Translation and Non-Translation into Various Languages, Particularely English.' www.fut.es/~apym/on-line/rates/rates.html

Raghavan, Chakravarthi. *Recolonization: GATT, the Uruguay Round and the Third World*. London: Zed Books, 1990.

Randall, Marilyn. *Pragmatic Plagiarism: Authorship, Profit, and Power*. Toronto: University of Toronto Press, 2001.

Renoliet, Jean-Jacques. *L'UNESCO oubliée: La Société des Nations et la coopération intellectuelle 1919–1946*. Paris: Publications de la Sorbonne, 1999.

Review of *Smilla's Sense of Snow*. *Publisher's Weekly*, 28 June 1993.

Ricketson, Sam. *The Berne Convention for the Protection of Literary and Artistic Works: 1886–1986*. London: Centre for Commercial Law Studies, 1987.

Robb, Graham. *Victor Hugo*. London: Picador, 1997.

Rose, Carol. *Property and Persuasion: Essays on the History, Theory, and Rhetoric of Ownership*. Boulder, CO: Westview Press, 1994.

– 'The Several Futures of Property: Of Cyberspace and Folk Tales, Emission Trades and Ecosystems.' 83 *Minnesota Law Review* 129 (November 1998).

Rose, Mark. 'The Author as Proprietor: *Donaldson v. Becket* and the Geneaology of Modern Authorship.' *Representations* 23 (summer 1988): 51–85.

– *Authors and Owners: The Invention of Copyright*. Cambridge, MA: Harvard University Press, 1993.

RosettaBooks LLC. 'Random House and RosettaBooks, LLC Settle Litigation and Set E-book Licensing Alliance.' Press release, 4 December 2002.

Rouet, François. *Le Livre: Mutations d'une industrie culturelle*. Paris: La Documentation Française 5105, 2000.

Ryan, Michael P. *Knowledge Diplomacy: Global Competition and the Politics of Intellectual Property*. Washington: Brookings Institution Press, 1998.

Salles, Alain. 'Les descendants de Victor Hugo veulent interdire la suite des Misérables.' *Le Monde*, 29 April 2001.

Samuelson, Pamela. 'Digital Information, Digital Networks, and the Public Domain.' Paper presented at the Conference on the Public Domain, Duke University, Durham, NC, 9–11 November 2001.

– 'Towards a New Politics of Intellectual Property.' *Communications of the ACM* 44, no. 3 (March 2001): 98–9.

Sanjek, David. 'Don't Have to DJ No More.' In *The Construction of Authorship: Textual Appropriation in Law and Literature*, ed. Woodmansee and Jaszi, 343–60.

Sarat, Austin, and Thomas R. Kearns, eds. *Law in the Domains of Culture*. Ann Arbor: University of Michigan Press, 1998.

Sassen, Saskia. *Globalization and Its Discontents: Essays on the New Mobility of People and Money*. New York: New Press, 1998.

– 'The Spatial Organization of Information Industries: Implications for the Role of the State.' In *Globalization: Critical Reflections. International Political Economy Yearbook*, ed. James H. Mittelmann, 33–52. Boulder, CO: Lynn Rienner Publishers, 1996.

Satterlee, Thom. 'A Case for Smilla.' *Translation Review* 50 (1996): 13–17.

Saunders, David. *Authorship and Copyright*. London: Routledge, 1992.

Schäffner, Christina. 'Introduction: Globalization, Communication, Translation.' In *Translation in the Global Village*, ed. Christina Schäffner, 1–10. Clevedon: Multilingual Matters, 2000.

Schiffrin, André. *The Business of Books: How International Conglomerates Took Over Publishing and Changed the Way We Read*. London: Verso, 2000.

– 'The Corporatization of Publishing.' In *Corporate Power in the United States*, ed. Joseph Sora, 145–52. New York: Wilson, 1998.

– 'The Eurocrash on Books.' *The Nation*, 31 December 2001.

Schou, Søren. 'Danmark set nedefra: Modtagelsen af Peter Høegs forfatterskab i de tysksprogede lande.' In *Lys og Blade: sider af upplysningens litteratur: til Povl Schmidt*, ed. John Norregard Frandsen, 299–306. Odense: Odense Universitetsforlag, 1995.

Schwartz, John. '2 Copyright Cases Decided in Favor of Entertainment Industry.' *New York Times*, 29 November 2001.

Sell, Susan. *Power and Ideas: North-South Politics of Intellectual Property and Antitrust*. New York: SUNY Press, 1998.

Sengupta, Mahasweta. 'Translation as Manipulation: The Power of Images and the Images of Power.' In *Between Languages and Cultures*, ed. Anuradha Dingwaney and Carol Meier, 159–74. Pittsburgh: University of Pittsburgh Press, 1995.

Shammel, Wayne, and Dave Stephenson. 'Protecting American Indian Intellectual Property in the Twenty-First Century: The Case of the Cow Creek Tribe and the Indian Motorcycle.' *Cultural Survival Quarterly*, 24, no. 4, http://www.culturalsurvival.org/publications/csq/csqarticle.cfm ?id=0DB3AB93-F83A-4579-B25D-2CE275446961&region id=6&sub region id=21&issue id=23.

Sherman, Brad. 'From the Non-Original to the Ab-Original: A History.' In *Of*

Authors and Origins: Essays on Copyright Law, ed. Sherman and Strowel, 111–30.

Sherman, Brad, and Lionel Bentley. 'Balance and Harmony in the Duration of Copyright: The European Directive and Its Consequences.' In *Textual Monopolies: Literary Copyright and the Public Domain*, ed. Parrinder and Chernaik, 15–37.

Sherman, Brad, and Alain Strowel, eds. *Of Authors and Origins: Essays on Copyright Law*. Oxford: Clarendon Press, 1994.

Shook, David. 'Wanted at AOL: Another Bob Pittman.' *Business Week*, 19 July 2002.

Siwek, Stephen E. 'Executive Summary.' In *Copyright Industries in the U.S. Economy – The 2002 Report*. Washington: The International Intellectual Property Alliance, 2002.

Software and Information Industry Association (SIIA). 'Five Years: $59.2 Billion Lost.' Press release, 24 May 2000.

Simon, David. 'Keepers of the Word.' *The Nation*, 25 December 2000.

Simonds, W.E. 'Report on the International Copyright Bill of the House Committee on Patents.' In *The Question of Copyright: A Summary of Copyright Laws at Present in Force in the Chief Countries of the World*, ed. G.E.O. Haven Putnam. New York: G.P. Putnam and Sons, 1891.

Sinacore-Guinn, David. *Collective Administration of Copyrights and Neighboring Rights: International Practices, Procedures, and Organizations*. Boston: Little, Brown and Company, 1993.

Skow, John. 'A Big Hit, A Small Miss.' *Time*, 13 September 1993.

Smiers, Joost. 'Copyrights: A Choice of No-Choice for Artists and Third World Countries: The Public Domain Is Losing Anyway.' www.constantvzw.com/copy.cult/cjs1.html

Smith, Douglas K., and Robert C. Alexander. *Fumbling the Future: How Xerox Invented, Then Ignored, the First Personal Computer*. New York: William Morrow and Company, 1988.

Smith, Nina, and Marceline White. 'Freedom to Craft a Future? The Impact of Trade Liberalization on Grassroots Craftswomen.' http://www.womensedge.org/trade/craftwomen.htm

Snell-Hornby, Mary. 'Communicating in the Global Village: On Language, Translation, and Cultural Identity.' In *Translation in the Global Village*, ed. Christina Schäffner, 11–28. Clevedon: Multilingual Matters, 2000.

Solberg, Thorvald. *International Copyright in the Congress of the United States, 1837–1886*. Boston: Press of Rockwell and Churchill, 1886.

Stallman, Richard. 'Why Software Should Be Free.' In *Intellectual Property:*

Moral, Legal, and International Dilemmas, ed. Adam D. Moore, 283–97. Lanham: Rowman and Littlefield, 1997.

Stallybrass, Peter, and Allon White. *The Politics and Poetics of Transgression*. Ithaca, NY: Cornell University Press, 1986.

Stanger, Alison. 'In Search of The Joke: An Open Letter to Milan Kundera.' *New England Review* 18, no. 1 (winter 1997): 93–100.

Strange, Susan. *States and Markets*. 2nd ed. London: Pinter, 1994.

Strömholm, Stig. 'Droit Moral – The International and Comparative Scene from a Scandinavian Viewpoint.' *International Review of Industrial Property and Copyright Law* 14, no. 1 (1983): 343–84.

Strowel, Alain. 'Droit d'Auteur and Copyright: Between History and Nature.' In *Of Authors and Origins: Essays on Copyright Law*, ed. Sherman and Strowel, 235–53.

Svedjedal, Johan. 'Den svenska bokmarknaden.' In *Den Svenska Litteraturen*, Vol. 7, ed. Lars Lönnroth and Hans-Erik Johannesson, 11–37. Stockholm: Bonniers, 1990.

Tebbel, John. *Between Covers: The Rise and Transformation of American Book Publishing*. New York: Oxford University Press, 1987.

– *The Creation of an Industry, 1630–1865*. Vol. 1 of *A History of Book Publishing in the United States*. New York: Bowker, 1975.

– *The Expansion of an Industry, 1865–1919*. Vol. 2 of *A History of Book Publishing in the United States*. New York: Bowker, 1975.

Thal Larsen, Peter. 'The Year the Giants Chose to Merge.' *Financial Times*, 9 May 2001.

Thorvall, Kerstin. 'Välsvarvad hjältinna.' *Dagens Nyheter*, 11 July 1994.

Trolle, Karin. *Miss Smilla's Feeling for Snow: The Making of a Film by Bille August*. London: Harvill Press, 1997.

Tunstall, Jeremy, and David Machin. *The Anglo-American Media Connection*. Oxford: Oxford University Press, 1999.

'Uhørt Høeg-succes.' *Politiken*, 16 October 1993.

Union des Associations Internationales. *Les Congrès Internationaux de 1681 à 1899*. Brussels: Union des Associations Internationales, 1960.

– *Yearbook of International Organizations 1998/9*. Brussels: Union des Associations Internationales, 1998.

United Nations Conference on Trade and Development (UNCTAD). *World Investment Report 1999: Foreign Direct Investment and the Challenge of Development*. New York and Genva: UNCTAD, 1999.

– *World Investment Report 2000: Cross-border Mergers and Aquisitions and Development*. New York and Geneva: UNCTAD, 2000.

- *World Investment Report 2001: Promoting Linkages*. New York and Geneva: UNCTAD, 2001.
- *Statistical Profiles of the Least Developed Countries 2001*. Geneva: UNCTAD, 2001.

United Nations Economic and Social Council (ECOSOC). 'Discrimination against Indigenous Peoples.' Study on the Protection of the Cultural and Intellectual Property of Indigenous Peoples by Erica-Irene Daes, Special Rapporteur of the Subcommission on Prevention of Discrimination and Protection of Minorities and Chairperson of the Working Group on Indigenous Populations. ECOSOC Document E/CN.4/Sub.2/1993/28. New York and Geneva: ECOSOC, 1993.

United Nations Educational, Scientific and Cultural Organization (UNESCO).
- Action Plan for the Safeguarding of Intangible Cultural Heritage, as approved by the international experts on the occasion of the International Round Table on 'Intangible Cultural Heritage – Working Definitions.' Piedmont, Italy, 14–17 March 2001. UNESCO Document 161 EX/15. Paris: UNESCO, 2001.
- *International Flows of Selected Cultural Goods 1980–98*. Paris: UNESCO, 2000.
- *Many Voices, One World: Communication and Society Today and Tomorrow: Towards a New More Just and More Efficient World Information and Communication Order*. Paris: UNESCO, 1980.
- Recommendations on the Safeguarding of Traditional Culture and Folklore adopted by the General Conference at its twenty-fifth session. Paris, 15 November 1989. www.unesco.org/culture/laws/paris/html eng/page1.shtml
- *Statistical Yearbook 1999*, Paris, UNESCO, 1999.
- Stockholm Action Plan on Cultural Policies for Development (1998). http://www.unesco.org/culture/laws/stockholm/html eng/actionpl3.shtml

United States Trade Representative (USTR). 2002 'Special 301' Report. Washington: USTR, 2002.

Vaidhyanathan, Siva. *Copyrights and Copywrongs: The Rise of Intellectual Property and How It Threatens Creativity*. New York: New York University Press, 2001.

Venuti, Lawrence. *The Scandals of Translation: Towards an Ethics of Difference*. London: Routledge, 1998.
- *The Translator's Invisibility: A History of Translation*. London: Routledge, 1995.

Venuti, Lawrence, ed. *The Translation Studies Reader*. London: Routledge, 2000.

Verrier, Richard. 'Messier Likely to Fend Off Ouster Bid.' *Los Angeles Times*, 23 April 2002.

Vivendi Universal. 'Closing Off Sale of Houghton Mifflin.' Press Release, 31 December 2002.
– 'Creation of Vivendi Universal, a Global Communications Giant.' Press release, 8 December 2000.
– 'Seagram's Spirits and Wine Business Sold to Diaego and Pernod Ricard.' Press release, 19 December 2000.
– 'Vivendi Universal reports strong first quarter consolidated financial results.' Press release, 29 April 2002.
Wallerstein, Immanuel. *The Modern World-System*. 2 vols. New York: Academic Press, 1974.
Wasserstein, Bruce. *Big Deal: 2000 and Beyond*. New York: Time Warner, 2000.
Weber, Daniel. 'Culture or Commerce? Symbolic Boundaries in French and American Book Publishing.' In *Rethinking Comparative Cultural Sociology: Repertoires of Evaluation in France and the United States*, ed. Michèle Lamont and Laurent Thévenot, 127–47. Cambridge: Cambridge University Press, 2000.
Wells Branscomb, Anne. *Who Owns Information? From Privacy to Public Access*. New York: Basic Books, 1994.
Wennö, Nicholas. 'Staten stäms av filmbolag. Tvistefråga. "Är fröken Smillas känsla för snö en svensk film" eller inte?' *Dagens Nyheter*, 13 January 1999.
Westman Tullus, Barbro. 'Peter Høeg önskar ingen bättre Smilla.' *Svenska Dagbladet*, 28 February 1997.
Whiteside, Thomas. *The Blockbuster Complex: Conglomerates, Show Business, and Book Publishing*. Middletown: Wesleyan University Press, 1980.
Whitney, Gretchen. 'International Book Production Statistics.' In *International Book Publishing: An Encyclopedia*, ed. Philip G. Altbach and Edith S. Hoshino, 163–86. London: Fitzroy Dearborn, 1997.
Williams, John. Book Review of *Miss Smilla's Feeling for Snow: New Statesman and Society*, 3 September 1993.
Williams, Raymond. *Keywords: A Vocabulary of Culture and Society*. London: Fontana, 1976.
Woodmansee, Martha. *The Author, Art, and the Market: Rereading the History of Aesthetics*. New York: Columbia University Press, 1993.
– 'The Cultural Work of Copyright: Legislating Authorship in Britain, 1857–1842.' In *Law in the Domains of Culture*, ed. Sarat and Kearns, 65–96.
– 'The Genius and the Copyright: Economic and Legal Conditions of the Emergence of the "Author."' *Eighteenth-Century Studies* 17 (summer 1984): 425–48.
Woodmansee, Martha, and Peter Jaszi, eds. *The Construction of Authorship: Textual Appropriation in Law and Literature*. Durham: Duke University Press, 1994.

World Intellectual Property Organization (WIPO). 'The Attempts to Protect Expressions of Folklore and Traditional Knowledge.' WIPO International Forum on 'Intellectual Property and Traditional Knowledge: Our Identity, Our Future.' Muscat, 21–2 January 2002. WIPO Document WIPO/IPTK/MCT/02/INF.5. Geneva: WIPO, 2002.

– 'Elements of a *Sui Generis* System for the Protection of Traditional Knowledge.' Intergovernmental Committee on Intellectual Property and Genetic Resources, Traditional Knowledge and Folklore, Third Session, Geneva, 13–21 June 2002. WIPO document WIPO/GRTKF/IC/3/8. Geneva: WIPO, 2002.

– *Intellectual Property Needs and Expectations of Traditional Knowledge Holders: WIPO Report on Fact-Finding Missions on Intellectual Property and Traditional Knowledge 1998/1999.* Geneva: WIPO, 2001.

– 'Matters Concerning Intellectual Property and Genetic Resources, Traditional Knowledge and Folklore.' WIPO General Assembly, Twenty-Sixth (12th Extraordinary Session), Geneva, 25 September–3 October 2000. WIPO Document WO/GA/26/6. Geneva: WIPO, 2000.

– 'Preliminary Systematic Analysis of National Experiences with the Legal Protection of Expressions of Folklore.' Intergovernmental Committee on Intellectual Property and Genetic Resources, Traditional Knowledge and Folklore, Fourth Session, Geneva, 9–17 December 2002, WIPO document WIPO/GRTKF/IC/4/3. Geneva: WIPO, 2002.

– Report. Intergovernmental Committee on Intellectual Property and Genetic Resources, Traditional Knowledge and Folklore, Second Session, 10–14 December 2001. WIPO Document WIPO/GRTKF/IC/2/16. Geneva: WIPO, 2001.

– *WIPO Intellectual Property Handbook: Policy, Law and Use.* Geneva: WIPO, 2001.

WIPO Copyright Treaty (1996). http://www.wipo.int/clea/docs/en/wo/wo033en.htm

WIPO-UNESCO. Model Provisions for National Laws on the Protection of Expressions of Folkore against Illicit Exploitation and Other Prejudical Actions. (1982). http://www.wipo.org/globalissues/laws/

World Trade Orgainzation (WTO). Doha Ministerial Declaration. Adopted on 14 November 2001. WTO Document WT/MIN01/DEC/1. Geneva: WTO, 2001.

– Proposal on Protection of the Intellectual Rights of the Traditional Knowledge of Local and Indigenous Communities. Communication from Cuba, Honduras, Paraguay, and Venezuela. WTO Document WT/GC/W/329. Geneva: WTO, 22 September 1999.

XEROX Corporation. 'Now! Office Copying Enters the Age of Automation: Copying Costs Dramatically Cut!' *Fortune*, March 1960, 167–72. (Advertisement)
– 'Now X Marks the Spot.' *Fortune*, July 1961, 25. (Advertisement)
– *The Story of Xerography.* http://a1851.g.akamaitech.net/f/1851/2996/24h/cache.xerox.com/downloads/usa/en/s/Storyofxerography.pdf
– 'What Xerox Gives You for Your Nickel.' *Fortune*, June 1963, 60–1. (Advertisement)
– 'Which Is the $2,800 Picasso? Which Is the 5c Xerox 914 Copy?' *Fortune*, September 1963, 224–5. (Advertisement)
– *Xerox Online Factbook 2002–2003.* http://www.xerox.com/go/xrx/template/019d.jsp?view=Factbook&id=Historical&Xcntry=USA&Xlang=en_US.
Zern, Leif. 'En berättelse med skräddarsydd kostym: Peter Høeg svarar på alla tillrop, men hans roman saknar något.' *Dagens Nyheter*, 4 July 1994.

Cases

American Geophysical Union v. Texaco, Inc., 802 F. Supp. 1 (S.D.N.Y), 60 F. 3d 913.
Basic Books, Inc. v. Kinko's Graphics Corp., 758 F. Supp. 1522 (S.D.N.Y.). (1991)
John Bulun Bulun v. R & T Textiles Pty Ltd., 1082 FCA. (1998)
Campbell v. Acuff-Rose Music Inc., 510 U.S. 569. (1994)
Eldred v. Ashcroft., 239 F. 3d 372, *affirmed.* (2003)
Hugo contre SA Plon, TGI Paris, 1ère chambre, 1ère section, 12 septembre. (2001)
Milpurrurru v. Indofurn Pty Ltd. No. DG4 of 1993 FED No. 975/94 Copyright (1994) 54 FCR 240 (1994) 130 ALR 659. (1994)
Random House Inc. v. RosettaBooks LLC., 150 F. Supp. 2d 613 (S.D.N.Y.). (2001)
San Fransisco Arts & Athletics, Inc. v. United States Olympic Committee, 483 U.S. 522. (1987)
Sony Corp. v. Universal City Studios, Inc., 464 U.S. 417. (1984)
Stowe v. Thomas, 23 F. Cas. 201. (1853)
Suntrust Bank v. Houghton Mifflin Co., 136 F. Supp. 2d 1357, 268 F. 3d 1257. (2001)
Williams & Wilkins Co. v. United States, 487 F. 2d 1345, *affirmed by an equally divided Court*, 420 U.S. 376. (1975)
Yumbulul v. Reserve Bank of Australia, No. D G26 of 1989 Fed No. 448 Trade Practices – Aborigines – Copyright 21 IPR 481. (1991)

INDEX

Action Plan for the Safeguarding of the Intangible Cultural Heritage, 112

Adamantopoulos, Konstantinos, 176n8

Agreement on Trade Related Aspects of Intellectual Property Rights (TRIPS): absence of provisions for traditional knowledge in, 113–14; developing and least developed countries coming into compliance with, 107, 112, 178n34; lack of moral rights in, 123; opposition to article 27(b) of, 113; protection of computer programs and compilation of data in, 107–8; scope and importance of, 6–7, 106; and the WTO trade framework, 106, 122, 139, 145. *See also* World Trade Organization (WTO)

Alford, William P., 150n19

Alliance Against Counterfeiting and Piracy (AACP), 93

Altbach, Philip G., 152n30

American Geophysical Union v. Texaco Inc., 70–3, 165n59

Anderson, Benedict, 155n43

Aoki, Keith, 150–1n21

AOL Time Warner, 85–6, 97–9

Arendt, Hannah, 144, 188nn91–2

Association Littéraire et Artistique Internationale (ALAI): accused of catering only to French interests, 39, 137; early conferences of, 34–5; famous early members of, 33; formation of, 32, 156nn56, 58; as promoting national literatures, 33–5; and the question of translation, 38–9, 54–5, 157–8n3; and relationship to Victor Hugo, 32–4

Association of American Publishers Inc. (AAP), 93, 174n94

Assouline, Pierre, 128

Australia, copyright cases in, 116–24, 181n81

authorship: associated with the nation-state, 20, 35; and gender, 5; and the impact of technology, 57, 66–8, 73–4; and originality, 5, 57; related to the author as legal subject, 4–5; in relationship to translation, 38–40, 49, 53, 56, 57; as a 'transdiscursive' function, 5; and value, 149n1

Bagdikian, Ben H., 86, 171n47
Balzac, Honoré de, 16, 17, 55
Barlow, John Perry, 143, 144
Barnet, Richard J., 85, 168–9n27
Barron, Anne, 119
Barthes, Roland, 73, 152n38
Basic Books, Inc. v. Kinko's Graphics Corp., 72–3
Battelle Memorial Institute, 60–1
Benjamin, Walter, 27, 67
Benkler, Yochai, 136
Berne Convention for the Protection of Literary and Artistic Works (1886): article 6(bis) [moral rights clause] of, 117, 123, 132; article 15 (4) of the Stockholm Act of, 111; bilateral treaties preceding the, 17; and developing nations, 107–8, 111; and the United States, 55, 92–4, 108; Diplomatic Conferences preceding the, 55, 157n71; initial signatories of, 36; length of protection in, 10, 186n57; reproduction rights in, 74; revisions of, 107; three main pillars of, 152n29; translation treated in, 39–40, 49, 55, 137–8, 157n1
Bertelsmann, 77, 85–6, 89, 98, 170n43
Bettig, Ronald V., 152n34, 176n85
Bollier, David, 150n10, 185n46
Bourdieu, Pierre, 56, 153n9
Boyd White, James, 153n39, 157n2
Boyle, James, 10, 109, 133, 152n34, 176n123
Brazil, 92
Bronfmann, Edgar, Jr., 97–8
Brooks, John, 62, 68, 69, 83, 164n51
Bulwer-Lytton, Edward George, 17
Burrell, Robert, 178n30
Business Software Alliance (BSA), 91

Calhoun, Craig, 188n91
Campbell v. Acuff-Rose Music, Inc., 131
Canada, 91, 94, 105–6, 118
Canal+, 86, 97
Carlson, Chester F., 6, 58–61, 144, 162n3
Caron, Christoph, 132
Casanova, Pascale, 15, 33
Castells, Manuel, 151n22, 177n17
Cavanaugh, John, 85, 168–9n27
Cérésa, François, 127–9
Chatterjee, Rimi B., 160n45
China, 88, 91, 105, 106, 115
Clay, Henry, 21
conglomeratization: definition of, 76; in history, 77, 167n6; of publishing, 76–89; of telecommunications, 96, 175n104
Congrès Littéraire International (1878), 14–37, 125–9, 155n45
content: definition of, 89; as valuable resource for media conglomerates, 78, 96, 176n123
convergence: definition of, 78, 96, 167n10; as part of the WIPO Copyright Treaty, 96
Coombe, Rosemary J., 133, 150–1n21, 152n34, 178n33, 179n43
copier, the: and the dissemination and control of knowledge and information, 70, 72–3; early predecessors to, 59, 162n6; as enabling sampling, 73–4; as a 'killer of books,' 58; leading to new legislation and control, 69, 74–5; in relation to print culture, 66–8
Copyright Clearance Center (CCC), 71–2
(Sonny Bono) Copyright Term

Extension Act (CTEA), 10, 132, 135, 151n25; copyright, *see* intellectual property rights; as different from *droit d'auteur*, 7; extension of in the European Union, 10, 135, 151n25, 186n59; preceded by privileges, 4, 149n3; questioned as incentive, 71, 165–6n63; as a subcategory of intellectual property rights, 6–7; and 'work-for-hire' principle, 7, 48, 150n14
Cosette ou le temps des illusions, 9, 127–9
cultural policy, 145–7, 189n102
cultural studies, 182n98

Danius, Sara, 45–6
Das, Sonia, 165n60
David, F., 41, 47–50, 54
Defoe, Daniel, 17
Dellon, Hope, 130
Dessauer, John, 83, 163n8
developing countries: asking for exceptions in adhering to international agreements, 55, 95, 107–8, 138; as holders of valuable resources, 110–14; policies of in regard to intellectual property rights, 103–5, 107–8, 177n14; TransNational Corporations from, 88, 173n63
Dickens, Charles, 17, 21
Dietz, Adolf, 183–4n11
Digital Millennium Copyright Act (DMCA), 108, 141
Dingwaney, Anuradha, 158n15
Dinwoodie, Graeme B., 144, 186n51
Disney Corporation, 85, 86, 90, 134
domain public. *See* public domain
'domain public payant,' 127, 137, 183–4n11, 187n69

Drahos, Peter, 90, 178n32
droit d'auteur, 7, 146
Droz, Numa, 35
Druon, Maurice, 128
Dumas, Alexandre, 17
Dyssegaard, Elisabeth, 41, 42, 44

Eisenstein, Elisabeth, 164n47
Eldred v. Ashcroft, 135, 145, 186nn61, 63, 64
Eldred, Eric, 135, 145
Electronic Frontier Foundation, 142, 143
enclosure movement, 133
English (language): as a 'clearinghouse' language, 54, 161n63; dominating translations globally, 40, 52–4, 138–9, 161n68; possible reasons for success of, 162n78
Epstein, Jason, 167n7
European Union, 10, 77, 106, 135, 141, 151n25
Exposition Universelle. *See* World Fairs

fair use: codification of in section 107 of the 1976 U.S. Copyright Act, 69–71, 130–1, 140; and translation, 168n58
Farrar, Straus and Giroux, 41, 43, 49
Feather, John, 149n3, 153–4n16
Felman, Shoshana, 13
Felten, Edward, 141, 187n82
Fish, Stanley, 153n39
Flaubert, Gustave, 17
folklore: alternative terms for, 112; definition and scope of, 111–12; economic losses and piracy of, 114–15, 180n73; gendered aspects of, 115; and heritage, 110, 179n48;

protection of through copyright,
111. *See also* traditional knowledge
Foucault, Michel, 4, 152n32
Fouché, Pascale, 167–8n15
Fourtou, Jean-Réné, 98
France: cultural policy in, 146; and
the cultural universalism of Paris,
25–9; linguistic policies of, 56,
162n78; nineteenth-century cultural hegemony of, 16, 23–4, 29,
31, 39–40, 55–6; securing exceptions for cultural industries in
GATT, 106; seeking to include
translations in the Berne Convention, 55; setting the agenda in
early international agreements, 23;
similarities and differences with
United States in regard to intellectual property rights and cultural
hegemony, 56; TransNational
MediaCorporations from, 86
free trade, 8, 100–24; as foundation
for intellectual property rights,
100; as the 'grand narrative' of
globalization, 122; disfavouring
developing nations, 138
Free Trade Agreement (FTA), 106
Frøken Smillas fornemmelse for sne.
See *Smilla's Sense of Snow*

Gaines, Jane M., 109, 152n34, 154n33
Gallo, Max, 128
Gana Okediji, Ruth, 138, 165n58,
185n47
Garcia Canclini, Nestor, 189n104
Geller, Paul Edward, 7
General Agreement on Tariffs and
Trade (GATT). *See* World Trade
Organization (WTO)
General Agreement on Trade in
Services (GATS), 106

General Electric (GE), 77, 92
General System of Preferences
(GSP), 92
Giddens, Anthony, 34
Gilroy, Paul, 45
Ginsburg, Jane C., 150n15, 188n87
globalization, 9–11, 137–40; and
nineteenth-century internationali-
zation, 29–30; representation of,
10; spatiality of, 9
Goldstein, Paul, 150n11, 174n100
Gone With the Wind, 129–31, 135
Greco, Albert, 88–9, 168n26
Group of 77, 103–4
Gründ, Alain, 81
Gulf + Western, 76

Habermas, Jürgen, 144, 188n91
Hall, Stuart, 12, 42, 157n74, 182n98
Harlequin Enterprises, 48
Harvey, Edwin R., 187n69
Harvill Press, 47–50
Hatch, Orrin, 186n60
Hemmungs Wirtén, Eva, 155nn43, 49,
160n44
Herman, Edward S., 170n39, 171n47
Hesse, Carla, 149n3
Hetzel, Pierre-Jules, 16, 153–4n13
Hobsbawm, Eric, 162n77
Homestead, Melissa J., 19, 149n5,
157n2
Houghton Mifflin, 83, 87, 98, 129–30
Hugo, Charles, 15
Hugo, Lauretta, 127, 128
Hugo, Pierre, 128–9, 132
Hugo, Victor: as an advocate of the
public domain, 125–9; compared
with Voltaire and André Gide as
public intellectual, 20; death and
funeral of, 36; iconic status of,
14–15; and opening speech at the

1878 Congrès Littéraire International, 18–30, 125–9; and relationship with ALAI, 32–5; and relationship with book market, 16–18
Hugo contre S A Plon, 127–9, 132
Hunchback of Notre Dame, 134
Høeg, Peter, 5, 40–1, 43–4, 48–53, 139, 159n30

Instituto Nacional de Biodiversidad (INBio), 113
intellectual property rights: as a critical feature of globalization, 10–11, 137–40; definition of, 7, 150n16; expansion of, 10, 108–9, 133, 185nn45, 49; and gender, 5, 115, 149n5; international periodization of, 90, 173n73; as a regime favouring Western resources, 100–24; as related to cultural export/import, 40, 55–6, 89–93, 137; relationship to authorship, 5; rights in, 7; serving the interests of the nation-state, 10–11, 137–8; Swedish term for, 8; and technology, 6, 31–2, 140–2, 165n57
Intelsat, 32
InterGovernmental Organizations (IGOs): early examples of, 31; explosive growth of, 102
International Bank for Reconstruction and Development (IBRD). *See* World Bank
International Bureau of Weights and Measures, 31
International Commission for the Study of Communication Problems. *See* MacBride Report
International Federation of Reproduction Rights Organizations (IFRRO), 74

International Intellectual Property Alliance (IIPA), 90–1
International Labour Office (ILO), 31
International Monetary Fund (IMF), 102
International Publishers Association (IPA), 81
International Telecommunication Union (ITU), 31, 96
International Telegraph Union. *See* International Telecommunication Union (ITU)
International Trade Organization (ITO), 102

Jackson, John, H., 176n6, 182–3n102
Janke, Terri, 181n81
Jazsi, Peter, 150n14, 152n34
John Bulun Bulun v. R & T Textiles Pty Ltd., 119–21
Jones, Steve, 8

Kaplan, Alice, 152n36
Kapor, Mitch, 143
Kearns, Thomas R., 152n34
Klein, Naomi, 183n103
Korda, Michael, 167n7
Kornei, Otto, 59
Krüger, Mechthild, 159n31
Kundera, Milan, and English-language translation of *The Joke*, 48–9

Lagardère, 86, 87, 171n54
Lange, David, 143, 185nn45, 49
Least Developed Countries (LDCs). *See* developing countries
Lefevere, André, 42
Lehman, Bruce, 176–7n13, 177n20
Leithauser, Brad, 44, 47

Lessig, Lawrence, 134, 185n45, 187n80
Litman, Jessica, 134, 165n55
Loseley, David, 189n102

MacBride Report, 104
Malmkjær, Kirsten, 49, 50, 51
Maskus, Keith E., 176n8
Massey, Doreen, 13, 140, 151n22
Maurice, Paul, 132
May, Christopher, 100, 152n34
McChesney, Robert W., 170n39, 171n47
McLeod, Kembrew, 166n71, 178n33, 182n100
McLuhan, Marshall, 66–7, 73, 75, 141
McSherry, Corinne, 166n68
Meier, Carol, 158n15
mergers and acquisitions (M&As), 76–7, 80, 86, 96
Mérimée, Prosper, 17
Merryman, John Henry, 185n43
Messier, Jean-Marie, 97–8
Mexico, 88, 92, 105–6, 115
Michon, Jacques, 161n73
Middelhoff, Thomas, 98, 167n8
Milpurrurru v. Indofurn Pty Ltd., 116–19
Misérables, Les, 15, 16, 18, 22, 128
Miss Smilla's Feeling for Snow. See Smilla's Sense of Snow
Mitchell, Margaret, 8, 129–32
Mollier, Jean-Yves, 153n13, 161n73, 168n25
Moore, Michael, 106, 114
moral rights: in the Berne Convention, 117; in France, 7, 129, 132, 185n43; as possible protection for traditional knowledge, 123

Moretti, Franco, 23–4, 150–1n21, 155n37
Morley, David, 10

Nader, Ralph, 61
Negativland, 136, 186n65
New International Economic Order (NIEO), 103–4
New World Information and Communication Order (NWICO), 104
Nilsson, Sven, 189n102
Noguez, Dominique, 128–9, 132
non-governmental organizations (NGOs), 102, 124
Norseng, Mary Kay, 45
North American Free Trade Agreement (NAFTA), 88, 105–6, 115, 123
Notre-Dame de Paris, 15, 18, 22, 134
Nunberg, Geoffrey, 162n2
Nunnally, Tiina, 41, 47–50, 54

Ohman, Richard, 79
Olson, Peter, 87, 172n56
Oppenheim, Charles, 142
Organization for Economic Co-Operation and Development (OECD), 104
Organization of the Petroleum Exporting Countries (OPEC), 103
Otto, Diane, 104

Paramount Communications, 76
Parkhurst Ferguson, Priscilla, 23
'piracy': in crafts, 114–15; described as linked to organized crime and terrorism, 92–3, 174n90; financial losses to the U.S. 'core copyright industries' due to, 90–1; as a strategy legitimized by nineteenth-century U.S. publishers,

55, 93–5, 174–5n102; successful
nineteenth-century writers as
victims of, 17, 21; and U.S. trade
policy, 89–92, 106, 138
Porsdam, Helle, 153n39
Posner, Richard A., 153n39
Primo Braga, Carlos Alberto, 177n15
print culture: centrality of, 3–4, 13;
and conglomeratization, 76–99;
import/export of, 53–4; spatiality
of, 150–1n21, 155n43; technology
and, 66–8, 72–5, 140–5; and translation, 38, 52–3. See also authorship
Provisional Congress of the Confederacy, 93
public domain, 9, 125–37, 143–8;
balancing private rights, 133–6,
183n6; cultural policy and, 145–7;
definition of, 125; described as the
American West, 143; differences
in views of between Europe and
United States, 144; Disney Corporation's use of, 134; as limited to
the nation-state, 143; as a prerequisite for authorship, 134; problems in conceptualizing, 133–4;
represented as an 'innovation
commons,' 143–4; rivalrous and
non-rivalrous resources of, 134;
traditional knowledge and, 109,
136–7; Victor Hugo's view of,
125–7, 132
publishing: comparison between
French and U.S., 80–1; conglomeratization of, 76–99, 169n38;
contribution of to the economy of
Transnational MediaCorporations,
87–8, 172n56; and e-books, 81;
French structure of, 87, 169n28,
171–2n55; three segments of, 84;

traditional structure and imagery
of, 79–81, 168n16,25
Pym, Anthony, 161n65

Randall, Alice, 8, 129
Randall, Marilyn, 182n100
Random House, 81, 85, 87, 89
Random House Inc. v. RossettaBooks
LLC, 81, 168n23
Recommendation on the Safeguard-
ing of Traditional Culture and
Folklore, 111
Renoliet, Jean-Jacques, 177n17
Reproduction Rights Organizations
(RROs), 74
Ricketson, Sam, 49, 150n7, 157n1,
173n73, 178n37, 186n57
Ripley, Alexandra, 130
Rose, Carol, 136, 140, 188n88
Rose, Mark, 5, 153–4n16
Ryan, Michael P., 151n28

Samuelson, Pamela, 147
San Francisco Arts & Athletics Inc. v.
U.S. Olympic Committee, 108
Sand, George, 16–17, 55
Sanjek, David, 166n71
Sarat, Austin, 152n34
Sassen, Saskia, 151n22
Satterlee, Thom, 47, 49, 51
Saunders, David, 154n18
Scarlett: The Sequel to Margaret
Mitchell's Gone With the Wind,
130
Schiffrin, André, 80, 89, 167n7,
168n26
Scott, Sir Walter, 17
Seagram, 86, 87, 88, 97
Secure Digital Music Initiative
(SDMI), 141

Sell, Susan, 174n88, 177n15
Sengupta, Mahasweta, 160n45
Sherman, Brad, 119, 152n34, 181n76, 182n93
Simon and Schuster, 76, 84, 87
Sinacore-Guinn, David, 166n72
Sklyarov, Dimitry, 141–2
Smilla's Sense of Snow: describing the process of globalization, 139; and fictitious F. David as translator of *Miss Smilla's Feeling for Snow*, 41, 47, 49, 50, 54, 160n57; global success of, 41, 43, 158n13; movie by Bille August, 46–7, 159n35; narrative structure of, 45; postcolonial aspects of, 44–6, 159nn31, 33; reading of by the online Book Group List, 50–1; reviews of, 43–4, 159n23; story and setting of, 42; Tiina Nunnelly's translation of, 47; translation of compared with *Miss Smilla's Feeling for Snow*, 47–52, 161n63
Snell-Hornby, Mary, 162n78
Société des Auteurs, Compositeurs et Èditeurs de Musique (SACEM), 74
Société des gens de lettres de France, 14, 126, 128, 153n1
Software and Information Industry Association (SIIA), 91
Sony Corp. v. Universal City Studios, Inc., 70
Stallman, Richard, 144, 179n38
Stallybrass, Peter, 100, 109
Stanger, Alison, 48–9
Statute of Anne, the, 17
Stockholm Action Plan on Cultural Policies for Development, 179n48
Stowe v. Thomas, 19, 49, 157n2
Stowe, Harriet Beecher, 19, 49, 94

Strange, Susan, 11, 13, 152n32
Strömholm, Stig, 150n13
Strowel, Alain, 152n34
Sue, Eugene, 17
Suntrust Bank v. Houghton Mifflin Co., 129–32, 184n28
Svedjedal, Johan, 161n68
Swedish Union of Authors, 74

Tagore, Rabindranath, 48
Tebbel, John, 93
traditional knowledge, 100–24, 136–7; customary protection of, 118; definition and scope of, 110–12; incompatability with current intellectual property regimes, 109, 116–24, 136–7, 182n100; and suggestions for a sui generis system protecting, 123–4, 183n104; within the WTO framework and TRIPS, 113–14, 122–4; work done by UNESCO and WIPO on, 107–13. *See also* folklore
'transediting,' 48, 160n44
translation, 38–56; and authorship and intellectual property rights, 38–40, 53, 56, 157n2; in the Berne Convention, 39, 40, 49, 55, 137–8, 157n1; and cultural imperialism, 39–40, 41, 52–6, 137–8, 158n15; differences between nineteenth-century French and English, 23–4, 155n37; economy of, 49, 160n49; importance of, 38; 'invisibility' of, 40; as a major incentive behind early international agreements, 5, 38–9, 55, 157n1, 157–8n3; statistics on, 52, 161n68
transnational corporations (TNCs); 87–8, 147, 172n58
Transnational Media Corporations

(TNMCs), 6, 87–9, 96; based outside the United States, 86; financial losses of, 97–9; relationship and alliances between, 86, 171n45
Twain, Mark, 21

Uncle Tom's Cabin, 19, 49, 94
Union des Associations Internationales, 27, 102
United Nations Conference for Trade and Development (UNCTAD), 77, 103, 104
United Nations Economic and Social Council (ECOSOC), 102
United Nations Educational, Scientific, and Cultural Organization (UNESCO): controversies regarding NIEO and NWICO in, 104–5, 147; statistics on translation from, 40, 52, 53; work on traditional knowledge by, 110–12, 114
United States: and the Berne Convention, 55, 92–4, 108; contribution of core copyright industries to the economy of, 90–2; dissatisfaction with UN system, 102, 104, 177n17; launching trade policy and intellectual property rights in the 1980s, 90–3, 102–3, 138; as a pirate- and developing nation in the nineteenth-century, 55–6, 93–5, 138, 174–5n102; as representative of a cultural imperialism similar to the French, 56; statistics on cultural exports of, 89–90
United States Trade Representative (USTR), 91–2
Universal Postal Union, 31
Universal Radiotelegraph Union, 32
upphovsrätt. *See* droit d'auteur

Vaidhyanathan, Siva, 21
Venuti, Lawrence, 40, 158nn12, 16, 160nn49, 57
Viacom, 84, 85, 86, 87,
Vivendi Universal, 77, 86–7, 97–9

Waldman, Guido, 47, 48, 50
Wallerstein, Immanuel, 156n53
Weber, Daniel, 80, 168n21
Wells Branscomb, Anne, 150n10
White, Allon, 100, 109
Whiteside, Thomas, 168n24, 169n30
Williams & Wilkins Co. v. The United States, 68–73
Williams, Raymond, 120
Wind Done Gone, The, 8, 129–32, 135
Woodmansee, Martha, 152n34, 157n68, 187n81
Wordsworth, William, 21, 154n30
World Bank, 102
World Fairs, 14, 19, 25–6, 154n22
World Intellectual Property Organization (WIPO), 8, 100–24; Copyright Treaty (WTC), 96, 107, 141; and fact-finding missions (FFM) on traditional knowledge, 110–11, 122; Global Intellectual Property Issues Division of, 107; Intergovernmental Committee on Intellectual Property and Genetic Resources, Traditional Knowledge, and Folklore, 112–13; and work regarding traditional knowledge, 107–14, 178n35
WIPO-UNESCO Model provisions for National Laws on the Protection of Folklore Against Illicit Exploitation and other Prejudicial Actions, 111–12, 115, 124
World Investment Report, 86, 87, 88
World Trade Organization (WTO):

1999 Seattle Ministerial Meeting
of, 107, 113–14, 178n34, 180n69,
70; 2001 Qatar Ministerial Meeting
of, 114; Dispute Settlement Body
(DSB) of, 106, 107; GATT and
background to, 102–6. *See also*
Agreement on Trade Related
Aspects of Intellectual Property
Rights (TRIPS)

xerography: critiqued by Marshall
McLuhan, 66, 73, 75; first successful experiment with, 59–60, 162–
3n7; as an invention nobody
wanted, 60

Xerox, 57–75, 144; acquiring publishers, 83–4; adding 'scorch eliminators' to copiers from, 61; breakthrough with the model 914, 61–4;
and ContentGuard, Inc., 75, 141;
early competitors to, 62; early history of, 60–1, 163n8; in the movie
9 to 5, 63; 'lost decade of,' 64–6;
1960s success of, 64; and 1972
Federal Trade Commission suit,
65; PARC, 65, 144; TV commercials promoting copiers from, 62–3

Yumbulul v. Reserve Bank of Australia,
116–18

STUDIES IN BOOK AND PRINT CULTURE

General editor: Leslie Howsam

Bill Bell, et al., *Where Is Book History? Essays in the Emergence of a Discipline*

Hazel Bell, *Indexes and Indexing in Fact and Fiction*

Heather Murray, *Come, bright Improvement! The Literary Societies of Nineteenth-Century Ontario*

Joseph A. Dane, *The Myth of Print Culture: Essays on Evidence, Textuality, and Bibliographical Method*

William A. Johnson, *Bookrolls and Scribes in Oxyrhynchus*

Christopher J. Knight, *Uncommon Readers: Denis Donoghue, Frank Kermode, George Steiner, and the Tradition of the Common Reader*

Eva Hemmungs Wirtén, *No Trespassing: Authorship, Intellectual Property Rights, and the Boundaries of Globalization*

Siân Echard and Stephen Partridge, eds, *The Book Unbound: Editing and Reading Medieval Manuscripts and Texts*